Alaska

John J. Horton is Deputy Librarian of the University of Bradford and currently Chairman of its Academic Board of Studies in Social Sciences. He has maintained a longstanding interest in the discipline of area studies and its associated bibliographical problems, with special reference to European Studies. In particular he has published in the field of Icelandic and of Yugoslav studies, including the two relevant volumes in the World Bibliographical Series.

Robert A. Myers is Associate Professor of Anthropology in the Division of Social Sciences and Director of Study Abroad Programs at Alfred University, Alfred, New York. He has studied post-colonial island nations of the Caribbean and has spent two years in Nigeria on a Fulbright Lectureship. His interests include international public health, historical anthropology and developing societies. In addition to *Amerindians of the Lesser Antilles: a bibliography* (1981), *A Resource Guide to Dominica, 1493-1986* (1987) and numerous articles, he has compiled the World Bibliographical Series volumes on *Dominica* (1987), *Nigeria* (1989) and *Ghana* (1991).

Ian Wallace is Professor of German at the University of Bath. A graduate of Oxford in French and German, he also studied in Tübingen, Heidelberg and Lausanne before taking teaching posts at universities in the USA, Scotland and England. He specializes in contemporary German affairs, especially literature and culture, on which he has published numerous articles and books. In 1979 he founded the journal *GDR Monitor*, which he continues to edit under its new title *German Monitor*.

Hans H. Wellisch is Professor emeritus at the College of Library and Information Services, University of Maryland. He was President of the American Society of Indexers and was a member of the International Federation for Documentation. He is the author of numerous articles and several books on indexing and abstracting, and has published *The Conversion of Scripts and Indexing and Abstracting: an International Bibliography*, and *Indexing from A to Z*. He also contributes frequently to *Journal of the American Society for Information Science*, *The Indexer* and other professional journals.

Ralph Lee Woodward, Jr. is Professor of History at Tulane University, New Orleans. He is the author of *Central America, a Nation Divided*, 2nd ed. (1985), as well as several monographs and more than seventy scholarly articles on modern Latin America. He has also compiled volumes in the World Bibliographical Series on *Belize* (1980), *El Salvador* (1988), *Guatemala* (Rev. Ed.) (1992) and *Nicaragua* (Rev. Ed.) (1994). Dr. Woodward edited the Central American section of the *Research Guide to Central America and the Caribbean* (1985) and is currently associate editor of Scribner's *Encyclopedia of Latin American History*.

VOLUME 183

Alaska

Marvin W. Falk

Compiler

CLIO PRESS

OXFORD, ENGLAND · SANTA BARBARA, CALIFORNIA
DENVER, COLORADO

in Publication Data

raphical Series;

II. Series
016.9798

ISBN 1–85109–141–6

ABC-CLIO Ltd.,
Old Clarendon Ironworks,
35A Great Clarendon Street,
Oxford OX2 6AT, England.

ABC-CLIO Inc.,
130 Cremona Drive,
Santa Barbara,
CA 93116, USA.

Designed by Bernard Crossland.
Typeset by Columns Design and Production Services Ltd., Reading, England.
Printed and bound in Great Britain by Bookcraft (Bath) Ltd., Midsomer Norton.

THE WORLD BIBLIOGRAPHICAL SERIES

This series, which is principally designed for the English speaker, will eventually cover every country (and many of the world's principal regions), each in a separate volume comprising annotated entries on works dealing with its history, geography, economy and politics; and with its people, their culture, customs, religion and social organization. Attention will also be paid to current living conditions – housing, education, newspapers, clothing, etc. – that are all too often ignored in standard bibliographies; and to those particular aspects relevant to individual countries. Each volume seeks to achieve, by use of careful selectivity and critical assessment of the literature, an expression of the country and an appreciation of its nature and national aspirations, to guide the reader towards an understanding of its importance. The keynote of the series is to provide, in a uniform format, an interpretation of each country that will express its culture, its place in the world, and the qualities and background that make it unique. The views expressed in individual volumes, however, are not necessarily those of the publisher.

VOLUMES IN THE SERIES

1 *Yugoslavia*, Rev. Ed., John J. Horton
2 *Lebanon*, Rev. Ed., C. H. Bleaney
3 *Lesotho*, Shelagh M. Willet and David Ambrose
4 *Zimbabwe*, Rev. Ed., Deborah Potts
5 *Saudi Arabia*, Rev. Ed., Frank A. Clements
6 *Russia/USSR*, Second Ed., Lesley Pitman
7 *South Africa*, Rev. Ed., Geoffrey V. Davis
8 *Malawi*, Rev. Ed., Samuel Decalo
9 *Guatemala*, Rev. Ed., Ralph Lee Woodward, Jr.
10 *Pakistan*, David Taylor
11 *Uganda*, Robert L. Collison
12 *Malaysia*, Ian Brown and Rajeswary Ampalavanar
13 *France*, Rev. Ed., Frances Chambers
14 *Panama*, Eleanor DeSelms Langstaff
15 *Hungary*, Thomas Kabdebo
16 *USA*, Sheila R. Herstein and Naomi Robbins
17 *Greece*, Richard Clogg and Mary Jo Clogg
18 *New Zealand*, R. F. Grover
19 *Algeria*, Rev. Ed., Richard I. Lawless
20 *Sri Lanka*, Vijaya Samaraweera
21 *Belize*, Second Ed., Peggy Wright and Brian E. Coutts
23 *Luxembourg*, Carlo Hury and Jul Christophory
24 *Swaziland*, Rev. Ed., Balam Nyeko
25 *Kenya*, Robert L. Collison
26 *India*, Rev. Ed., Ian Derbyshire
27 *Turkey*, Merel Güçlü
28 *Cyprus*, Rev. Ed., P. M. Kitromilides and M. L. Evriviades
29 *Oman*, Rev. Ed., Frank A. Clements
30 *Italy*, Lucio Sponza and Diego Zancani
31 *Finland*, J. E. O. Screen
32 *Poland*, Rev. Ed., George Sanford and Adriana Gozdecka-Sanford
33 *Tunisia*, Allan M. Findlay, Anne M. Findlay and Richard I. Lawless
34 *Scotland*, Eric G. Grant
35 *China*, Peter Cheng
36 *Qatar*, P. T. H. Unwin
37 *Iceland*, John J. Horton
38 *Nepal*, John Whelpton
39 *Haiti*, Rev. Ed., Frances Chambers

40 *Sudan*, Rev. Ed., M. W. Daly
41 *Vatican City State*, Michael J. Walsh
42 *Iraq*, Second Ed., C. H. Bleaney
43 *United Arab Emirates*, Frank A. Clements
44 *Nicaragua*, Rev. Ed., Ralph Lee Woodward, Jr.
45 *Jamaica*, K. E. Ingram
46 *Australia*, Second Ed., I. Kepars
47 *Morocco*, Rev. Ed., Anne M. Findlay and Allan M. Findlay
48 *Mexico*, Rev. Ed., George Philip
49 *Bahrain*, P. T. H. Unwin
50 *The Yemens*, G. Rex Smith
51 *Zambia*, Anne M. Bliss and J. A. Rigg
52 *Puerto Rico*, Elena E. Cevallos
53 *Namibia*, Stanley Schoeman and Elna Schoeman
54 *Tanzania*, Colin Darch
55 *Jordan*, Ian J. Seccombe
56 *Kuwait*, Frank A. Clements
57 *Brazil*, Solena V. Bryant
58 *Israel*, Second Ed., C. H. Bleaney
59 *Romania*, Andrea Deletant and Dennis Deletant
60 *Spain*, Second Ed., Graham J. Shields
61 *Atlantic Ocean*, H. G. R. King
62 *Canada*, Ernest Ingles
63 *Cameroon*, Mark W. DeLancey and Peter J. Schraeder
64 *Malta*, John Richard Thackrah
65 *Thailand*, Michael Watts
66 *Austria*, Denys Salt with the assistance of Arthur Farrand Radley
67 *Norway*, Leland B. Sather
68 *Czechoslovakia*, David Short
69 *Irish Republic*, Michael Owen Shannon
70 *Pacific Basin and Oceania*, Gerald W. Fry and Rufino Mauricio
71 *Portugal*, P. T. H. Unwin
72 *West Germany*, Donald S. Detwiler and Ilse E. Detwiler
73 *Syria*, Ian J. Seccombe
74 *Trinidad and Tobago*, Frances Chambers
76 *Barbados*, Robert B. Potter and Graham M. S. Dann
77 *East Germany*, Ian Wallace
78 *Mozambique*, Colin Darch
79 *Libya*, Richard I. Lawless
80 *Sweden*, Leland B. Sather and Alan Swanson
81 *Iran*, Reza Navabpour
82 *Dominica*, Robert A. Myers
83 *Denmark*, Kenneth E. Miller
84 *Paraguay*, R. Andrew Nickson
85 *Indian Ocean*, Julia J. Gotthold with the assistance of Donald W. Gotthold
86 *Egypt*, Ragai N. Makar
87 *Gibraltar*, Graham J. Shields
88 *The Netherlands*, Peter King and Michael Wintle
89 *Bolivia*, Gertrude M. Yeager
90 *Papua New Guinea*, Fraiser McConnell
91 *The Gambia*, David P. Gamble
92 *Somalia*, Mark W. DeLancey, Sheila L. Elliott, December Green, Kenneth J. Menkhaus, Mohammad Haji Moqtar, Peter J. Schraeder
93 *Brunei*, Sylvia C. Engelen Krausse and Gerald H. Krausse
94 *Albania*, William B. Bland
95 *Singapore*, Stella R. Quah and Jon S. T. Quah
96 *Guyana*, Frances Chambers
97 *Chile*, Harold Blakemore
98 *El Salvador*, Ralph Lee Woodward, Jr.
99 *The Arctic*, H. G. R. King
100 *Nigeria*, Robert A. Myers
101 *Ecuador*, David Corkhill
102 *Uruguay*, Henry Finch with the assistance of Alicia Casas de Barrán
103 *Japan*, Frank Joseph Shulman
104 *Belgium*, R. C. Riley
105 *Macau*, Richard Louis Edmonds
106 *Philippines*, Jim Richardson
107 *Bulgaria*, Richard J. Crampton
108 *The Bahamas*, Paul G. Boultbee
109 *Peru*, John Robert Fisher
110 *Venezuela*, D. A. G. Waddell
111 *Dominican Republic*, Kai Schoenhals
112 *Colombia*, Robert H. Davis
113 *Taiwan*, Wei-chin Lee
114 *Switzerland*, Heinz K. Meier and Regula A. Meier
115 *Hong Kong*, Ian Scott

116 *Bhutan*, Ramesh C. Dogra
117 *Suriname*, Rosemarijn Hoefte
118 *Djibouti*, Peter J. Schraeder
119 *Grenada*, Kai Schoenhals
120 *Monaco*, Grace L. Hudson
121 *Guinea-Bissau*, Rosemary Galli
122 *Wales*, Gwilym Huws and D. Hywel E. Roberts
123 *Cape Verde*, Caroline S. Shaw
124 *Ghana*, Robert A. Myers
125 *Greenland*, Kenneth E. Miller
126 *Costa Rica*, Charles L. Stansifer
127 *Siberia*, David N. Collins
128 *Tibet*, John Pinfold
129 *Northern Ireland*, Michael Owen Shannon
130 *Argentina*, Alan Biggins
132 *Burma*, Patricia M. Herbert
133 *Laos*, Helen Cordell
134 *Montserrat*, Riva Berleant-Schiller
135 *Afghanistan*, Schuyler Jones
136 *Equatorial Guinea*, Randall Fegley
137 *Turks and Caicos Islands*, Paul G. Boultbee
138 *Virgin Islands*, Verna Penn Moll
139 *Honduras*, Pamela F. Howard-Reguindin
140 *Mauritius*, Pramila Ramgulam Bennett
141 *Mauritania*, Simonetta Calderini, Delia Cortese, James L. A. Webb, Jr.
142 *Timor*, Ian Rowland
143 *St. Vincent and the Grenadines*, Robert B. Potter
144 *Texas*, James Marten
145 *Burundi*, Morna Daniels
146 *Hawai'i*, Nancy J. Morris and Love Dean
147 *Vietnam*, David Marr and Kristine Alilunas-Rodgers
148 *Sierra Leone*, Margaret Binns and Tony Binns
149 *Gabon*, David Gardinier
150 *Botswana*, John A. Wiseman
151 *Angola*, Richard Black
152 *Central African Republic*, Pierre Kalck
153 *Seychelles*, George Bennett, with the collaboration of Pramila Ramgulam Bennett
154 *Rwanda*, Randall Fegley
155 *Berlin*, Ian Wallace
156 *Mongolia*, Judith Nordby
157 *Liberia*, D. Elwood Dunn
158 *Maldives*, Christopher H. B. Reynolds
159 *Liechtenstein*, Regula A. Meier
160 *England*, Alan Day
161 *The Baltic States*, Inese A. Smith and Marita V. Grunts
162 *Congo*, Randall Fegley
163 *Armenia*, Vrej Nersessian
164 *Niger*, Lynda F. Zamponi
165 *Madagascar*, Hilary Bradt
166 *Senegal*, Roy Dilley and Jerry Eades
167 *Andorra*, Barry Taylor
168 *Netherlands Antilles and Aruba*, Kai Schoenhals
169 *Burkina Faso*, Samuel Decalo
170 *Indonesia*, Sylvia C. Engelen Krausse and Gerald H. Krausse
171 *The Antarctic*, Janice Meadows, William Mills and H. G. R. King
172 *São Tomé and Príncipe*, Caroline S. Shaw
173 *Fiji*, G. E. Gorman and J. J. Mills
174 *St. Kitts-Nevis*, Verna Penn Moll
175 *Martinique*, Janet Crane
176 *Zaire*, Dawn Bastian Williams, Robert W. Lesh and Andrea L. Stamm
177 *Chad*, George Joffé and Valérie Day-Viaud
178 *Togo*, Samuel Decalo
179 *Ethiopia*, Stuart Munro-Hay and Richard Pankhurst
180 *Punjab*, Darshan Singh Tatla and Ian Talbot
181 *Eritrea*, Randall Fegley
182 *Antigua and Barbuda*, Riva Berleant-Schiller and Susan Lowes with Milton Benjamin
183 *Alaska*, Marvin W. Falk

Contents

Introduction

Alaska is the 49th state of the union; like the 50th, Hawaii, it shares no common borders with the 'lower 48'. Its geography, climate, history and economic development set it apart. It has many similarities with Northern and Western Canada, but it looks to Washington, DC and Seattle for those things that Canadians may find in Ottawa or Toronto. It is the only region of North America to have had a colonial era under Russia; elsewhere other European powers dominated, such as England, France, Spain or Holland. Alaska is also a major tourist destination. All of this has helped shape publications about Alaska.

Geography

Alaska is the size of a subcontinent, situated at the extreme Northwest of North America between Canada and the former Soviet Union. With 586,412 square miles, Alaska has almost one-fifth of the total area of the rest of the states put together. There are 33,904 miles of tidal shoreline, more that the rest of the United States combined. Alaska's Little Diomede Island in the Bering Strait is less than three miles from Big Diomede, which is Russian territory. The greatest distance from east to west is 2,200 miles and from north to south, 1,200 miles.

The mountains of Alaska continue the Rocky Mountain and Pacific coastal ranges and include seventeen of the twenty highest peaks in the United States. To the north is the Brooks Range, forming a continental divide between waters flowing toward the Arctic Ocean and waters flowing west into the Bering Sea. It is about 600 miles long, and its highest point is 9,239 feet, with most peaks between 3,000 and 5,000 feet. Despite being the highest mountain range north of the Arctic Circle, there is little glaciation. Between the Brooks Range and the Alaska Range to the south are several lower ranges and foothills. The Alaska Range forms an arc about 600 miles long from

Canada to the Aleutian Range. It is rugged with numerous glaciers, and includes Mt. McKinley, at 20,320 feet the highest mountain in North America. The Aleutian range, starting on the Alaska Peninsula, contains over seventy volcanoes. It is about 1,500 miles long and is mostly submerged, forming the Aleutian Island chain. South of the Alaska Range are the Talkeetnas and the Wrangell Mountains (each covering an area of about 100 by 70 miles). Most of the Wrangells are covered with a large ice cap. The Kenai mountains cover much of the Kenai Peninsula and average between 2,000 and 4,000 feet above sea level. The Chugach mountains are to the east and north, averaging between 7,000 and 8,000 feet. To the south, the St. Elias chain (200 by 100 miles) runs along the coast through the Southeast region of Alaska. This range contains some of the world's largest glaciers and some of the highest mountains in North America: Mt. Logan (in Canada), 19,850 ft.; Mt. St. Elias, 18,008 ft.; and numerous other peaks higher than any other mountains in the United States, outside Alaska.

Alaska has more than three million lakes, 94 of which are larger than 10 square miles in surface area. The largest of these are Lake Iliamna (315 square miles) and Naknek (242 square miles). In a land with very few roads and highways, navigable rivers are used extensively to move bulk freight and fuel during the ice-free months. The largest and the longest river in Alaska is the Yukon, which originates in Canada and flows 1,875 miles into the Bering Sea (1,400 of this distance is in Alaska). Five of the ten largest rivers in Alaska are tributaries to the Yukon. They are: the Porcupine (555 miles), the Koyukuk (554 miles), the Tanana (314 miles), the Innoko (463 miles), and Birch Creek (312 miles). The 540-mile-long Kuskokwim River parallels the Yukon, emptying into the Bering Sea in western Alaska. The remainder of the ten longest rivers are the Colville (428 miles), emptying into the Arctic Ocean; the Noatak (396 miles), emptying into Kotzebue Sound; and the Kobuk (347 miles), which also has its mouth in the Kotzebue area.

Alaska has five distinct climatic zones: Temperate Oceanic, Subtemperate, Maritime Arctic, Interior Continental, and High Arctic or Polar. It ranges from semi-arid arctic landscapes with average annual temperatures well below freezing and annual precipitation of less than five inches, to a moderate coastal rain forest climate with a mean annual temperature of 47 degrees and over 200 inches of precipitation. The record high is 100 degrees Fahrenheit set in the Interior in 1915, and the record low is −80 degrees set in 1971 on the North Slope. The climate is controlled by a number of factors which include the northerly latitude, mountains which divide one climatic zone from another and the Japanese current which brings warm water northwards.

Permafrost, or permanently frozen subsoil, covers much of Interior and almost all of Arctic Alaska. In fact, about 85 per cent of the entire state is in the arctic circumpolar permafrost zone. Permafrost can reach depths of several thousand feet, and even when the surface few feet melt, it keeps water from passing through to the sub-strata all year round. By limiting the absorption of precipitation, it keeps a great deal of water at the surface even in arid regions, supporting tundra and taiga ecosystems and numerous lakes. Permafrost does not allow normal construction and development techniques. Buildings placed on permafrost with an inadequate thermal shield will melt the permafrost and the structure will begin to sink. In addition, many natural processes slow down or stop, such as the decomposition of human wastes. Disturbance of the insulating surface vegetation on tundra with its underlying permafrost can lead to rapid erosion as the exposed area melts.

Most of the US volcanoes are in Alaska. Over half of the seventy volcanoes of the Aleutian chain have been active in historic times. There are volcanoes elsewhere too, such as on the Alaska Peninsula and in the Wrangell Mountains. One of the largest eruptions ever recorded was on the Alaska Peninsula in 1912. It spread ash up to 700 feet deep over an extensive area and created what is known as the Valley of Ten Thousand Smokes, now a national monument.

Alaska has the world's third greatest concentration of glaciation, following the Antarctic and Greenland. Glaciers cover more than 15,000 square miles. One, the Malaspina Glacier, covers an area larger than the state of Rhode Island. In all, ice-fields and glaciers together cover 28,800 square miles, almost 5 per cent of Alaska's surface area. Most of the glaciation is in areas of heavy snowfall, near the coast or in regions where moisture-laden coastal winds cross high mountains, primarily in Southeastern and Southcentral Alaska in the Saint Elias, Chugach and Kenai mountains.

Alaska regions

The Southeast region (or Panhandle) is a narrow strip, 25 to 50 miles wide, running about 500 miles along the coast, and sharing a common border with the Canadian province of British Columbia and the Yukon Territory. Average precipitation varies from 80 to 100 inches annually. The Alexander Archipelago, which hugs the coast, contains about 11,000 islands, rocks, and reefs. Of this number, about 1,000 are named islands. Fishing and timber are supplemented by tourism as the chief industries. It is a land with numerous fjords, glaciers, islands and forest – the Tongass National Forest covers 16 million acres – and its picturesque scenery has drawn visitors and cruise ships for many generations. In addition to scheduled and charter air service, the area is served by the Alaska Marine Highway, a system of state-owned ferries. The present state capital, Juneau, is located in this region. Other major settlements include Ketchikan, Sitka, Wrangell, and Petersburg. There are about 25 smaller communities.

The Southcentral region is the population centre of the state. Alaska's largest city, Anchorage, is the state's primary business and transportation centre; over half of all state and federal civilian employees active in Alaska are also based there. Valdez is the terminus of the Trans-Alaska Pipeline. The Matanuska Valley just north of Anchorage was the location of a major agricultural resettlement programme in the 1930s and it remains the largest dairy and truck farming region in the state. Kodiak and Afognak islands are included in this region; the centre of early Russian-American settlement, these islands remain a major fishing centre. The Kenai Peninsula and Prince William Sound are very scenic. Precipitation in this area is about 17 inches, but snowfall is much heavier at higher elevations and the average annual precipitation can be as high as 80 inches along some coastal areas.

Both the Alaska Peninsula and the Aleutian Chain are sparsely populated. The Aleutians are generally treeless and subject to high winds and fog, but they are situated in the midst of one of the world's richest fisheries, where the nutrients and warm water of the Japanese Current meet the shallow and productive Bering Sea. Some sheep and cattle are raised on a few islands. The region is cool in the summer and annual precipitation is usually between 28 and 70 inches, depending on location. Bristol Bay, on the north side of the Alaska Peninsula, has one of the world's most productive salmon fisheries. It is a transition area between the Alaska Peninsula, the Interior and Western Alaska.

Western Alaska includes the Kuskokwim and Yukon delta area and extends to about 200 miles inland. It starts above Bristol Bay to the south and includes the Seward Peninsula to the north. Most of the area is tundra, covered by many lakes and few trees. The major centres are Nome on the Seward Peninsula and Bethel on the Kuskokwim River. There is reindeer herding on Seward Peninsula, but the primary economic activities are commercial fishing and subsistence hunting and fishing.

Interior Alaska enjoys a continental climate. Much of it is semi-arid with 11 inches of annual precipitation in Fairbanks, the largest city. Winters are cold with temperature dropping to as low as −72 degrees Fahrenheit, but it is also the warmest part of Alaska during the summer. The region has both boreal forests below 2,000 ft (taiga) and tundra environments. Most of the state's gold placer mining activity is in this region. The state's largest coal-mining facility is in Healy. Fairbanks serves as the regional distribution hub and is the location of the University of Alaska's research campus. There is a small amount of farming near Fairbanks. A major grain-farming effort at Delta has met with very limited success because of the lack of a viable market, and interest in the agricultural potential of areas near Nenana and Fort Yukon have yet to bear fruit.

On the Arctic Slope, the average temperature reaches only 30 and 40 degrees during the short summer. The region starts in the south with the northern foothills of the Brooks Range and proceeds north across the arctic coastal plain. Prudhoe Bay oil and gas fields are here, as are a number of other fields currently under development or exploration. The administrative centre for the region is Barrow, the northernmost town in the United States. Transportation and trade in the Southwestern Arctic is based in Kotzebue. A substantial part of the state's petroleum investment is in the North Slope production facilities and the pipeline, which provides a substantial tax base for the North Slope Borough.

There are several major islands in the Bering Sea north of the Aleutians. The Pribilof Islands have rookeries, where the world's largest fur-seal herd gathers each year. To the Northeast is Nunivak Island where a thriving musk-ox herd is the basis for the native quiviut handicraft industry (the soft underfur of the musk-ox is used for weaving warm garments). Saint Lawrence Island is directly south of the Bering Strait and Little Diomede is situated in the strait itself.

Natural resources

Alaska has traditionally been seen as a vast storehouse of natural resources both renewable (such as timber) and non-renewable (such as minerals). Alaska is also seen as a last refuge for wilderness and for subsistence-based village life. Conflicting land-use values have created a contentious political environment which is shaping resource policy in Alaska by both national and state government.

Where gold was once Alaska's primary mineral revenue source, it is now oil; the total Alaska reserves are unknown and exploration is continuing. Oil was first exploited commercially near Cordova at Katalla in 1902. The National Petroleum Preserve Number Four was created in 1923 covering 37,000 square miles, but despite extensive exploration, especially in the 1940s and 1950s, nothing has ever really come of it. Oil was discovered in 1957 on the Kenai Peninsula, where the Swanson and other fields were developed. In 1968, the Prudhoe Bay discovery was made. It has revolutionized Alaskan society directly and indirectly through the construction of the 800-mile Trans-Alaska Pipeline. It has acted as a catalyst for many legal, economic and social changes such as those brought by the Native Claims Settlement Act. In addition, it has proved the major revenue source for the state. However, developers have not always had free reign. Efforts to drill exploratory wells in the Arctic National Wildlife Refuge – not far from the Prudhoe Bay oil fields, already in production – have been blocked in the US Congress for more than a decade.

Most commercial logging takes place in the almost six million acres of commercial stands in the Southeast Region with its coastal rain forest. In contrast, the Interior forest of about 106 million acres with its slower rate of tree growth has been exploited only by small local sawmills. Western hemlock and Sitka spruce are the two leading species of value for harvesting. There is substantial Japanese investment in Alaska's timber industry.

Alaska's commercial fish production is the highest in value of all the states. From the 1880s up to the early 20th century, Alaska had the world's largest salmon fishery and there was extensive whaling before the First World War. In 1990, Alaska's commercial catch was valued at $1.5 billion. It has six of the top ten US ports judged by value of fish landed (Dutch Harbor, Kodiak, Petersburg, Kenai, Ketchikan and Cordova). In addition to the US fishing fleet, large fleets have been operated in these waters by Japan and the former Soviet Union, and smaller fleets are operated by Taiwan, South Korea and Poland. Since the adoption of the 200-mile limit, foreign fishing within these boundaries is controlled by the North Pacific Fisheries Council and the US Department of State. Foreign vessels began being phased out in 1988. Major commercial species include salmon, herring, pollack, halibut, king crab, tanner crab, Dungeness crab, and shrimp.

On land, Alaska has a reputation for massive amounts of fish and wildlife. For the most part, this is an illusion: the total wild biomass (total mass of all living creatures added together) is less than half that of Texas, a much smaller and more heavily developed area. There is a great deal of migration and animal species are sometimes heavily concentrated, giving the appearance of great abundance. This is the case with massive salmon runs (salmon actually do most of their growing while at sea) or enormous herds of caribou. At other times game may be heavily concentrated due to food sources, such as bear along a salmon stream.

There are a number of large land animals to be found in Alaska. There are thirteen major caribou herds, many of which range over hundreds of miles. Of these the Porcupine and Fortymile caribou herds are shared with Canada. Moose exist from the Panhandle to the Colville River in the north. Caribou and moose are the two largest sources of wild meat for Alaskans. Other large herbivorous animals thrive in more limited geographical areas. These include the bison transplanted to Alaska in the 1920s (four major herds at Delta Junction, McCarthy, Healy and the Copper River drainage); Sitka blacktail deer (coastal areas as far north as Kodiak and Afognak islands); elk (transplanted in 1928 to Raspberry and Afognak islands); musk-ox (re-introduced into Alaska at Nunivak and Barter islands); Dall sheep and mountain goat.

The fur bearers have provided the basis for Alaska's oldest traditional industry. They include beaver, coyote, arctic fox, red fox, lynx, bear, wolf, marmot, marten, mink, muskrat, land (river) otter and sea otter. Non-commercial species include arctic hare, snowshoe hare, a variety of squirrels and porcupine.

Marine mammals include whales, sea lions, seals (harbour, ringed, ribbon, bearded and elephant) and porpoises.

There are at least 395 species of birds in Alaska, the most numerous being waterfowl. Alaska serves as a major breeding ground for millions of ducks and geese. Some travel great distances, such as the arctic tern, which travel from the Antarctic every year. Cranes and swans also migrate. The world's heaviest concentration of bald eagles occurs in Southeast Alaska, but perhaps the most typical of the year-round species is the raven, used as an important symbol for a variety of native traditions.

Most commercial fish species are also valued as sport fish. The most famous is the king salmon; the record size is 91 pounds. Halibut can be as large as 400 pounds. Other species includes the Arctic char, Arctic grayling, burbot, dolly varden, kokanee, ling cod, northern pike, rockfish, sheefish, salmon (silver, red, pink, chum), trout (steel head, brook, cut-throat, lake, rainbow) and white fish.

Population

At the time when the Russians first made contact with Alaska's native peoples, there were an estimated 60,000 Eskimo, Aleuts and Indians living in Alaska. One widely accepted theory holds that all of the aboriginal people of North America came from Asia, across the

Bering Land Bridge which at one time united Alaska and Northeast Asia. They then migrated southward across North and South America and developed highly differentiated cultures.

Eskimos inhabited the area from the Arctic down the coast to south of Prince William Sound, including Kodiak. At the time of contact, there were more than 20 groupings with a total population of about 30,000 people. There are three major language groups: Inupiaq in the north, Siberian and Central Yup'ik in western Alaska and Sugpiaq to the south. Most lived by the coast and hunted sea mammals, but there were extensive inland groups as well, primarily caribou hunters. Their culture and technology were highly adapted to the environment. Much of this technology was later adopted by others, such as explorers coming into the region. Eskimo populations continue to occupy most of their original territory and a number have become urban dwellers as well.

Aleuts populated a portion of the Alaska Peninsula and the Aleutian Island chain. It is difficult to estimate the number of pre-contact Aleuts because of profound changes wrought by early contact with fur merchants from Siberia, who began using Aleut hunters soon after the Second Bering Expedition of 1741. Initial exploitation was severe and there was a substantial drop in the population which accompanied the unintended introduction of foreign diseases. Through a system of hostage holding, hunters were compelled to accompany Russian merchants great distances from their homes, and in time they became closely allied with the Russians.

The Athabascans mostly occupied the interior of Alaska, but some also lived on the coast, in the Cook Inlet region. In order to follow the shifting game concentrations, they were more nomadic than other coastal peoples. There are many Athabascans in Canada too. The Athabascan language is very closely related to the Navajo of the Southwestern United States. There are at present approximately 7,000 Athabascans in Alaska.

The largest population of Southeast Indians are the Tlingits. Numbering about 12,000, they dominated commerce between coastal areas and the Indians of the nearby Canadian interior. They have a totem culture with a highly developed clan structure.

About a thousand Tsmishians live on Annette Island. They migrated there from British Columbia under the leadership of Anglican Father William Duncan, in 1887. More than 700 Haidas live in Alaska. They emigrated from farther south in the 1700s, primarily to the southern part of Prince of Wales Island. They share many elements of culture with other tribes of the Pacific Northwest Coast.

Although Alaska has one of the smallest populations in the US, it has been growing very rapidly since the Second World War. The first census was conducted in 1880, counting a population of 33,426. The census of 1890 showed 32,052; 1900 – 63,592; 1910 – 64,356; 1920 – 55,036; 1929 – 59,278; 1939 – 72,524; 1950 – 128,643; 1960 – 226,167; 1970 – 302,583; 1980 – 401,851; and 1990 – 550,043. Half of the state's population lives in Anchorage with a population of 226,338.

The land

There has been very little land in private ownership in Alaska, but this situation is changing rapidly. Even today, only about 160,000 acres have been cleared or built on, including all cities, farms, mines and petroleum development. In order to provide an economic base for the new state, the Statehood Act granting statehood in 1959 allowed Alaska to select a total of 103 million acres for its own. The selection and transfer has never been completed, as the Department of Interior refused to allow that to happen before withdrawals for study of 'National Interest Land' and native withdrawals. In 1972, a suit resulted in the transfer of 41 million acres. In 1978, the Secretary of Interior withdrew about 114 million acres from most public use and President Jimmy Carter designated 56 million acres as National Monuments under the 1906 Antiquities Act. These withdrawals were modified by the Alaska National Interest Lands Conservation Act of 1980 which, in total, affected 131 million acres of land in Alaska.

The Alaska Native Claims Settlement Act was passed by the federal government in 1971 as compensation for loss of lands historically occupied by natives and to resolve various pending legal questions regarding the ownership of Alaska's lands. Native regional corporations were formed to administer the settlement assets which were $900 million and 44 million acres of land. There are twelve regional corporations within Alaska and one in Seattle for natives resident outside Alaska. The settlement applies only to those living at the time of the settlement. Subsequent congressional amendments allow corporations to provide shares to those born later, if they choose to do so. Shares in native corporations and the conveyed lands could not be sold for a period of 20 years after passage of the legislation, and this provision too has been extended. Native corporations play an active role in corporate enterprise within the state, engaging in such business as banking, fishing fleets, hotels, geological exploration companies, regional airlines, and construction firms. A number of village corporations were also eligible for land selections and function in much the same way as the regional corporations. The corporations must balance the needs of their region and its development against the need to preserve the corporate assets and make a profit.

The Alaska native regional corporations, and the areas that they serve are as follows: Ahtna Incorporated, the Copper River Basin; Aleut Corporation, the Aleutian Islands; Arctic Slope Regional Corporation, Arctic Alaska; NANA Regional Corporation, the Kotzebue area; Bering Straits Native Corporation, the Seward Peninsula; Bristol Bay Native Corporation, the Bristol Bay area; Calista Corporation, Yukon-Kuskokwim Delta; Chugach Natives Incorporation, Prince William Sound; Cook Inlet Region, Inc., Cook Inlet region; Doyon Limited, Interior Alaska; Koniag, Kodiak region; Sealaska Corporation, Southeast Alaska; and the 13th Regional Corporation, natives living outside Alaska.

The Alaska road network is small. There is a total of 6,048 miles of roads, forest roads and highways maintained by the state, local government, the military and National Parks. The state has one railroad, the Alaska Railroad, which runs 470 miles from Seward and Whittier through Anchorage to Fairbanks. The White Pass and Yukon Route is only partially in Alaska, running between Skagway, Alaska, and Whitehorse, Yukon Territory. Built at the turn of the century, it has lost its mining-related freight business and now serves the tourist industry. Since the only means of reaching much of the state is by air, Alaska has six times as many pilots as the per capita national average.

Communications

Alaska is served by a variety of communication media. Newspaper coverage is on a regional basis. Anchorage is served by the state's largest daily paper, the *Anchorage Daily News*. Other major daily newspapers include the *Fairbanks Daily News-Miner*, the *Juneau Empire*, the *Ketchikan Daily News*, the *Kodiak Daily Mirror*, the *Peninsula Clarion* from the Kenai Peninsula, and the *Daily Sitka Sentinel*. There are a number of once- and twice-weekly papers. Regional twice-weeklies and bi-weeklies include *The Bering Straights* in Nome, the *Cheechako News* in Kenai, the *Chugach-Eagle River Star*, the *Copper Valley Views*, *Cordova Times*, *The Delta Paper* in Delta Junction, *Homer News*, *Kodiak Times* in Kodiak, *Kusko Courier* in McGrath, the *Lynn Canal News* from Haines, the *Mukluk News* in Tok, the *Nome Nugget*, *The Frontiersman* in Palmer, the *Petersburg Pilot*, the *Seward Phoenix Log*, the *Southeastern Log* from Ketchikan, the *Valdez Vanguard*, the *Valley Sun* from Wasilla, and the *Wrangell Sentinel*. Special-interest periodicals include the *Alaska Fisherman's Journal* (monthly), *Alaska Woman*, *Alaska Geographic* (quarterly), and *Alaska Magazine*. There are also a number of hobby and industry publications. The largest of these is *Alaska Journal of Commerce*. Alaska has no law school of its own, but legal questions are debated in the *U.C.L.A.–Alaska Law Review* twice yearly.

The state depends on modern communication systems to tie its scattered population together. Satellite communication along with traditional radio contacts keep remote areas in touch with medical centres and provide information and entertainment. There are public and commercial television stations in Anchorage, Fairbanks, Juneau, Sitka, and Bethel. These are frequently extended in coverage through 'translators' in nearby smaller communities. Cable television has made its appearance in the larger communities and there are over sixty commercial and public radio stations throughout the state. After an initial trial period, the state's Television Demonstration Project is being expanded commercially to bring simultaneous broadcasts to the state via satellite and to bring television to remote locations through satellites, with receiving dishes located in villages.

Education

Until very recently, Alaskan education in general has been struggling with inadequate resources with which to address the needs of a widely scattered population. During the Russian-American era, there were several company schools in addition to those established by the Orthodox Church. A number of them provided at least some instruction in native languages. The Church schools continued on a diminished scale well after the sale in 1867. Before and during the gold-rush years other churches combined with the Federal government to provide an expanding educational system and the Presbyterian missionary, Sheldon Jackson, became the US Commissioner of Education for Alaska. In later years the Bureau of Indian Affairs established schools in the larger native communities with boarding schools to accommodate those from the smaller villages. Through a landmark legal settlement known as the Molly Hooch case, the state is required to provide education in localities where as few as sixteen students live, so that boarding schools became a thing of the past, except for Mt. Edgecumbe near Sitka, which is maintained as an alternative to village education. All B.I.A. (Bureau of Indian Affairs) schools have been transferred to the state.

Alaskans aged from 7 to 16 are guaranteed free education by the state constitution. Students can enrol in a correspondence school course, either through a local school district or through the state's centralized correspondence study programme. The State Board of

Education sets state-wide policy and locally there are 52 school districts with elected school boards for the approximately 550 public schools in the state. Larger urban areas such as Anchorage and Fairbanks have school districts very much like those found elsewhere. Rural education, however, is organized according to Rural Education Attendance Areas. Many of these are extremely large: the North Slope Borough is larger than the entire state of Minnesota, but has fewer than 1,100 pupils in all grades of school; the Yukon Flats area is also bigger than many states but has a total of 301 students.

The University of Alaska was founded as the Alaska Agricultural College and School of Mines in 1917. It admitted its first students in 1922, and it changed its name to the University of Alaska in 1935. The 1960s and 1970s saw the move away from a central campus located in Fairbanks to a state-wide system of higher education. There are at present three major units based at Fairbanks, Anchorage and Juneau, with smaller local campuses and learning centres administered through them, except for a semi-autonomous community college campus at Valdez. The research emphasis of the University is on the problems and phenomena of the Arctic and sub-Arctic. It maintains close communication with other such research efforts in Canada, Greenland, Iceland, the United Kingdom, Scandinavia and Siberia. Areas of special interest include geophysics, marine science, mineral industries, biological science, resource management and agriculture. There are two private institutions of higher learning currently active in the state: Alaska Pacific University in Anchorage and Sheldon Jackson Junior College in Sitka.

Alaska is rich in archaeological sites, a number of which are now on the National Register of Historic Places. The oldest monuments of the historical period include Russian buildings in Kodiak, Sitka and scattered localities served by the Orthodox Church. Other historic monuments include the Aleutian battlefields from the Second World War, left largely as they were. There are a number of old mining operations still to be seen such as the Independence Mine at the state historical park in Hatcher Pass, Skagway and the Chilkoot Trail areas preserve the flavour of the Gold Rush as do a number of structures of that era in towns from Ketchikan to Fairbanks. Large parts of Fort Egbert at Eagle have been restored by the federal government and National Trust for Historic Preservation. The *Sternwheeler Nenana*, the largest wooden boat of its kind is the centrepiece of a municipal park, Alaskaland, containing a number of structures moved there from old Fairbanks. A number of roadhouses and similar buildings from throughout Alaska are now on the National Register of Historic Places.

Recreation

Following the passage of the 1980 Alaska National Interest Lands Act, a total of 51,209,354 acres were placed under the National Park Service administration. In addition, a total of 76,058,785 acres of National Wildlife Refuge land are under the administration of the US Fish and Wildlife Service, many of the refuges created before the 1980 law. The State of Alaska administers five state parks, fifty highway waysides, five recreation areas, four historic sites, two trail systems and one wilderness park. The Bureau of Land Management maintains the White Mountain National Recreation Area and the Steese National Conservation area. There are twenty-six National Wild and Scenic Rivers.

Alaska's best-known state sport is dog mushing. The most famous event is the annual Iditarod Trail Sled Dog Race which commemorates the emergency delivery of diphtheria serum to Nome during the 1925 epidemic. The race was promoted by Joe Redington, Sr., of Knik and first run in 1973. The route covers about 1,200 miles from Anchorage to Nome and has taken from just under 11 days to 20 days for the winning times. It sometimes takes more than an additional week before all finishers have completed the course. There are other major and minor mushing events that are closely followed in Alaska, including the Yukon Quest between Fairbanks and Whitehorse in the Yukon Territory, Canada, the Anchorage Fur Rendezvous, and the North American Championship Sled Dog Races in Fairbanks. There are downhill ski facilities near Juneau, Anchorage and Fairbanks. Cross-country ski racing is growing in popularity. Snow machines are popular as recreational as well as utility vehicles.

Government

As the highest official in an imperial chartered company, Russian-American Company managers took on many government duties. Following the merchant Baranov's retirement as Chief Manager, a series of Russian naval officers were sent to head the company in Alaska. The managers of the Russian-American Company were: Alexander Andreevich Baranov (1790-1818); Leontii Andreanovich Hagemeister (1818); Semen Ivanovich Yanovskii (1818-20); Matvei Ivanovich Muraviev (1820-25); Peter Egorovich Chistiakov (1825-30); Baron Ferdinand P. von Wrangell (1830-35); Ivan Antonovich Kupreianov (1835-40); Adolph Karlovich Etholen (1840-45); Michael Dmitrievich Tebenkov (1845-50); Nikolai Yakovlevich Rosenberg (1850-53); Alexander Ilich Rudakov (1853-54); Stepan Vasilievich

Voevodskii (1854-59); Ivan Vasilievich Furuhjelm (1859-63); and Prince Dmitrii Maksutov (1863-67).

During the years between Alaska's purchase and territorial status under the Organic Act of 1884, Alaska was governed by a series of military and custom officials. After 1884, the following were presidentially appointed territorial governors: John Kinkead (1884-85); Alfred P. Swineford (1885-89); Lyman E. Knapp (1889-93); James Sheakley (1893-97); John G. Brady (1897-1906); Wilford B. Hoggat (1906-9); Walter E. Clark (1909-13); John F. Strong (1913-18); Thomas Riggs, Jr. (1918-21); Scott C. Bone (1921-25); George A. Parks (1925-33); John W. Troy (1933-39); Ernest Gruening (1939-53); B. Frank Heintzelman (1953-57); and Mike Stepovich (1957-58).

The following governors were elected following statehood: William A. Egan (1959-66); Walter J. Hickel (1966-69); Keith H. Miller (succeeded Hickel, 1969-70); William A. Egan (1970-74); Jay S. Hammond (1974-82); Bill Sheffield (1982-86); Steve Cowper (1986-90); Walter J. Hickel (1990-94); and Tony Knowles (1994-).

The following were non-voting delegates to Congress before statehood: Frank H. Waskey (1906-7); Thomas Cale (1907-9); James Wickersham (1909-17); Charles A. Sulzer (1917 – contested election); James Wickersham (1918 – seated as delegate); Charles A. Sulzer (1919 – died before taking office); George Grigsby (1919 – seated as a delegate in a special election); James Wickersham (1921 – seated as delegate, having contested election of Grigsby); Dan A. Sutherland (1921-30); James Wickersham (1931-33); Anthony J. Dimond (1933-44); and E. L. Bartlett (1944-58).

The following have been US senators since statehood: E. L. Bartlett (1959-68); Ernest Gruening (1959-68); Mike Gravel (1968-80); Ted Stevens (1968-); and Frank Murkowski (1980-).

The following were the members of the US House of Representatives for Alaska: Ralph Rivers (1959-66); Howard Pollock (1966-70); Nicholas Begich (1970-72); and Don Young (1973-).

The Alaska constitution provides for a bicameral legislature with 20 senators and 40 representatives. The constitution differs from those of other states most significantly in granting more power to the governor, who retains line-item veto authority over appropriations. Regional and local government is provided by boroughs and municipalities; there are no counties. Boroughs can be quite large; some are bigger than many states in the 'Lower 48'. Areas outside of boroughs are part of the 'unorganized borough' for which the state legislature acts as borough assembly.

At the time when the lease sale for Prudhoe Bay occurred, Alaska was very nearly bankrupt because of its inadequate tax base. By the time the Trans-Alaska Pipeline began production, the state had a solid income. However, the fear remained that as the Prudhoe fields began to decline there would not be enough money to continue essential state services. In 1976, voters approved a constitutional amendment which established the Alaska Permanent Fund. It provides that: 'At least 25 percent of all mineral lease rentals, royalties, royalty sale proceeds, Federal mineral revenue sharing payments, and bonuses received by the state shall be placed in a Permanent Fund. . .'. The Alaska Permanent Fund Corporation was established in 1980 to manage the fund. The legislature has channelled additional revenues into the Fund and the total went over twelve billion dollars in 1991. Dividends on earned interest were to be paid to Alaskans based on length of residency. Tied up for several years in court battles, this plan was finally ruled unconstitutional by the US Supreme Court in 1982. A back-up plan, paying $1,000 to all with at least six months' residency was put into effect for 1982, and since then annual dividends to Alaska residents have fluctuated, depending on the earnings of the fund and the number of residents submitting applications.

The state constitution provides for local government through boroughs. They exercise powers of taxation and education on an area-wide basis. In addition, first- and second-class boroughs must exercise planning and zoning functions. Other services such as police protection and utilities may be provided either area-wide or in smaller areas such as service districts. Unified municipalities are one of the many options for local government. The borough and all incorporated cities within it are on a one-man-one-vote principle for the election of assemblies. School boards are elected at large. A variety of local forms of government are possible, including a directly elected mayor; a mayor elected by and from the assembly or council; or a city manager form in which the mayor is not actively engaged in administration. The following is a list of organized boroughs, with the size in square miles and an indication of the cities within the borough: Municipality of Anchorage, 1,884 square miles (Anchorage, Girdwood, Glen Alps); Bristol Bay, 1,200 square miles; Fairbanks North Star, 7,500 square miles (Fairbanks, North Pole); Haines, 2,620 square miles; Juneau City and Borough, 3,100 square miles; Kenai Peninsula, 14,697 square miles (Kenai, Homer, Seldovia, Seward, Soldotna, Kachemak); Ketchikan Gateway, 1,250 square miles (Ketchikan, Saxman); Kodiak Island, 5,400 square miles (Akhiok, Kodiak, Larsen Bay, Old Harbor, Ouzinkie, Port Lions); Matanuska-Susitna, 20,544 square miles (Palmer, Wasilla); North Slope, 88,281 square miles (Anaktuvuk Pass, Barrow, Kaktovik, Point Hope,

Wainwright); Sitka City and Borough, 2,900 square miles. The North Slope Borough is the world's largest municipal government in terms of area, covering an area larger than the state of Utah.

History

The outside world first learned of Alaska following the 1741 voyage of exploration led by Vitus Bering, a Dane in the service of Russia. Earlier voyages such as those by Semen Dezhnev in 1648 or Mikhail Gvodzev in 1730 had remained unknown in Europe and others such as Bering's own 1728 voyage through Bering Strait had not sighted the Alaskan mainland because of fog. Exploitation of the rich furs available in the Aleutians began almost immediately, and by 1799 the Russian-American Company began operating as a monopoly. It also served as the government in Alaska. Firmly established by its colourful first governor, Alexander Baranov (1790-1818), it made excellent profits for a time, based on the China fur trade. Mineral deposits were found, but only minimally exploited. For a variety of reasons, trade eventually became unprofitable and Russian America was sold to the United States in 1867. The Russian era had established the Russian Orthodox Church in much of Alaska, had led to the discovery and mapping of the coast by the Russians and others such as Captain James Cook, and had founded a number of permanent settlements. Extensive scientific observations were made, and the rich written heritage which chronicles this era is now becoming available to English-speakers through several extensive translation projects. The Russians had developed education and had established written forms for a number of native languages based upon the Cyrillic alphabet.

The actual exploration and communication of results was a multinational affair. Many foreign nationals were in the Russian service, such as Vitus Bering himself – a Dane. Others included the Englishman Joseph Billings, who commanded a major expedition and Georg Steller, a young German scientist. Other nationals sailing under their own flags included James Cook and George Vancouver from Great Britain; Jean François de La Perouse from France; American traders like Joseph Mears from the United States; and Spanish explorers such as Alejandro Malaspina and Juan Francisco de la Bodega y Quadra. Combining this with the efforts of eminent Russian explorers such as Alexander Kashevarov and Lieutenant Lavrentii Zagoskin, the map of Alaska and the Far North Pacific became clear within a relatively short period.

American activity in the newly acquired land did not immediately fill the void left by the departure of the Russian-American Company with its many governmental and economic activities. Most of the skilled Russian population left following the sale. Sealing in the Pribilof Islands and whaling brought ships north, but, except for trading activity, interaction with Alaskans was limited. Salmon brought fishermen and commercial canneries were established, beginning in 1878, but most of the cannery crews were brought in and relatively few native Alaskans found employment in the industry. A series of gold discoveries in and near Alaska brought prospectors and miners. This movement flourished from the 1880s until the First World War. Juneau, Nome and Fairbanks were all established as gold-mining centres as well as many other towns long since abandoned and nearly forgotten. Alaska passed from direct rule by the army, navy and customs service to a limited form of civil government with the Organic Act of 1884 and Alaska's first governor was appointed by the President of the United States.

In many ways, the Klondike Gold Rush of 1897-1900 in neighbouring Canada was a watershed. The small number of resident miners in the north were joined by others, many rank amateurs. Some went on to later strikes in Alaska. With them came much publicity in American papers, with all the attendant romance of adventure. There was a crying need for more supplies, a greater military presence and better civil government – especially an expanded judiciary.

In 1900, the Civil Code for Alaska was passed. In 1906, Alaska was allowed to elect a non-voting delegate to Congress. The capital was moved to Juneau from Sitka and in 1912 a Second Organic Act established Alaska as a territory, creating its first legislature. In 1922, President Warren Harding came to drive the last spike in the Alaska Railroad, establishing the first modern alternative to river and trail travel to the interior. The development of a pioneer air service soon followed. During the Depression, development was materially aided by a number of new settlers brought to the Matanuska Valley by the United States government to farm in 1936.

The Second World War provided another watershed in Alaska's history. Fighting took place in the Aleutians. The United States and Canada reacted to what might have become a major new front by establishing a road to Alaska in 1942 known as the Alcan Highway, and other supply measures such as the Canol project to tap Canadian crude oil at Norman Wells. New military bases and the ferrying of lend-lease aid to the Soviet Union brought renewed activity and increased population. This activity continued after the war as radar stations and other installations were maintained against the new threat from the Soviet Union. The increased population and the growing political maturity of the Territory led to a major statehood drive. This was finally realized in 1959 when Alaska became the 49th state.

A number of natural disasters troubled the new state, the greatest of which were the 1964 earthquake and the 1967 Fairbanks flood. The 1964 Good Friday earthquake destroyed much of Anchorage, the largest city, and brought devastating tidal waves upon a number of coastal communities such as Valdez and Kodiak. Not all was hard going, however. Military spending had been the mainstay of the economy. In the 1960s, British investments in petroleum and Japanese investments in the lumber industry had helped expand the state's economy. The short-to-medium financial future of the state was secured through oil discoveries, most significantly on Kenai Peninsula and at Prudhoe Bay on the Alaska Arctic Coast. A giant lease sale in 1969 was to begin the construction of the Trans-Alaska Pipeline. However, the question of who owned the land to be crossed by the pipeline and what their rights were had to be settled first. This was done through the Alaska Native Claims Settlement Act of 1971. Actual construction began only in 1974, directed by the Alyeska Pipeline Service Company owned by a consortium of eight oil companies. The 789-mile pipeline began pumping oil from Prudhoe Bay towards the shipping terminal at Valdez on 20 June 1977. The total cost of the project was over twelve billion dollars.

Alaska and Alaskana

The literature on Alaska has been profoundly affected by the marketplace. Alaskans have traditionally purchased books at a brisk rate, but since the state has so few residents, the in-state market is relatively small. This has meant that, in order to be commercially successful, publications must appeal to those outside the state. Themes that emphasize the exotic or that appeal to armchair tourists are perennial favourites. At the same time, there is a substantial amount of small-press activity and self-publishing going on within the state. These products usually lack the marketing that would lead to wide distribution, so that they are often hard to acquire, especially outside Alaska.

The number of publications on Alaska depends on the definition of what constitutes a publication. This is especially true for what are traditionally considered to be near-print or grey literature categories. For the specialist, these are frequently very important, since the information they contain is often not available anywhere else. These are typically in the form of administrative studies developed to support agency decision-making, produced either in-house or through grant-funded research. If one includes the most important of these publications, but eliminates brochures and other ephemera, there are probably some 50,000 monographic titles on Alaska. Access to citations for most of these is available through regional electronic bibliographical utilities such as the Western Library Network. These citations have been repackaged on CD-ROMs (PolarPac, WLN's LaserCat) and widely distributed. Through shared cataloguing, much of this information is available throughout the country on OCLC and other commonly available utilities utilized by modern libraries. Access to many of these libraries may be gained through the Internet. But where to start?

Most general subject periodical indexes such as Academic Abstracts, Science Citation Index, ERIC, Humanities Index and Social Science Index, contain some Alaskana. However, there are generally few references. The Rasmuson Library maintains an electronic periodical index, BibAPR (Bibliography of Alaska and the Polar Regions), as a part of its GNOSIS on-line public access catalogue. This is available electronically and on the PolarPac CD-ROM disk.

This bibliography is designed to provide guidance to anyone approaching the literature on Alaska. It is highly selective, and designed to provide access to titles that are in print or that are most likely to be held by major libraries outside Alaska. Where there are many choices for a particular topic, a decision was made to select some and reject many. Others might have chosen differently.

Acknowledgements

I wish to thank Katherine Arndt, Terrence Cole and David Hales for their comments on earlier versions of this manuscript. Blue Roesbery has assisted in the construction of the index.

Marvin W. Falk
April 1995

The State and Its People

1 **Alaska, a pictorial history.**
Claus-M. Naske, L. J. Rowinski. Norfolk, Virginia: Donning, 1983. 271p. bibliog.

This is a casual and broad general history extensively illustrated with both historical and recent photographs.

2 **Alaska: the land, the people, the cities.**
Michael Macy. New York: Mallard Press, 1991. 128p.

This photographic presentation is accompanied by a minimal amount of text.

3 **Alaska: reflections on land and spirit.**
Edited by Robert Hedin, Gary Holthaus. Tucson, Arizona: University of Arizona Press, 1989. 322p.

Twenty-two essays form this anthology of non-fiction. The contributions range from journal entries to meditations to scientific observations. A number of well-known contributors, both living and dead, are represented, including John McPhee, Pierre Berton and John Muir. The two editors are both poets and their interest in style and elegance is reflected in their choices.

4 **Alaskans: life on the last frontier.**
Ron Stickland. Harrisburg, Pennsylvania: Stackpole, 1992. 288p.

A skilfully woven narrative about the lives of 63 Alaskans, the book is based upon interviews that were begun in 1989. There is indeed a diverse cast of characters.

5 **The Alaskans.**
Keith Wheeler. Alexandria, Virginia: Time-Life Books, 1977. 240p. bibliog. (Old West Series).

This is a popular, richly illustrated introduction to the history of Alaska. It takes its flavour from the Time-Life 'Old West Series', which depicts in its other volumes topics such as cattlemen, rustlers and gold rushes.

6 **Alaska's magnificent park lands.**
Washington, DC: National Geographic Society, 1984. 199p. 14 maps.

This is a pictorial introduction, but not a guide, to the national parks and preserves in Alaska which include Glacier Bay National Park and Preserve; Wrangell-St. Elias National Park and Preserve; Kenai Fjords National Park; Denali National Park and Preserve; Lake Clark National Park and Preserve; Katmai National Park and Preserve; Aniakchak National Monument and Preserve; Yukon-Charlie Rivers National Preserve; Bering Land Bridge National Preserve; Cape Krusenstern National Monument; Kobuk Valley National Park; Noatak National Preserve; and Gates of the Arctic National Park and Preserve.

7 **Alaska's national parks.**
Photographed by Fred Hirschmann, text by Kim Heacox. Portland, Oregon: Graphic Arts Publishing, 1990. 157p. map.

This is a visual tour of each of the seventeen national parks, preserves or monuments conducted through the lens of a master photographer.

8 **Coming into the country.**
John McPhee. New York: Farrar, Straus and Giroux, 1977. 438p. (Also available in paperback).

Many Alaskans consider this to be the best contemporary account of Alaska written by an outsider. It is especially strong on the fascination of finding one's self through experiencing the wilderness. Several of the developments about which McPhee wrote, from the perspective of 1977, such as the transfer of the Alaskan capital from Juneau to Willow, have not come to pass.

9 **Divided twins: Alaska and Siberia.**
Yevgeny Yevtushenko, photographs by Boyd Norton and Yevgeny Yevtushenko, translated by Antonina W. Boris. New York: Viking Studio Books, 1988. 224p.

This is an illustrated comparison of the peoples, wildlife and landscapes of the regions on both sides of the Bering Strait. The text is published in both English and Russian. There have been extensive exchanges and visits between the two regions in the past several years and there is now a regularly scheduled air service.

10 **Edges of the earth: a man, a woman, a child in the Alaskan wilderness.**

Richard Leo. New York: H. Holt, 1991. 303p.

Leo depicts life on a wilderness homestead that was established near Denali Park during the 1980s. It is one of the latest of this genre, which flourished during the enthusiastic homesteading era which directly followed the Second World War.

11 **The last light breaking: personal essays from arctic Alaska.**

Nick Jans. Anchorage: Alaska Northwest, 1993. 219p. map. bibliog.

These are 23 essays by someone looking for adventure and the status of 'an arctic hero,' who stayed for almost 15 years. He writes about nature, the landscape and people – especially the Inupiat Eskimo.

12 **One man's wilderness: an Alaskan odyssey from the journals and photograph collection of Richard Proenneke.**

Sam Keith. Anchorage: Alaska Northwest, 1973. 108p. (*Alaska Geographic*, vol. 1, no. 2).

This journal of a middle-aged man building a cabin by himself in the wilderness is accompanied by photographs of the area and of the wildlife living there, and explains the progress of cabin construction.

13 **Southeast Alaska.**

Nancy Zimmerman, foreword by James A. Michener. Portland, Oregon: Graphic Arts Center Publishing Company, 1988. 160p.

This large-format book of images by a master photographer depicts the life and scenery of Southeast Alaska.

Geography

General

14 **Alaska and its resources.**

William H. Dall. Boston: Lee and Shepard, 1870. 627p. map. bibliog.

This book, in various editions, was almost the only general description of Alaska available to the reading public for many years. Dall was one of a handful of American experts on Alaska, having served with the Western Union Telegraph project during the 1860s, prior to Alaska's sale to the United States. While the volume has a number of factual errors, it provides an overview of what was known of Alaska before the gold rushes altered this new American possession.

15 **Alaska's great interior.**

Edited by Robert A. Henning. Edmonds, Washington: Alaska Geographic, 1978. 96p. (*Alaska Geographic*, vol. 5, no. 3).

With the Alaska Range to the south and the Brooks Range to the north, the Interior is a large region with a northern continental climate. This compilation of contributions by Interior writers describes the area and its largest settlement, Fairbanks.

16 **Alaska's Konyag country: Kodiak from sea otter settlement to king crab capital.**

Yule Chaffin, Trisha Hampton Krieger, Michael Rostad. Kodiak, Alaska: Chaffin Incorporated, 1983. 269p. bibliog.

A general description of the physical geography, economy, and population of Kodiak and surrounding islands, with a strong historical component.

17 **The Aleutian islands: their people and natural history.**
Henry Bascom Collins, Austin H. Clark, Egbert H. Walker. Washington, DC: Smithsonian Institution, 1945. 131p. bibliog. (Smithsonian Institution. War Background Studies, no. 21).

This concise introduction includes lists of mammals, birds and plants that are native to the islands.

18 **The Aleutians.**
Edited by Lael Morgan. Edmonds, Washington: Alaska Geographic, 1980. 224p. (*Alaska Geographic*, vol. 7, no. 3).

The Aleutian chain of islands is over 1,000 miles long. This is the most thorough of the Geographic Series on Alaska's regions, covering such topics as the geological evolution of the islands, their many active volcanoes, the region's tsunamis and earthquakes, its weather, flora and fauna and, above all, its human population throughout history.

19 **Bristol Bay Basin.**
Edited by Robert A. Henning. Edmonds, Washington: Alaska Northwest, 1978. 96p. (*Alaska Geographic*, vol. 5, no. 3).

Bristol Bay's primary economic activity has always been fishing and fish processing. It is sparsely settled, and has a diverse landscape, from forest to tundra, with some very large lakes, especially Iliamna and Lake Clark.

20 **Cook Inlet country.**
Edited by Robert A. Henning. Edmonds, Washington: Alaska Northwest, 1977. 144p. (*Alaska Geographic*, vol. 5, no. 1).

Cook Inlet has the Alaska Peninsula on one side and the Kenai Peninsula on the other, with the city of Anchorage at the head of navigation. This region is important as a major tourist destination, commercial centre, and petroleum source. It contains over half of the state's population and includes the Matanuska-Susitna valleys, the largest of Alaska's modest agricultural areas.

21 **Environmental atlas of Alaska.**
Charles W. Hartman. Fairbanks, Alaska: Institute of Water Resources, Engineering Experiment Station, University of Alaska, 1984. rev. ed. 95p. maps.

Climatic conditions, light, engineering considerations and a general description of the physical aspects of Alaska are presented.

22 **The geography and geology of Alaska; with a summary of existing knowledge.**
Alfred Hulse Brooks. Washington, DC: GPO, 1906. 327p. 9 maps. bibliog.

Although it is out of date, this geography was written by a geologist who worked and explored very extensively during the gold rush and who became head of the United

States Geological Survey in Alaska. It gives a glimpse of the extent of geographical knowledge during that era and the response to the need for information occasioned by the gold rush.

23 **Glacier Bay: old ice, new land.**
William Boehm. Edmonds, Washington: Alaska Geographic, 1975. 134p. (*Alaska Geographic*, vol. 3, no. 1).

A heavily pictorial introduction, this is an exploration of Glacier Bay National Monument. Ancient and modern glaciers have created a striking landscape rich in plant and animal habitat. A substantial variety of marine and fresh water systems exist as well, including deep-water channels, straits, fjords, bays, saltwater estuaries, tide flats, rivers, streams, ponds and lakes.

24 **The Gulf of Alaska: physical environment and biological resources.**
Edited by Donald W. Hood, Stephen T. Zimmerman. Washington, DC: Alaska Office, Ocean Assessments Division, National Oceanic and Atmospheric Administration, US Department of Commerce. 655p. maps. bibliog.

A substantial collection of articles contributed by more than thirty leading experts in the field, this work covers the physical environment, biological resources and issues and perspectives. It is copiously illustrated with charts, over 80 maps and diagrams. Each subject article includes its own list of bibliographical references.

25 **Introductory geography and geology of Alaska.**
Leo Mark Anthony, Tom A. Tunley. Anchorage: Polar Publishing Company, 1976. 273p. maps. bibliog.

This is a pre-college-level textbook that includes a brief history of mining in Alaska.

26 **Islands of the seals: the Pribilofs.**
Edited by Robert A. Henning. Anchorage: Alaska Geographic, 1982. 123p. maps. (*Alaska Geographic*, vol. 9, no. 3).

Saint Paul and Saint George islands were discovered by the Russians, who moved a small population of Aleut natives there to conduct fur seal harvests. The annual fur harvests continued under the direction of the US government up to the time this book was published, but since then have ceased. Verdant wildlife colonies exist on the islands, and many tourists come to view and photograph birds, seals and sea lions.

27 **Kodiak, island of change.**
Compiled and edited by Nancy Freeman. Edmonds, Washington: Alaska Geographic, 1977. 96p. (*Alaska Geographic*, vol. 4, no. 3).

An overview, this introduction to Kodiak covers a variety of topics from the geological events creating the island, through such natural phenomena as the weather, wildlife and climate, to history and the then current economic situation.

28 **The Kotzebue Basin.**
Edited by Robert A. Henning. Anchorage: Alaska Geographic, 1981. 184p. maps. (*Alaska Geographic*, vol. 8, no. 3).

The Kotzebue Basin is drained by the Noatak, Kobuk and several smaller rivers. It is right at the Arctic Circle. The coast hosts populations of fish and marine mammals. The region has a variety of diverse ecosystems, and an ancient Eskimo culture with prehistoric remains going back at least 10,000 years. It contains all or part of the Bering Sea Land-Bridge National Preserve, the Selawik National Wildlife Refuge, the Gates of the Arctic National Park and Preserve, the Noatak National Preserve, the Kobuk Valley National Park, and the Cape Krusenstern National Monument.

29 **Living in the polar regions.**
Theodore A. Rees Cheney. New York: F. Watts, 1987. 95p. bibliog.

Aimed at a juvenile readership, it compares the relationship between geography and culture on the North Slope, Alaska; a valley in northeastern Siberia; and Hudson Bay.

30 **A photographic geography of Alaska.**
Edited by Robert A. Henning. Anchorage: Alaska Geographic, 1983. 192p. maps. (*Alaska Geographic*, vol. 7, no. 2).

This is a general, popular introduction to the six regional geographies of Alaska: Southeast, South-Central, Interior, Alaska Peninsula and the Aleutians, Bering Sea, and Arctic.

31 **Sitka and its ocean/island world.**
Edited by Pat Roppel. Anchorage: Alaska Geographic, 1982. 128p. (*Alaska Geographic*, vol. 9, no. 2).

Sitka (New Archangel) was the capital of Russian America and, for a brief period, the Territory of Alaska. It has since become a regional centre, with fishing, a pulp mill, Sheldon Jackson College, tourism, and a coastguard station as its principal industries.

32 **The Stikine River.**
Edited by Robert A. Henning, Marty Loken. Edmonds, Washington: Alaska Geographic, 1979. 95p. (*Alaska Geographic*, vol. 6, no. 4).

The mouth of the Stikine is near Wrangell, Alaska, which has served as the supply and transfer point for river traffic for over 100 years. The river itself drains a portion of British Columbia. Today the river is considered to be a prime wilderness canoeing and rafting area.

33 **Wrangell-Saint Elias International Mountain Wilderness.**
Gered Wright, Gil Mull, George Herben. Anchorage: Alaska Geographic, 1981. 144p. map. (*Alaska Geographic*, vol. 8, no. 1).

The Wrangell-Saint Elias National Park and Preserve was created in 1980. It borders the Chugach National Forest and Tongass National Forest in Alaska, and the Kluane National Park in the Yukon Territory, Canada. It contains the highest coastal mountains in the world. This 20-million-acre region also has massive glaciers, and a variety of other geomorphic features such as mud volcanoes. There remains physical evidence of the extensive mining activity that once thrived there.

Geology

34 **Guidebook to permafrost and Quaternary geology along the Richardson and Glenn highways between Fairbanks and Anchorage, Alaska.**
Edited by Troy L. Péwé, R. D. Reger. Fairbanks, Alaska: Division of Geological & Geophysical Surveys, Department of Natural Resources, State of Alaska, 1983. 263p. maps. bibliog.

Originally prepared for an international conference (Fourth International Conference on Permafrost, 18-22 July 1983, University of Alaska), this guide covers a major portion of Central and South-Central Alaska that is accessible by road. The geology and vegetation is significantly different in many ways from that depicted in a sister publication on the road to the Arctic (see item no. 35). It is extensively illustrated with drawings, charts, maps and photographs. It graphically illustrates the effects of human activity on vegetation and permafrost. Areas covered include the middle Tanana River Valley, the Delta River area, Alaska Range, Copper River basin, Matanuska glacier, the Upper Cook Inlet region, and the Matanuska Valley.

35 **Guidebook to permafrost and related features along the Elliott and Dalton highways, Fox to Prudhoe Bay, Alaska.**
Edited by Jerry Brown, R. A. Kreig. Fairbanks, Alaska: Division of Geological & Geophysical Surveys, Department of Natural Resources, State of Alaska, 1983. 230p. maps. bibliog.

This guide was originally produced for a major international conference (Fourth International Conference on Permafrost, 18-22 July 1983, University of Alaska). It is a highly detailed log of the route from near Fairbanks north along the pipeline haul road corridor. It is written in a clear and precise manner. It includes explanations of processes, numerous illustrations and strip maps. Topics include climate, physiography, permafrost, hydrology (including pingos), geology, vegetation, soils, and cirque glaciation.

36 **Physiographic divisions of Alaska.**
Clyde Wahrhaftig. Washington, DC: GPO, 1965. 52p. maps. bibliog. (Geological Survey Professional Paper 482).

New classifications of the geographical and geological (physiographical) regions became necessary because of the quantities of new information that became available from the 1940s to the 1960s. Boundaries are drawn based primarily upon topology. This is the standard reference work.

37 **Placer deposits of Alaska: an inventory of the placer mines and prospects of Alaska, their history and geologic setting.**
Edward H. Cobb. Washington, DC: GPO, 1973. 213p. 55 maps. bibliog. (Geological Survey Bulletin 1374).

Despite its age, this is still the best general reference to Alaska's mining districts, with specific locations, and citations to the specialized literature.

38 **Quaternary geology of Alaska.**
Troy L. Péwé. Washington, DC: GPO, 1975. 145p. 19 maps. bibliog. (Geological Survey Professional Paper 835).

This is an extensively illustrated study for both a lay and professional readership of glaciological and geological processes which have formed Alaska's landscape. It also covers changes in the distribution of plants and animals.

39 **Riches from the earth: a geologic tour along the Dalton Highway, Alaska.**
Edited by William R. Diel, Arthur Banet, Jr. Anchorage: Alaska Natural History Association, 1993. 128p. bibliog.

Specially drawn illustrations and colour photographs depict geological processes in a manner readily understood by non-geologists. The Dalton Highway runs from Fairbanks, across the Yukon River, and through the Brooks Range to Prudhoe Bay on the Arctic coast. The highway has also been called the 'Haul Road'. The usefulness of this volume transcends its limited geographical coverage in the explanation of such phenomena as Quaternary glaciation, permafrost degradation, ice-rich sediments, pingos, granite tars, the role of aquifers in ice overflows, ice lenses, layers of horizontal ground ice, yardangs, raised-edge polygons, petroleum formations and stratigraphical sections, and dinosaur bone locations.

40 **Roadside geology of Alaska.**
Cathy Connor, Daniel O'Haire. Missoula, Montana: Mountain Press Publishing Company, 1988. 250p. 44 maps. bibliog.

This is a guide for laymen, covering areas accessible by the Alaska Marine Highway (state-owned ferry system) and the road network. It includes illustrations of the effects of geological events such as earthquakes, tsunamis, glacial action and volcanoes. It should be used with caution, however, as it does not enjoy a good reputation among geologists.

Special features

41 **Alaska's glaciers.**
Bruce Molnia. Anchorage: Alaska Geographic, 1982. 144p. maps. (*Alaska Geographic*, vol. 9, no. 1).

Molnia explains how a glacier functions, and describes its parts. He then describes the various types of glaciers and how they change through time, including the effects of the Ice Ages upon Alaska's geology. Alaska's glaciers are categorized and described in their substantial variety, and information is provided on how and where to view them. Special cautions are suggested when approaching and travelling on them.

42 **Alaska marine ice atlas.**
Joseph C. LaBelle, James L. Wise. Anchorage: Arctic Environmental Information and Data Center, 1983. 302p. maps. bibliog.

Sea ice conditions, tide maps, and distribution of ice flow by month are some of the topics presented. Climatic data and the relationship of climate to ice is shown in great detail.

43 **Handbook for the Alaskan prospector.**
Ernest Wolff. Fairbanks, Alaska: Mineral Industry Research Laboratory, School of Mineral Industry, University of Alaska, 1969. 2nd ed. 460p. bibliog.

This frequently reprinted and popular general guide to the geology and mineralogy of gold-bearing regions gives details of prospecting techniques, equipment and procedures.

44 **Permafrost and its effect on life in the North.**
Troy L. Péwé. Corvallis, Oregon: Oregon State University Press, 1966. 40p. map. bibliog.

Péwé's classic explanation of the impact of permafrost was first published in a volume of proceedings in 1957. Topics include the role of permafrost in preserving prehistoric animal remains, such as now extinct bison species and the mammoth. The profound influence of permafrost upon both vegetation and man-made structures is also explained.

45 **Volcanoes of North America: United States and Canada.**
Edited by Charles A. Wood, Jurgen Kienle. Cambridge, England; New York: Cambridge University Press, 1990. 354p.

About one-third of the book is devoted to Alaska. It provides data for each volcano.

Maps and gazetteers

46 **Alaska atlas and gazetteer.**
Freeport, Maine: DeLorme Mapping, 1992. 156p. 135 maps.

A bound set of 11 by 15.2 inch reproductions of United States Geological Survey topographical maps which cover the more densely populated regions of the state at a scale of 1:300,000 and for the less populated portions at a scale of 1:1,400,000. It is accompanied by an index of place-names and physical features.

47 **Alaska place names.**
Alan Edward Schorr. Juneau: Denali Press, 1991. 4th ed. 191p.

This is a compilation of twenty-five years of Alaska place-name decisions made by the United States Board of Geographic Names. It serves as a supplement to Orth (item no. 53), and it includes both new names and additions and corrections to earlier work.

48 **Alaska regional profiles.**
Linda Selkregg. Anchorage: University of Alaska, Arctic Environmental Information and Data Center, 1974-76. 6 vols. 1,000+ maps and illustrations. bibliog. (Sponsored by the Office of the Governor of Alaska in Co-operation with the Joint Federal-State Land Use Planning Commission for Alaska).

This set of volumes provides the most comprehensive coverage available of Alaska's physical geography and land use. Each large-format, loose-leaf, volume covers a particular region: vol. 1, *Southcentral*; vol. 2, *Arctic*; vol. 3, *Southwest*; vol. 4, *Southeast*; vol. 5, *Northwest*; vol. 6, *Yukon*. The coverage of the natural environment includes climate, topography, geology, soils and biotic communities; the man-made environment includes history, government, services, transportation and community facilities. Although dated, this set of volumes still serves as the basic resource inventory reference work for Alaska. It has served resource managers and land planners throughout the 1970s and 1980s. Each volume contains a very extensive bibliography.

49 **Alaskan maps: a cartobibliography of Alaska to 1900.**
Marvin W. Falk. New York: Garland, 1983. 245p. 5 maps. bibliog.

A cartobibliography of approximately 1,300 maps of Alaska, arranged by year of first publication. It includes manuscript maps if they were subsequently published in facsimile. Citations include references to other major map bibliographies. Reproductions and facsimile reprints are noted (if any) and there are numerous annotations explaining the historical significance of individual maps.

50 **Atlas geograficheskikh otkrytii v Sibiri i v Severo-Zapadnoi Amerike, XVII-XVIII vv.** (Atlas of geographical discoveries in Siberia and North-Western America, XVII-XVIII centuries.)
Aleksei V. Efimov. Moscow: Nauka, 1964. 134p. 194 maps. bibliog.

The colonization of Siberia by Russia led to a number of discoveries. This atlas reproduces the most significant manuscript maps depicting the emerging knowledge of

Siberia and the North Pacific. This includes Alaska during the years immediately preceding, and following, the two Bering expeditions. A summary of the foreword and a list of maps are printed in English.

51 **Atlas of the Northwest coasts of America; with hydrographic notes.**
Compiled by Captain 1st Rank Mikhail Dmitrievich Teben'kov, translated from the Russian and edited by Richard A. Pierce. Kingston, Ontario: Limestone Press, 1981. 109p. 39 maps. (Alaska History, vol. 21).

This is the last and the best known of the great published atlases of Russian America. Teben'kov spent 25 years in Alaska, first as a naval officer and eventually as the Chief Manager of the Russian-American colony. The copper plates were engraved in Sitka and then transported by Teben'kov to St. Petersburg for publication in 1852. This atlas continued to be used for many years and was taken as a model for the new maps published by both the US Coast and Geodetic Survey and the British Hydrographic Office in subsequent years.

52 **The cartography of the Northwest Coast of America to the year 1800.**
Henry R. Wagner. Berkeley, California: University of California Press, 1937. 2 vols. 40 maps. bibliog. Reprinted, Amsterdam: Nico Israel, 1968.

This cartobibliography is one of the classics in the history of cartography. Wagner, the author of a number of works on the history of the American west, provides an extensive narrative, followed by a cartobibliography which cites 911 maps, with annotations including information on reproductions and the locations of originals. This is followed by an annotated list of place-names appearing on the maps that are still in use, and a list of obsolete place-names. The primary area of coverage is California, but Alaska is also treated, with 211 maps of interest. The ending date of 1800 precludes most of the published Russian maps and atlases of Alaska, and even within these date constraints a number of important Russian maps are not listed.

53 **Dictionary of Alaska place names.**
Donald J. Orth. Washington, DC: GPO, 1967. Reprinted with minor revisions in 1971. 1,084p. 12 maps. bibliog. (Geological Survey Professional Paper 567).

This is the most complete place-name reference for Alaska, based upon decisions of the United States Board of Geographic Names. Brief, but not entirely accurate, biographies of major explorers are included in the front matter.

54 **Early cartography of the Bering Strait region.**
Raymond H. Fisher. *Arctic*, vol. 37, no. 4 (Dec. 1984), p. 574-89. 26 maps. bibliog.

The best short description of the evolution of maps from before the Bering expeditions (1600s) through to the publication of maps from Captain Cook's third expedition (1780s).

55 **Geographic dictionary of Alaska.**
Marcus Baker, James McCormick. Washington, DC: GPO, 1906. 2nd ed. 690p. bibliog. (Geological Survey Bulletin 299).

There were several Alaska Coast Pilots and other government publications with smaller gazetteers printed from 1869 to 1902. However, there were conflicting and multiple place-names. Several years of effort by Marcus Baker and the newly created Board of Geographic Names standardized usage and provided short explanations of the origins of place-names. Baker published the first edition in 1902 (446p. Geological Survey Bulletin 187). McCormick completed the second edition, under way when Baker died. The second edition includes a useful history of exploration. Although Orth (q.v.) is an expansion of this early work, Baker and McCormick have many details not carried over to Orth.

56 **Images of pre-discovery Alaska in the work of European cartographers.**
Marvin W. Falk. *Arctic*, vol. 37, no. 4 (December 1984), p. 562-73. 13 maps. bibliog.

An analysis of the pre-Bering (1728 voyage) maps of the North Pacific and Alaska published in Europe.

57 **Klondike visions: dreams of a promised land.**
Terrence Cole. *Alaska Journal*, vol. 16 (1986), p. 82-93.

The term 'Klondike' as a place-name evoked particular visions that drew people to the gold rush and helped make it a popular literary theme. Many at the time thought it to be in Alaska, and the popular perception welded the Yukon and Alaska together.

58 **Shem Pete's Alaska: the territory of the Upper Cook Inlet Dena'ina.**
Compiled and edited by James Kari, James A. Fall. Fairbanks, Alaska: Alaska Native Language Center, University of Alaska and the CIRI Foundation, 1987. 330p. maps. bibliog.

An ethnogeography of upper Cook Inlet compiled from 32 Dena'ina and Ahtna informants in addition to Shem Pete. The area is divided into 16 distinct regions, treating 711 places and about 720 native place-names. It is extensively illustrated with historical and recent photographs, maps and charts.

59 **Tanaina country: Denaina elnena.**
James Kari, Priscilla Russell Kari, edited by Jane McGary, maps by Karen Pearson. Fairbanks, Alaska: Alaska Native Language Center, University of Alaska, 1982. 109p. maps. bibliog.

This is an ethnogeographical treatment of native Tanaina-language place-names and terminology.

Travel Guides

60 **Adventuring in Alaska.**
Peggy Wayburn. San Francisco: Sierra Club Books, 1988. rev. ed. 375p. bibliog.

This guide provides less detailed information on accommodation and services than many other publications, but it attempts to be more analytical and evaluative than most. The authors place a special emphasis upon natural phenomena.

61 **Alaska bicycle touring guide, including parts of the Yukon Territories and Northwest Territories.**
Alys Culhane, Pete Praetorius. Juneau: Denali Press, 1992. 2nd ed. 318p. 20 maps.

This volume is based upon an exploration of Alaska by bicycle undertaken in 1988. It divides routes into roughly fifty-mile segments, and provides information on conditions and terrain as well as accommodation and sight-seeing opportunities.

62 **Alaska paddling guide.**
Jack Mosby, David Dapkus. Anchorage: J & R Enterprises, 1986. 3rd ed. 113p. map.

A systematic guide to 110 float-, canoeing-, and kayaking-rivers and streams with descriptions including whitewater ratings, course sketches, access points, and a guide to the relevant United States Geological Survey topographical maps for each of the waterways.

63 **Alaska wilderness lodges.**
Kathy Doogan, illustrated by Diana Tillion. Anchorage: Alaska Northwest Books, 1992- . annual.

Just over fifty lodges are featured, with an emphasis on those which provide elegant, and usually expensive, accommodation. The volume does not provide a comprehensive list, but it does cover all regions of the state.

64 **Alaska wilderness milepost.**
Anchorage: Alaska Northwest Books, 1991. 6th ed. 454p. 11 maps.

This is an off-road companion to the older and well-established, road-based *Milepost* (q.v.). The publication is divided into broad regions and provides community-by-community coverage. It includes contact addresses for local government or the appropriate native corporation.

65 **Alaska's inside passage traveller.**
Ellen Searsby. Occidental, California: Windham Bay Press, 1991. 13th ed. 208p.

A guide aimed at budget-minded travellers who use the state's Alaska Marine Highway ferry system to tour Southeast Alaska.

66 **Alaska's parklands, a complete guide.**
Nancy Simmerman. Seattle, Washington: The Mountaineers, 1983. 336p. map. bibliog.

This guide covers 111 state and national parks, monuments, wildlife refuges, forests, wild and scenic rivers and recreation areas. Coverage for each is brief, but information on many of the less well known parks are difficult to find in any other commonly available publication. Extensively illustrated with black-and-white photographs and small sketch maps.

67 **Bed and breakfasts in Alaska: a directory.**
Mary Sherman, Skip Ray, John Roller, Dan L. Burton. Anchorage: Glacier House Publications, 1987. 93p. 49 maps.

The bed-and-breakfast concept for tourist accommodation has become widespread in Alaska only within the last decade. Local visitors' centres sponsored by chambers of commerce and telephone directories can also be of help in locating an alternative to a commercial hotel.

68 **Cruising guide to Prince William Sound.**
Jim Lethcoe, Nancy Lethcoe. Valdez, Alaska: Prince William Sound Books, 1984-85. 2 vols. 100+ maps. bibliog.

This is the most detailed guide available for the those interested in recreational boating in these waters. It provides extensive advice applicable to northern waters in general on how to deal with hypothermia and other emergencies. Approximately 100 selected anchorages are described in some detail and the reader's attention is drawn to local points of interest. Historical background essays and information about the natural habitat make this guide useful to both the general reader and the sailor.

69 **Fielding's Alaska and the Yukon.**
Robert W. Bone. New York: Fielding Travel Books, 1990. 363p. 19 maps.

Bone is a professional travel writer who provides an outsider's perspective on Alaska (he first visited the state in 1982). The information provided in this work is accurate and precise.

70 **Fodor's 94 Alaska.**
Edited by Alison Hoffman. New York: Fodor's Travel Publications, 1993. 290p.

Fodor's guide is for the tourist, including those from abroad (especially the British tourist), coming by plane or cruise-ship. Brief, sometimes overly written, introductions to Alaska by well-known authors (Stanton Patty, James Michener, John McPhee) lead the reader to the prosaic details of cruise-ship schedules and recommended restaurants.

71 **Gateway to gold: Skagway, the White Pass, & the Chilkoot trail past and present.**
Marina Loi McCready. Whitehorse, Yukon Territory: Studio North, 1990. 44p.

This is a pictorial walking guide to gold rush history in the small town at the head of Lynn Canal, one of the chief starting points for the overland journey to Dawson and the Klondike gold rush.

72 **Insight guide: Alaska.**
Edited by Janie Freeburg. Singapore: APA Publications, 1991. 335p. 7 maps.

A number of Alaskan writers have contributed chapters on particular aspects of Alaska such as natural history. These comprise the bulk of the book. A 'travel tips' section covers transportation, accommodation, and things to do and see.

73 **Let's go: the budget guide to the Pacific Northwest, Western Canada & Alaska 1992.**
Edited by Tim Whitmire in association with Harvard Student Agencies. New York: St. Martin's Press, 1991. 458p. annual.

A general regional guide which pays particular attention to inexpensive accommodation and travel. Alaska itself is covered in somewhat less than a quarter of the book but the information is concise and useful, if somewhat sharp-tongued.

74 **The Milepost.**
Bothell, Washington: Alaska Northwest Books, 1993. 656p. maps. bibliog. annual.

The most commonly used travel manual, this popular general travel guide emphasizes travel by road, but it also includes information on ferries and cruise-ships. It provides a mile-by-mile (or kilometre-by-kilometre in Canada) log for access routes through British Columbia, Alberta, and the Yukon Territory. Each highway in Alaska has its own chapter, with information on attractions, sport fishing, accommodation and side roads.

75 **Mountain bike Alaska: 49 trails in the 49th state.**
Richard Larson. Anchorage: Glacier House Publications, 1991. 120p. 50 maps.

The Southcentral area of Alaska is covered, including the Kenai Peninsula to the south of Anchorage, Anchorage parks and trails, and side trails for mountain bicycles as far north as the Alaska Range and Denali Park. Each trail is evaluated and includes a one-page topographical route map.

76 **Rving in Alaska: campgrounds & services.**
Richard D. Anderson. Anchorage: Billiken Press, 1991. 196p. maps.

This is a guide for those interested in 'rv' (recreational vehicle or motor home) camping. These large motorized caravans can be rented in Alaska's larger cities and increasing numbers of tourists arrive in them each year from elsewhere in North America.

Travel Narratives

First approaches (1648-1795)

77 **Account of a voyage of discovery to the north-east of Siberia, the Frozen Ocean and the North-east Sea.**
Gavriil A. Sarychev (Gawrila Sarytschew). Amsterdam: Nico Israel, 1969. 2 vols. (Reprint of the original 1806 London edition).

The Billings Expedition explored Alaskan waters from 1790 to 1792, although it took many additional years to cross Siberia and fit out the ships. The Englishman Billings had served with Captain Cook and then made a career in Russian service. Sarychev served under Billings and made a number of independent surveys in the Aleutians. Sarychev later edited the expedition report and became vice-admiral and chief Russian hydrographer.

78 **Account of the Russian discoveries between Asia and America to which are added the conquest of Siberia and the history of the transactions and commerce between Russia and China.**
William Coxe. New York: A. M. Kelley, 1970. Reprint of the 3rd ed., with supplement to *Russian Discoveries*. 454p. maps.

It was primarily through the four major editions of Coxe's account that English readers became acquainted with Russian activity in the North Pacific.

79 **The Alaska travel journals of Archibald Menzies, 1793-1794.**
Edited by Wallace M. Olson. Fairbanks, Alaska: University of Alaska Press, 1993. 247p. maps. bibliog.

Menzies served as a naturalist and surgeon with the Vancouver expedition. This portion of his personal and scientific account was not published with Lamb's edition of Vancouver's voyages (see item no. 115). It relates a number of details regarding how the Vancouver expedition conducted surveys, the smaller boats leaving the two mother ships for days at a time as they explored inlets and around islands. There are a number of native encounters with the Tanaina, Tlingit and Haida Indians. Menzies' text is accompanied by an appendix listing the botanical collections made by Menzies and mentioned in his journal, compiled by a plant ecologist, John F. Thilenius.

80 **The art of Captain Cook's voyages. Volume three: the voyage of the *Resolution* and *Discovery* with a descriptive catalog of all known original drawings and paintings of peoples, places, artefacts and events and original engravings associated with the voyage.**
Rüdiger Joppien, Bernard Smith. London: Yale University Press, 1988. 2 vols.

The chief artist for Cook's third voyage was John Webber, whose drawings are as important for the South Seas as for Alaska. Each drawing is reproduced, and extensively annotated. In many cases there are a number of variations for one scene. For example, there may be a pen and ink drawing; a pen, wash and water-colour; and a published engraving of the same scene. Webber's work is most valuable for its rendering of ethnographic detail. There is a full description of the engraving and publication of this material after Webber's return to England.

81 **Bering and Chirikov: the American voyages and their impact.**
Edited by O. W. Frost. Anchorage: Alaska Historical Society, 1992. 456p. maps.

This volume of edited proceedings brings together papers by leading authorities from North America, Western Europe, and Russia. The meeting, held in Anchorage, commemorated the 250th anniversary of Bering's 1741 voyage of discovery to Alaska.

82 **Bering's search for the strait: the First Kamchatka Expedition 1725-1730.**
Evgenii G. Kushnarev, edited and translated by E. A. P. Crownhart-Vaughan. Portland, Oregon: Oregon Historical Society, 1990. 214p. 5 maps. bibliog. (North Pacific Studies Series, 15).

This is a new examination of Bering's first voyage by the Scientific Secretary of Russia's Central Naval Museum, employing previously unused documentation.

83 **Bering's successors, 1745-1780; contributions of Peter Simon Pallas to the history of Russian exploration toward Alaska.**
Compiled by Peter Simon Pallas, edited and translated by James Masterson, Helen Brower. Seattle, Washington: University of Washington Press, 1948. 96p. maps.

The accounts in this collection are taken from the German serial, *Neue Nordische Beytraege* (1781-83) edited by Peter S. Pallas. They are English translations of Pallas's translations into German from the Russian originals, and include Pallas's editorial notes and his essay 'Commentary on the Discoveries that Have Been Made in the Eastern Ocean Between Siberia and America' (p. 19-46). The English translations first appeared in *Pacific Northwest Quarterly*, vol. 38, nos. 1 and 2 (January and April 1947).

84 **Bering's voyages: an account of the efforts of the Russians to determine the relation of Asia and America.**

Frank A. Golder. New York: American Geographical Society, 1922. 2 vols. Reprinted, New York: Octagon Books, 1968. 12 maps.

This has long been considered the classic English account of the two Bering voyages. The first volume includes translations of the log-books and official reports of both the first (1725-30) and second (1733-42) expeditions. The second volume is Leonhard Stejneger's translation of Georg Steller's journal of the second sea portion of the second expedition. Steller is often considered to be the first scientist to describe Alaskan phenomena.

85 **Bering's voyages: the reports from Russia.**

Gerhard Friedrich Müller, translated with commentary by Carol Urness. Fairbanks, Alaska: University of Alaska Press, 1986. 221p. 23 maps. bibliog. (Rasmuson Library Historical Translation Series, vol. III).

Müller was one of the first members of the newly created Russian Academy of Sciences. He accompanied the Bering expedition as far as Kamchatka and spent many years in Siberia researching its history. This new translation of Müller's account includes extensive contributions by Urness, placing the events and controversies in context with explanations of the text's history and influence through time.

86 **Bering's voyages: whither and why.**

Raymond H. Fisher. Seattle, Washington: University of Washington Press, 1977. 217p. maps. bibliog.

Widely regarded as the best work on this question, it is a carefully reasoned and thoroughly researched revisionist explanation of the true goals of the two voyages led by Vitus Bering which resulted in the discovery of Alaska in 1741. Fisher argues that Peter the Great had more in mind than a simple question of geography and that the ultimate establishment of Russian America was more than an accidental by-product of the two Kamchatka expeditions.

87 **A chronological history of the discovery of the Aleutian Islands.**

Vasilli Nikolaevich Berkh. Kingston, Ontario: Limestone Press, 1974. 127p. (Materials for the Study of Alaska History, 5).

Translated from the Russian edition of 1823, this is one of the standard references for early, and obscure, voyages that are otherwise not well documented. There is an earlier, but not widely distributed translation of this work by the Works Progress Administration done in 1938.

88 **Early visitors to southeastern Alaska: nine accounts.**

Edited by Robert N. DeArmond. Anchorage: Alaska Northwest, 1978. 214p. maps. bibliog.

This compilation contains short observations by James Cook, 1778; Captain George Dixon, 1787; Captain Nathaniel Portlock, 1787; Captain Richard Cleveland, 1799; Captain John D'Wolf, 1805-6; Captain Camille de Roquefeuil, 1818; Commander Edward Belcher, 1837; Sir George Simpson 1841-42; and Captain Richard Collinson, 1850.

89 **Exploration in Alaska: Captain Cook commemorative lectures.**
Edited by Antoinette Shalkop. Anchorage: Cook Inlet Historical Society, 1980. 219p. 13 maps. bibliog.

This lecture series was established to celebrate the bicentennial of Captain Cook's voyage in Alaskan waters. Extensively illustrated topics include an examination of technical and human aspects of exploration in the 18th century, information on other explorers, including those from Russia and Spain, and related topics concerning Alaska Natives. This is an excellent introduction for anyone interested in an overview.

90 **Flood tide of empire: Spain and the Pacific Northwest, 1543-1819.**
Warren L. Cook. New Haven, Connecticut; London: Yale University Press, 1973. 620p. bibliog.

This is an expanded PhD dissertation on why the Spanish were unable to exploit successfully their claims to the entire Pacific Northwest beyond California, including Alaska. It is exceptionally well documented.

91 **Georg Wilhelm Steller: the pioneer of Alaska natural history.**
Leonhard Stejneger. Cambridge, Massachusetts: Harvard University Press, 1936. 623p. maps. bibliog.

Georg Steller was the naturalist assigned to Bering's ship on the voyage of discovery to Alaska in 1741. This is the best known of the accounts of his work. One of the most important episodes on the return voyage is the winter spent destitute on Bering Island, during which Bering died. Steller himself died as he was returning overland to St. Petersburg, and his descriptions of natural phenomena were published posthumously. These included the first descriptions of a number of species, including the Steller sea cow, a manatee which became extinct a few years later.

92 **Goldenberg's Gvozdev: the Russian discovery of Alaska in 1732.**
L. A. Goldenberg, edited by James L. Smith. Anchorage: White Stone Press, 1990. 156p. bibliog.

This is a translation of a book first published in Russian in 1985. Gvozdev was a land surveyor who participated in elements of the Great Northern Expedition of which Bering's 1728 and 1741 voyages were a part. In 1732, he landed on the Seward Peninsula in one of the expedition's ships, thus actually reaching North America nine years before Bering and Chirikov.

93 **John Ledyard's journal of Captain Cook's last voyage.**
John Ledyard, edited by James K. Munford. Corvallis, Oregon: Oregon State University, 1963. 264p. 5 maps. bibliog.

Ledyard's original journal, or rather account, was written after the voyage ended, but it was rushed into print in 1783, before the official 1784 voyage account was published in London (see item no. 117). He was an American in British service, serving Cook as a corporal of marines. This modern edition is furnished with extensive explanatory notes, a useful preface and introduction, illustrations that were not in the original edition, and a helpful, if brief, bibliography. The original edition was instrumental in luring numbers of 'Boston Men' into the Alaska fur trade.

94 **Journal of a voyage with Bering, 1741-1742.**
Georg Wilhelm Steller, edited by O. W. Frost, translated by Margritt A. Engel. Stanford, California: Stanford University Press, 1988. 252p. 4 maps. bibliog.

In a substantial introduction, Frost places this new version of the journal in context through a consideration of earlier works by and about Steller. Steller was a prolific natural scientist who accompanied Bering on his voyage of discovery. Many, if not most, of his manuscript reports have, however, been lost. This journal is a translation of the copy of the German journal deposited at the Library of Congress in 1917 by the American historian Frank Golder.

95 **The journal of Tomas de Suria of his voyage with Malaspina to the Northwest Coast of America in 1791.**
Edited with an introduction by Donald C. Cutter. Fairfield, Washington: Ye Galleon Press, 1980. 90p.

This was originally translated by Henry R. Wagner in the *Pacific Historical Review* in 1936 and in a very limited and now scarce edition issued by the Arthur H. Clark Company. The Malaspina voyage was a Spanish scientific circumnavigation, much like the British Cook expeditions. It had the best trained scientific crew of any of the Spanish voyages to Alaska. Tomas de Suria was a Mexican who joined the expedition to replace another artist who had left. His was the only unofficial journal kept on the expedition. A few of his drawings are reproduced.

96 **The journals of Captain James Cook of his voyages of discovery . . .**
Compiled by James Cawte Beaglehole. Cambridge, England: Cambridge University Press, 1955. 4 vols. (Hakluyt Society. Extra Series 34-36).

Beaglehole has brought together the the various journals in a scholarly edition which has become the standard work. Any serious study of Cook's voyages must include this along with the original published accounts.

97 **The life of Captain James Cook.**
John Cawte Beaglehole. Stanford, California: Stanford University Press, 1974. 760p. maps. bibliog.

There are many biographies of this most famous British explorer, but this remains the standard in terms of where Cook went and what he did. A New Zealander, Beaglehole made a life's work of Cook and his expeditions. His modern scholarly edition of the journals of Cook's three major voyages (see above) prepared him for this effort, which was nearly completed when he died. Although only a part of this work deals with the Alaska portion of Cook's third voyage, Cook's importance in the exploration of the North Pacific makes a study of his life worthwhile for anyone interested in the exploration of Alaska.

98 **Malaspina and Galiano: Spanish voyages to the Northwest Coast, 1791 and 1792.**
Donald C. Cutter. Seattle, Washington: University of Washington Press, 1991. 160p. 6 maps. bibliog.

This work was published to accompany an exhibition with the same title, mounted at the Vancouver Maritime Museum in 1991. Malaspina's was the most scientifically ambitious of all of the Spanish voyages to Alaskan waters, done in the manner of the British Cook or the French LaPerouse expeditions. The commentary is accompanied by photographs of artefacts collected, and reproductions of drawings and maps made on the voyage.

99 **Memoirs and travels.**
Mauritius Augustus Benyowskii. London: G. G. J. and J. Robinson, 1780. 2 vols.

Exiled in Kamchatka as a Polish prisoner of war, Benyowskii participated in a revolt and fled with 96 others to Macao, claiming to have sailed to the Bering Strait, Kodiak Island, the Aleutians and the Kuriles on the way. Much of this colourful tale is improbable and should be used with caution. It was very popular, with editions and translations issued in Holland, Germany, Poland, Sweden and France.

100 **The men with wooden feet: the Spanish exploration of the Pacific Northwest.**
John Kendrick. Toronto: NC Press, 1985. 168p. bibliog.

Kendrick is concerned with the process of exploration and his prose flows easily; however, his work lacks the scope and careful judgement of Warren Cook's *Flood tide of empire* (q.v.).

101 **Russian discoveries in the Pacific and North America in the eighteenth and nineteenth centuries.**
Alexander Andreev, translated by Carl Ginsberg. Ann Arbor, Michigan: published for the American Council of Learned Societies by J. W. Edwards, 1952. 214p.

This is a compilation of documents translated from the 1944 Russian edition. Subjects include early Cossack activities in the Aleutian Islands during the 1760s, the Golikov-Shelekhov fur trading company during the years 1785-90, and the journal of W. I. Korobitsyn, clerk of the Russian-American Company for the years 1795-1807.

102 **Russian expansion on the Pacific 1641-1850: an account of the earliest and later expeditions made by the Russians along the Pacific Coast of Asia and North America, including some related expeditions to the Arctic regions.**
Frank A. Golder. Cleveland, Ohio: Arthur H. Clark, 1914. 368p. 10 maps. bibliog.

About half of this pioneering study is related to developments leading up to Bering's second voyage. This includes the eastward expansion of the Russian fur trade into

Siberia and the occupation of Kamchatka. Nine appendices provide texts related to the Dezhnev and Bering voyages and to other exploration accounts.

103 **Russia in Pacific waters in 1715-1825; a survey of the origins of Russia's naval presence in the North and South Pacific.**
Glynn R. Barratt. Vancouver, Canada: University of British Columbia Press, 1981. 300p. maps. bibliog.

From Vitus Bering, who was a Dane in Russian service, to the 'collapse of hopes for Russian naval hegemony in the North Pacific', the Russian Navy was an important player, even though the Russian-American Company was a commercial venture. Barratt does not deal with non-Russian explorers or with merchant sailors except as they relate to the naval interests of Russia.

104 **The Russian expedition to America.**
Sven Waxell, translated by M. A. Michael from Johan Skalberg's Danish version. New York: Collier Books, 1962. 236p. maps. bibliog.

Lieutenant Sven Waxell was a Swede in Russian service assigned to Vitus Bering's second expedition (Second Kamchatka Expedition). He served in that capacity for sixteen years and was the only officer to have served (and survived) the entire expedition. He later wrote a voyage account for official submission, which he finished in German in 1756. It remained relatively unknown until a Danish translation was published in 1948. The first printing of this English translation was in 1952.

105 **Russians on the Pacific, 1743-1799.**
Raisa V. Makarova, translated by Richard A. Pierce, Alton S. Donnelly. Kingston, Ontario: Limestone Press, 1974. 301p. bibliog. (Materials for the Study of Alaskan History, no. 6).

This is an account of various private expeditions of Russian fur traders (*promyshlenniks*) which visited Alaska from the time of the second Bering expedition to the establishment of the government-mandated monopoly of the Russian-American Company. The records of these commercial small-scale enterprises are often scanty, but the only available source for this period. A chronology of voyages is included in the appendix as well as a lengthy contract of the Moscow merchant Vasilii Serebrennikov (1773). This is a translation from the Russian edition of 1968.

106 **Russian penetration of the north Pacific Ocean, 1700-1799: a documentary record.**
Edited and translated by Basil Dmytryshyn, E. A. P. Crownhart-Vaughan, Thomas Vaughan. Portland, Oregon: Oregon Historical Society, 1986. 557p. bibliog. (North Pacific Studies Series, no. 10).

A somewhat eclectic collection of reports and correspondence, it is part of a multi-volume series on historical sources for the study of Russian activity in the Russian Far East, the north Pacific and Alaska.

107 **Siberia and Northwestern America, 1788-1792: The journal of Carl Heinrich Merck, naturalist with the Russian scientific expedition led by Captain Joseph Billings.**
Carl Heinrich Merck, translated by Fritz Jaensch. Kingston, Ontario: Limestone Press, 1980. 215p. map. bibliog. (Materials for the Study of Alaskan History, no. 17).

Catherine the Great ordered the Billings expedition to further explore Alaskan waters in 1785. Merck, a physician, became the naturalist for the expedition. Most of his papers were scattered and lost until the 1930s. Merck describes ethnological as well as natural phenomena.

108 **The significance of Cook's third voyage to Russian tenure in the North Pacific.**
James R. Gibson. *Pacific Studies*, vol. 1 (1978), p. 119-46.

Cook's expedition met the Russians on the Aleutians and on the Kamchatka Peninsula. This is an assessment of their relationship, what information they exchanged, and what the British presence meant for the relatively small numbers of Russians established there. The Russians realized how vulnerable their establishment was to European vessels and the British became aware of the tremendous commercial potential of the fur trade with China.

109 **Surveyor of the sea: the life and voyages of Captain George Vancouver.**
Bern Anderson. Seattle, Washington: University of Washington Press, 1960. 274p. maps. bibliog.

Anderson's work emphasizes the mapping and surveying work of this most precise hydrographer. For some parts of Southeast Alaska, his maps and surveys remained the primary authority for 100 years.

110 **Vitus Bering: the discoverer of Bering Strait.**
Peter Lauridsen, translated from the Danish by Joulius Olson. Chicago, Illinois: S. C. Griggs and Co., 1889. 223p.

This is the first full-length biography of Bering published in English.

111 **The voyage of Semen Dezhnev in 1648: Bering's precursor with selected documents.**
Raymond H. Fisher. Cambridge, England: Hakluyt Society, 1981. 326p. 22 maps. bibliog.

Records of Dezhnev's voyage around the eastern tip of Asia through Bering Strait were discovered by Gerhard Friedrich Müller while conducting research in Siberia from 1733 to 1743. Later scholars, most notably the American Frank Golder, doubted the veracity of the voyage accounts. Fisher clearly establishes the account and reproduces the key documents in translation with full scholarly commentary.

112 **A voyage to America, 1783-1787.**
Grigorii Ivanovich Shelikhov, translated Marina Ramsay, edited with an introduction by Richard A. Pierce. Kingston, Ontario: Limestone Press, 1981. 161p. 3 maps. bibliog. (Alaska History, no. 19).

Shelikhov was a merchant who established the first permanent Russian settlement in Alaska. He was instrumental in the establishment of a monopoly trading company, which was formed after his death through the efforts of his wife and business partners. It then became the Russian-American Company. Pierce writes a most useful 35-page biography as the introduction. This voyage account includes information for those interested in ethnography as well as geography.

113 **A voyage to the North Pacific and a journey through Siberia, more than half a century ago.**
John D'Wolf. Fairfield, Washington: Ye Galleon Press, 1968. reprinted ed. 147p.

D'Wolf was a Yankee sea captain who was a business associate of Alexander Baranov, the Chief Manager of the Russian-American Company. He sold ships to the Russians, engaged in extensive trade, and even travelled overland across Siberia from Kamchatka to St. Petersburg. He became friends with a number of important individuals active in Alaska at the time, including Rezanov, Georg Langsdorff and Lieutenant Gavriil Davydov.

114 **A voyage of discovery to the north Pacific Ocean and round the world; in which the coast of North-West America has been carefully examined and accurately surveyed . . . 1790, 1791, 1792, 1793, 1794 and 1795.**
George Vancouver. London: Robinson and Edwards, 1798. 3 vols. and an atlas. maps.

Vancouver's official voyage report is a corner-stone of Alaska exploration and surveying. This is an essential source of information for Alaska, but also of interest for early observations in California, the Oregon country and British Columbia. There have been numerous subsequent editions and translations. This work should be used in conjunction with other sources edited by Lamb (see below) and the published journal of Archibald Menzies (see item no. 79).

115 **A voyage of discovery to the North Pacific and round the world, 1791-1795.**
George Vancouver, edited by W. Kaye Lamb. London: Hakluyt Society, 1984. 4 vols. (Works issued by the Hakluyt Society, 2nd ser. 163-66).

Lamb utilizes all of the then available private journals (the Menzies journal [see item no. 79] became available later) as well as official logs to produce the definitive account of this important voyage. Vancouver's survey of Southeast Alaska remained a major authority for nearly 100 years.

116 **A voyage round the world 1715-1788 . . .**
Jean Francois Galap de La Perouse, edited by M. L. A. Milet-Mureau. Amsterdam; New York: Nico Israel; Da Capo Press, 1969. reprinted ed. 2 vols. and an atlas. maps.

This is the first complete English edition first published in 1799 (the French was published in 1797). LaPerouse led an elaborate French expedition that included the Northwest Coast in its planned itinerary. The expedition was lost in the South Seas, but not before they sent copies of their Alaskan exploration records overland across Siberia to France. The exploration of the Lituyia Bay region was especially important.

117 **A voyage to the Pacific Ocean. Undertaken by command of His Majesty, for making discoveries in the northern hemisphere, to determine the position and extent of the west side of North America; its distance from Asia; and the practicability of a northern passage to Europe . . . 1776, 1777, 1778, 1779, and 1780.**
James Cook, James King. London: G. Nicoll & T. Cadell, 1784. 3 vols. and an atlas. maps.

A number of important discoveries were made, not only in Alaska but elsewhere in the Pacific (including the Hawaiian Islands). Cook himself was a highly trained surveyor, and his hydrographic charts are among the most influential of the eighteenth century. Artists accompanied the voyage, and the published illustrations are among the first widely distributed images on Alaska. The original, authorized expedition publication was preceded by others brought to press hastily to fill reader demand. This authorized version sold out almost immediately.

118 **Voyages made in the years 1788 and 1789 from China to the North West Coast of America.**
John Meares. Amsterdam; New York: Nico Israel; Da Capo Press, 1967. 372p. 10 maps. (Bibliotheca Australiana, no. 22).

This profusely illustrated work, first published in London in 1790, documents the experiences and discoveries of one of the early English traders to Alaska and the Pacific Northwest. He had encounters with the Russians on Kodiak Island and Cook Inlet. His ship was also involved in the Nootka controversy that nearly led to war between Spain and Britain.

119 **Voyages of enlightenment: Malaspina on the Northwest Coast 1791/1792.**
Alessandro Malaspina, translated and edited by Thomas Vaughan, E. A. P. Crownhart-Vaughan, Mercedes Palou de Inglesias. Portland, Oregon: Oregon Historical Society, 1977. 61p. 7 maps. bibliog.

This volume reproduces drawings made during Malaspina's voyage that are now a part of the Bauza Collection in the Museo de América in Madrid, Spain. They are especially concerned with natives encountered by the expedition.

Russian American era

Russian circumnavigations

120 **The Alaska diary of Adelbert von Chamisso, naturalist on the Kotzebue voyage 1815-1818.**
Translated by Robert Fortuine. Anchorage: Cook Inlet Historical Society, 1986. 69p.

The Kotzebue expedition was privately funded by Count Nikolai Rumiantsov to explore in and north of the Bering Sea and the western Pacific. Chamisso, a French-born German man of letters and science was appointed to be one of two naturalists for the expedition. He later became Curator of the Berlin Botanical Gardens. The text is accompanied by black-and-white reproductions of a number of illustrations created by the expedition's artist, Louis Choris. This publication is only of the Alaska portion of his diary. An edition covering the entire voyage has been published by the University of Hawaii Press (see below).

121 **Around the world on the 'Kamchatka', 1817-1819.**
Vasilli M. Golovnin, translated by Ella Lury Wiswell. Honolulu, Hawaii: University of Hawaii, 1979. 353p. map. bibliog.

This is translated from the Russian editions of 1822 and 1965, with additional commentary and appended material. Russian circumnavigations to Alaskan waters began in 1803 with an average of one a year for the next thirty years. Most had well-trained naval officers who were careful observers and many included trained scientists and artists. Fifteen of the original water-colours of Mihail Tikhanov, artist for this voyage, are reproduced in black and white. In addition to observations on Alaska, there are extensive sections on South America, the Hawaiian Islands, and the South Seas.

122 **The round the world voyage of Hiormonk Gideon, 1803-1809.**
Translated and edited by Lydia T. Black. Kingston, Ontario: Limestone Press, 1989. 186p. maps. bibliog. (Alaska History 32, Alaska State Library Historical Monograph, no. 9).

Gideon sailed with the Krusenstern Expedition and examined conditions that he found in Kodiak, especially regarding the situation of the natives in service to the Russian fur traders.

123 **Russian round-the-world voyages, 1803-1849, with a summary of later voyages to 1867.**
N. A. Ivanshintsov, translated from the Russian edition of 1872 by Glynn R. Barratt. Kingston, Ontario: Limestone Press, 1980. 156p. 13 maps. (Alaska History, no. 14).

This is a compilation of information on 34 voyages made up to 1849, with a brief account for each of them. Many of them are accompanied by a sketch-map of the voyage tracks. A shorter, single-paragraph, account is appended for each additional voyage up to 1864. A useful list of participants with names and ranks is appended with a brief mention of what happened to them in later life, if known.

124 **A voyage of discovery into the South Sea and Bering's Straits, undertaken in the years 1815-1818.**
Otto von Kotzebue. Amsterdam: Nico Israel, 1967. reprint of the 1821 ed. 3 vols. 15 maps. (Bibliotheca Australiana, no. 17-19).

Most Russian voyages to Russian America were sponsored by the government, the Russian-American Company or both. This voyage on the ship *Rurik* was fitted out and sent through the private funding of Count Rumiantsov. The English, Russian and German editions were all published within two years of each other. This was one of the most important expeditions to Alaska. A number of discoveries were made in the South as well as the North Pacific. The artist Louis Choris and naturalists Adelbert Chamisso and Johann Friedrich Escholtz were on board.

125 **A voyage around the world with the Romanzov exploring expedition in the years 1815-1818 in the brig *Rurik*, Captain Otto von Kotzebue.**
Adelbert von Chamisso, translated and edited by Henry Kratz. Honolulu, Hawaii: University of Hawaii Press, 1986. 375p. map. bibliog.

Chamisso moved in German scientific and literary circles before his voyage with the first Kotzebue expedition as the resident naturalist, and he continued his work as a botanist after he returned from the voyage. His job was to report on flora and fauna, but he also writes extensively on human encounters. Only a portion of Chamisso's account covers Alaskan topics, but there are extensive accounts of life aboard ship written by a non-sailor with literary talent. This is not a contemporary journal, but rather written long afterwards – in the 1830s.

126 **A voyage round the world 1826-1829. Vol. 1. To Russian America and Siberia.**
Frederic Litke with Friedrich Heinrich, Baron von Kittlitz, translated by Renee Marshall, Joan Moessner, edited by Richard A. Pierce. Kingston, Ontario: Limestone Press, 1987. 230p. maps. (Alaska History, no. 29).

This is a translation of the French edition of 1835 with a portion of a text by the expedition's ornithologist, von Kittlitz (*Denkwürdigkeiten einer Reise nach dem russischen America*, 1858) as an appendix (p. 121-89). Litke's voyage is important for the scientific work that was completed, for the extensive specimen collections made for St. Petersburg museums, and for the numerous drawings and sketches of life and landscape in Russian America. Some of the plates that were published in the original voyage atlas are reproduced here with explanations by Kittlitz. There are a number of observations concerning life in Russian America in both the Litke and the von Kittlitz texts.

127 **A voyage round the world in the years 1803, 4, 5, & 6, performed in the ship 'Neva'.**
Urey Lisiansky. Amsterdam: Nico Israel, 1968. reprint of the 1814 London ed. 388p. 8 maps. (Bibliotheca Australiana, no. 42).

The *Neva*, under the command of Captain Lisiansky, was the first in a long series of ships exploring and supplying Alaska as a part of the circumnavigation of the earth. A second ship, the *Nadezhda*, carried the expedition commander, Adam von Krusenstern. While Krusenstern stayed on the Asian side embroiled in a difficult voyage to Japan, Lisiansky sailed to Sitka where he aided in its recapture, following its destruction in an attack by Tlingit Indians. This is an important early account of Russian America. The English edition, which was translated by Lisiansky himself, contains maps and illustrations that were published in a separate, and now very rare, atlas in the Russian edition.

128 **Two voyages to Russian America, 1802-1807.**
G. I. Davydov, translated from the Russian edition of 1810-12 by Colin Bearne. Kingston, Ontario: Limestone Press, 1977. 257p. map. (Alaska History, no. 10).

The naval officers Davydov and Khvostov spent a number of years in the service of the Russian-American Company. Davydov's account is notable for its ethnographical content.

129 **Voyages and travels in various parts of the world, during the years 1803, 1804, 1805, 1806, and 1807.**
Georg Heinrich von Langsdorff. Amsterdam: Nico Israel, 1968. reprint of the London 1813-14 ed. 2 vols.

Langsdorff accompanied the Krusenstern expedition, serving as a physician and naturalist. He left the expedition in Kamchatka in 1805. He accompanied the Rezanov mission to California. His other observations include descriptions of the Pribilof Islands, Unalaska, Kodiak, Sitka, and an extensive journey across Siberia.

Northwest Passage and land exploration

130 **Civil and savage encounters: the worldly travel letters of an Imperial Russian navy officer, 1860-1861.**
Pavel Nikolaevich Golovin, translated and edited by Basil Dmytryshyn, Elizabeth Crownhart-Vaughan. Portland, Oregon: Oregon Historical Society, 1983. 175p.

These are the private letters of a well-placed naval officer. Golovin's official duty was to investigate and report on the operations and future prospects of the Russian-American company (q.v.). His account, published in Russia after his death, includes his travel to and from Alaska, and in such places as Germany, France, Great Britain, the eastern United States, Panama and the west coast. His description of life at Sitka includes local colour and social life. His description of a formal ball in the governor's mansion and his description of the growing madness of the director of the magnetic observatory are especially frank.

131 **Continental dash: the Russian-American Telegraph.**
Rosemary Neering. Ganges, British Columbia: Harsdal & Shubart, 1989. 230p. 4 maps. bibliog.

The Western Union Telegraph project was launched as an alternative to a trans-Atlantic cable to unite Europe and North America. The proposed route went up through what is now British Columbia and along the Yukon River valley before crossing Bering Strait to proceed across Siberia. The project lasted from 1864 to 1867, when another attempt was finally successful in laying cable across the Atlantic. Americans participating in this preliminary study phase of the project were able to learn about interior Alaska and Siberia. Several became leading US experts on Alaska during the following decades.

132 **Duflot de Mofras' travel on the Pacific coast.**
Eugene Duflot de Mofras, translated by Marguerite Eyer Wilber from the original French of 1844. Santa Anna, California: Fine Arts Press, 1937. 2 vols.

Duflot de Mofras was one of the best non-Russian observers of California and Russian America. The book includes an excellent description of the Russian colony at Fort Ross, California, and contains some excellently rendered cartography.

133 **Journal of H. M. S. *Enterprise*, on the expedition in search of Sir John Franklin's ships by Bering Strait, 1850-55.**
Richard Collinson, edited by T. B. Collinson. London: S. Low, Marston, Searle & Rivington, Ltd., 1889. 531p. 7 maps.

Collinson's account was published nearly forty years after his voyage, which had been a part of the massive search from both sides of the continent for John Franklin's expedition, from which he had not returned. Franklin's two ships, the *Erebus* and the *Terror*, had left England in 1845. During her part of the search, the *Enterprise* spent three years in the Arctic. The expedition was able successfully to sail along the entire northern coast of Alaska and into the Central Canadian Arctic.

134 **The journal of Rochfort Maguire, 1852-1854: two years at Point Barrow, Alaska, aboard H. M. S. *Plover* in the search for Sir John Franklin.**
Edited by John Bockstoce. London: Hakluyt Society, 1989. 2 vols. maps. bibliog.

The *Plover* was part of an eight-ship fleet operating via Barrow Strait in an attempt to rescue Sir John Franklin when he failed to return from his voyage in search of a Northwest passage. Bockstoce's 55-page introduction summarizes contacts between Eskimos and outsiders up to that date. Maguire's journal is rich in ethnographic detail, and is one of the first extended accounts of life at Point Barrow.

135 **A. F. Kashevarov's coastal explorations in Northwest Alaska, 1838.**
A. F. Kashevarov, translated by David Kraus, edited with an introduction by James W. VanStone. Chicago, Illinois: Field Museum of Natural History, 1977. 104p. 7 maps. bibliog. (Fieldiana: Anthropology, no. 69).

Kashevarov explored from Cape Lisburne along the coast to 30 miles east of Point Barrow. His party used small boats, because large ships had great difficulties with the combination of ice and shallow water. Kashevarov was born in Alaska and trained in St. Petersburg. He spent most of his career working for the Russian-American Company as a sailing officer or as a cartographer for the Hydrographic Office. His was the first expedition in this region to include an Inupiat-speaking interpreter.

136 **V. S. Khromchenko's coastal explorations in Southwest Alaska, 1822.**
V. S. Khromchenko, translated by David Kraus, edited with an introduction by James W. VanStone. Chicago, Illinois: Field Museum, 1973. 95p. 5 maps. bibliog. (Fieldiana: Anthropology, no. 64).

Khromchenko was accompanied by A. K. Etolin. Extensive coastal surveys were completed, including the first detailed examination of Nunivak Island and Golovnin Bay. Contacts with the region's Eskimos opened up the fur trade. The journal includes significant ethnographic observations.

137 **Life on the Yukon, 1865-1867.**
George R. Adams, edited by Richard A. Pierce. Kingston, Ontario: Limestone Press, 1982. 219p. bibliog. (Alaska History, no. 22).

Adams was a member of the scientific corps of the Collins Telegraph Expedition which was engaged in developing a route for the construction of a telegraph line that was to go through British Columbia and Alaska on its way to Siberia and, ultimately, Europe. The project was cut short by the successful transatlantic cable. The Yukon River basin was then little known to the outside world. While this account remained unpublished, other members of the expedition wrote many of the first English-language accounts of Alaska and parts of Siberia – these included Dall (q.v.), George Kennan, Richard Rush, Henry W. Elliott (q.v.) and Frederick Whymper (q.v.).

138 **Lieutenant Zagoskin's travels in Russian America, 1842-1844.**
Lavrentii A. Zagoskin, edited and translated by Henry N. Michael and Penelope Rainey from the 1956 Russian edition. Toronto, Canada: University of Toronto Press; Arctic Institute of North America, 1967. 358p. map. bibliog. (Arctic Institute of North America Anthropology of the North: Translations from Russian Sources, no. 7).

This is one of the leading sources for the study of the exploration of Alaska and the ethnography of the lower Yukon and Kuskokwim rivers. The book begins with a concise 32-page account of the life and works of Zagoskin, followed by various articles that Zagoskin had written, which set the scene for his main account: travel across Russia and Siberia to the eastern seaboard to voyage to Russian America on a company vessel and a vivid description of the Russian American headquarters settlement, Sitka. He writes a detailed account of the interaction between his party and native populations who had little previous direct contact with Russians. Appendices include a statistical table for the populations he contacted and native-language vocabularies. An 'index to names' consists of short biographies of individuals mentioned in the text. There is also a glossary of geographical place-names.

139 **Narrative of a voyage to the Pacific and Beering's Strait, to co-operate with the polar expeditions; performed in His Majesty's ship *Blossom* . . . in the years 1825, 26, 27, 28 . . . .**

Frederick W. Beechey. Amsterdam; New York: Nico Israel; Da Capo Press, 1969. reprinted ed. 2 vols.

Beechey's voyage contains a number of parts that do not directly relate to Alaska. For example, he visited Rio de Janeiro, Easter Island, Tahiti, California, Hawaii and Pitcairn Island where the mutineers from the *Bounty* had finally settled. For Alaska, there is important information on the Aleutian and Pribilof Islands, other islands in the Bering Sea and especially the northern coast of Alaska to beyond Point Barrow. There are a number of significant observations of Eskimo ways.

140 **The odyssey of a Russian scientist: I. G. Voznesenskii in Alaska, California and Siberia, 1839-1849.**

A. I. Alekseev, translated by Wilma C. Fullette, edited by Richard A. Pierce. Kingston, Ontario: Limestone Press, 1987. 139p. maps. (Alaska History, no. 30).

Voznesenskii collected specimens for the Russian Academy of Sciences in Kamchatka and Russian America. His extraordinary efforts spanned a number of years, and his activities provide insight into the nature and extent of science in pre-purchase Alaska. He made drawings depicting Russian America, 25 of which are reproduced in this volume.

141 **Russian exploration in Southwest Alaska: the travel journals of Petr Korsakovskiy (1818) and Ivan Ya. Vasilev (1829).**

Edited by James W. VanStone, translated by David H. Kraus. Fairbanks, Alaska: University of Alaska Press, 1988. 120p. 13 maps. bibliog. (Rasmuson Library Historical Translation Series, no. 4).

These are the first expeditions to the region occupied by Yupik-speaking Eskimos on the Nushagak River. VanStone has published widely on this region and conducted archaeological and ethnographic field-work there between 1964 and 1970.

142 **Travel and adventure in the Territory of Alaska, formerly Russian America – now ceded to the United States – and in various other parts of the North Pacific.**

Frederick Whymper. London: John Murray, 1868. 331p. map.

This work is especially useful for its description and the author's vivid illustrations of the Yukon valley, an area that was little known to the outside world before the work of the Collins Telegraph Expedition who were active at the very end of the Russian era in Alaska.

American era

Through the gold rush (1867-1910)

143 **Alaska: its southern coast and the Sitkan Archipelago.**
E. Ruhamah Scidmore. Boston, Massachusetts: D. Lathrop, 1885. 333p.

This is the first, and probably most widely read of the numerous early popular travel guides to southeast Alaska. These chapters first appeared as newspaper columns in St. Louis and New York. Scidmore visited Alaska during several summers and utilized the standard reference works in compiling her description. Although there are a number of errors of detail, her work gives a feel for Alaska in the 1880s.

144 **Alaska's Copper River: the 18th and 19th centuries.**
William S. Hanable. Anchorage: Alaska Historical Society for the Alaska Historical Commission, 1982. 99p. bibliog. (Alaska Historical Commission Studies in History, no. 21).

This is a useful, brief overview of a river that seemed to promise a major route from the coast at Prince William Sound to the interior of Alaska. Early Russian attempts failed and there was loss of life. The Lieutenant Allen expedition finally ascended the river in 1886 and it became the scene of considerable activity during the gold rush.

145 **The Alaskan voyage, 1881-1883: an expedition to the Northwest Coast of America.**
Johan Adrian Jacobsen, translated by Erna Gunther from the German text of Adrian Woldt. Chicago, Illinois: University of Chicago Press, 1977. 266p. bibliog.

Jacobsen, a Norwegian, travelled to Alaska in order to collect native artefacts for the Royal Berlin Ethnological Museum. He travelled widely, from the Haida Indians on the Queen Charlotte Islands of British Columbia, to the Yukon, and farther north to the Seward Peninsula and Kotzebue Sound. An amateur ethnographer, he made extensive observations of native life. There are many illustrations of artefacts that he collected.

146 **Blazing Alaska's trails.**
Alfred H. Brooks, compiled by L. Burton. Caldwell, Idaho: Caxton Printers, 1953. Reissued jointly by the University of Alaska and the Arctic Institute of North America in 1973. 528p. maps.

A collection of 27 essays written between 1914 and 1922 relating to Alaskan exploration. Brooks was director of the United States Geological Survey in Alaska and is the author of numerous technical government publications.

147 **The boundary hunters: surveying the 141st meridian and the Alaskan Panhandle.**
Lewis Green. Vancouver, British Columbia: University of British Columbia Press, 1982. 214p. bibliog.

Field work started in 1904 under very difficult conditions. The survey was not completed until sixteen years later.

148 **Chief Sesui and Lieutenant Herron: a story of who controls the bacon.**
William Schneider. *Alaska History*, vol. 1, no. 2 (1985), p. 1-18.

A small military exploring expedition that came through the upper Kuskokwim region in 1899 ran out of food. They were befriended by Chief Sesui and his people.

149 **Compilation of narratives of explorations in Alaska.**
Washington, DC: GPO, 1900. 856p. 20 maps.

This is a cornerstone of the literature of American early exploration. From the 1860s and throughout the gold rush, first a few, and then an increasing number of military exploring expeditions were sent to Alaska. This is a compilation of 51 accounts and sub-accounts. They are primarily accounts of land and river exploration, away from the coasts which were by then relatively well known. These explorers were looking for practical information: routes, food supply, agricultural potential and how best to manage this country which was rapidly filling with boom-and-bust mining settlements at the time this work was published.

150 **Exploration of Alaska, 1865-1900.**
Morgan B Sherwood. Fairbanks, Alaska: University of Alaska Press, 1992. 3rd printing. 207p. 10 maps. (The original 1965 edition was in the Yale Western Americana Series, no. 7).

This remains the standard one-volume history of the American exploration of Alaska from just before the purchase (the Western Union Telegraph expedition) through to the completion of the gold rush era reconnaissance expeditions. Writing from the perspective of the history of science, Sherwood details the work done by a variety of government agencies: the US Army, US Navy, Revenue Marine Service, Coast and Geodetic Survey, the US Geological Survey and the Smithsonian Institution.

151 **Harriman Alaska Expedition.**
Edited by C. Hart Merriam. Washington, DC: Smithsonian Institution, 1910-14. vols. I-V, VIII-XVI. 12 vols in 13. maps.

Edward Harriman, a railway magnate, decided to assemble an elaborate scientific cruise to Alaska aboard a large chartered yacht during the summer of 1899. He invited 25 leading experts on Alaska to form a scientific party to accompany him. He also brought along two photographers, two artists, stenographers, a medical staff, hunters, camp hands and 65 officers and crew. The scientific publications that resulted are classics in the field and were published over the course of the next two decades, the first two volumes by Doubleday, before the entire series shifted to the Smithsonian Institution. Volumes were published on history, glaciers, geology, botany, insects, crustaceans, molluscs, and other topics, each supported by hundreds of illustrations.

One volume of plates is devoted to starfish alone. For a history of the expedition see Goetzmann (item no. 157).

152 **In search of gold: the Alaska journals of Horace S. Conger 1898-1899.**

Edited by Carolyn Jean Holeski, Marlene Conger Holeski. Anchorage: Alaska Geographic Society, 1983. 331p. bibliog. (Alaska Historical Commission Studies in History, no. 28).

Conger was a 34-year-old pharmacist from Minnesota who was lured to the gold rush. He became a member of a party attempting to reach the gold-fields over the glacier at Valdez. They brought along thousands of pounds of supplies per person and a lot of gadgets of dubious value. The letters and diary entries are well edited and depict the adventure of a typical gold rush amateur who had the misfortune to choose a route that required glacier travel, in late winter, along with several thousand others. He prospected the relatively unproductive Chistochina district. Many of the miners who were with him died and he never did make it to real 'pay dirt'.

153 **In the Alaskan wilderness.**

George Byron Gordon. Philadelphia, Pennsylvania: John C. Winston Company, 1917. Reprinted by AMS in 1978. 247p. maps.

A journey made in 1907 by two brothers up the Kantishna from the Tanana River to Lake Minchumina, over the portage to the next watershed and down the Kuskokwim. Although portions of this route were well known, they were the first to complete the entire route.

154 **A journey to Alaska in 1868, being the diary of the late Emil Teichmann.**

Edited with an introduction by Oskar Teichmann. New York: Argosy-Antiquarian, 1963. 272p.

This is the travel diary – a reprint of a 1925 family-published limited edition work – of a young twenty-one-year-old businessman representing major London fur interests who travelled to Alaska in 1868 by way of the Isthmus of Panama and using a small chartered sailing boat. His is one of the first accounts of the period immediately following the establishment of American rule during a transition period when many Russians were still in Sitka. The portrait of the newly arrived American opportunists who came with the US military is not flattering.

155 **Lady Franklin visits Sitka, Alaska, 1870: the journal of Sophia Cracroft, Sir John Franklin's niece.**

Edited by Robert N. DeArmond. Anchorage: Alaska Historical Society, 1981. 134p. map.

This compilation provides a glimpse of Sitka in May and June 1870. Sitka had been the Russian headquarters and then became the American centre of government. Small as it was, it was for a long time the major settlement in Alaska. This early period is very poorly documented and a book such as this fills a real need. In addition to a transcription of the journal itself, there is a redrawn map of the Sitka townsite, with an appendix that inventories Sitka's buildings. The original map was made at the time of transfer by the Russian Commissioner, A. Pestchouroff, and is annotated by DeArmond, with notes about the ultimate fate of the buildings (most were destroyed by fire or torn down in an advanced state of disrepair). A second appendix reproduces the 1870 manuscript census, which enumerated 391 souls, not including the more than 100 soldiers stationed there at the time. Both of the visitors were well travelled and their comments reflect upon the rustic nature of this small settlement.

156 **Letters from Alaska: John Muir.**
Edited by Robert Engberg, Bruce Merrell. Madison, Wisconsin: University of Wisconsin Press, 1993. 115p. maps. bibliog.

This edition differs from the original 1915 publication (see item no. 165) in that it uses Muir's original dispatches to the *San Francisco Daily Evening Bulletin* newspaper rather than the version of these that Muir himself continued to revise until the end of his life.

157 **Looking far north: the Harriman expedition to Alaska 1899.**
William H. Goetzmann, Kay Sloan. Princeton, New Jersey: Princeton University Press, 1982. 244p. bibliog.

Railway millionaire Edward H. Harriman decided to travel to Alaska during the summer of 1899. He made an expedition of it, renting a large ship. He invited leading scientists, artists, photographers and literary men with an interest in Alaska to come along. The published results of this expedition (see item no. 151) are an important source for the study of Alaska. Goetzman examines the attitudes and assumptions of this crew of Victorian-era luminaries on board what they called a 'floating university'.

158 **Nome nuggets: some of the experiences of a party of gold seekers in northwestern Alaska in 1900.**
Leigh Hill French. New York: Montross Clarke & Emmons, 1901. 102p.

This account is by the leader of the Cape Nome Hydraulic Mining Company expedition.

159 **Our Arctic province: Alaska and the Seal Islands.**
Henry Wood Elliott. New York; London: Scribner; Sampson, Low, 1886. 473p. maps.

Elliott was sent to the Pribilof Islands as a government agent. He made the study of the 'Seal Islands' a personal cause and spent a number of years studying, making maps and drawings, and publishing about them in a number of government reports.

160 **Report of an expedition to the Copper, Tanana, and Koyukuk rivers . . . in the year 1885.**
Henry T. Allen. Washington, DC: GPO, 1887. 172p. 5 maps.

This was one of the most remarkable explorations of the American era. Earlier attempts to fully explore the Copper River basin completely had failed. Allen ascended the Copper River, moved to the Tanana basin and floated down to the confluence of the Tanana and Yukon, and then explored up the Koyukuk, another Yukon tributary. He had travelled about 1,500 miles in a single season. Allen's were the first maps of much of the interior of Alaska. This account was re-issued in the *Compilation of narratives* in 1900 (q.v.).

161 **Report of the operations of the US Revenue Steamer *Nunivak* on the Yukon River Station, Alaska 1899-1901.**
Washington, DC: GPO, 1902. 325p.

This steam riverboat was in service at the height of the gold rush along the Yukon. The report begins with a general description of the condition of Alaska and then proceeds to the details of life on the Yukon. The *Nunivak* overwintered in a slough on the river. The account is extensively illustrated.

162 **A summer in Alaska: a popular account of an Alaskan exploring expedition along the great Yukon River, from its source to its mouth . . . .**
Frederick Schwatka. St. Louis, Missouri: J. W. Henry, 1893. 418p. maps.

Lieutenant Schwatka was one of the best-known and popular Arctic and Alaskan explorers of his time. In this journey, he and his party went over the coastal range at the head of Lynn Canal to the headwaters of the Yukon after a voyage up the Inside Passage from the Vancouver Barracks, Washington Territory. This became the most common route used during the Klondike gold rush a few years later. He and his men constructed a raft which they used to float down the 2,000-mile length of the Yukon. Schwatka was not by any means the first to explore this country, but his illustrated account gives an excellent pre-gold rush overview of the upper and lower Yukon River valley.

163 **Ten thousand miles with a dogsled: a narrative of winter travel in interior Alaska.**
Hudson Stuck, reprinted edition edited by Terrence Cole. Lincoln, Nebraska: University of Nebraska Press, 1988. 410p.

A classic depiction of winter travel in interior Alaska. It describes some half dozen journeys made between 1904 and 1913 by the Episcopal Archdeacon in travelling to the various missions under his care. It was originally published by C. Scribner's Sons in 1914 with a second printing in 1916. A second edition was issued in 1927. It was also reprinted by Wolfe Publishing of Prescott, Arizona, in 1988.

164 **To the Chukchee Peninsula and to the Tlingit Indians 1881/1882: journals and letters by Aurel and Arthur Krause.**
Translated by Margot Kraus McCaffrey from the German edition of 1984 edited by Gerhard Krause, Ingeborg Krause, translation edited by Marvin W. Falk. Fairbanks, Alaska: University of Alaska Press, 1993. 230p. maps.

Two trained German scientists, the Krause brothers, were sent to the Chukchee Peninsula and Southwest Alaska by the Bremen Geographic Society to gather specimens and conduct studies. This is the human side of the expedition, which resulted in a number of scientific publications, most notably an ethnography of the

Tlingit Indians (see item no. 507). The account is accompanied by reproductions of hand-drawn sketches made during the expeditions.

165 **Travels in Alaska.**
John Muir. Boston, Massachusetts; New York: Houghton Mifflin, 1915. 327p.

This is an enduring and frequently reprinted classic of nature writing on Alaska. Muir first travelled to Alaska in 1879 and became fascinated with its glaciers. These descriptions end in 1890. He was the first to explore and write about Glacier Bay. His careful literary style lends itself well to descriptions of landscapes and flora, and to evocations of how it feels to travel through wilderness in a canoe.

166 **A Victorian earl in the Arctic: the travels and collections of the Fifth Earl of Lonsdale 1888-89.**
Shepard Krech, III. Seattle, Washington: University of Washington Press, 1989. 216p. bibliog.

The Earl spent a year in Alaska and Canada, hunting and collecting native artefacts. A major section of the book is devoted to the nature of his collecting and how it reflected his Victorian assumptions and attitudes.

167 **Voyages on the Yukon and its tributaries: a narrative of summer travel in the interior of Alaska.**
Hudson Stuck. New York: C. Scribner's Sons, 1917. 397p. map.

This was written as a companion to *Ten thousand miles with a dogsled* (q.v.). It depicts travel by the motor launch *Pelican* with a description of conditions along the rivers. Stuck is especially concerned with native conditions along his routes. There are also interesting descriptions of the country, the gold camps and settlements, and conditions experienced by the large commercial paddle-wheel steamboats plying these waters.

168 **The wilderness of Denali: explorations of a hunter-naturalist in northern Alaska.**
Charles Sheldon. New York; London: Charles Scribner's Sons, 1930. 412p. map.

In 1906 and 1908, Sheldon travelled to the area that is now Denali National Park. An observant naturalist as well as a hunter, his descriptions and advocacy were largely responsible for the publicity that led to the creation of a national park there in 1917.

169 **A winter circuit of our Arctic coast: a narrative of a journey with dog-sleds around the entire Arctic coast of Alaska.**
Hudson Stuck. New York; London: C. Scribner's Sons; T. Werner Laurie, 1920. 360p.

A veteran of many years of life in Alaska and many thousands of miles of travel, this is Archdeacon Stuck's fourth travel book. As with the others (q.v.), he describes the details and techniques of travel. This is an extremely long winter trip, taking very nearly six full months to complete. He travelled along the southern Brooks Range to the coast, and then followed it to Point Hope, Point Barrow and Herschel Island in Canada before turning southward to return to his home base in Fort Yukon. He describes the people he meets along the way, and he seems to have met most of the inhabitants of this sparsely populated country.

Post-gold rush (1911-)

170 **Across Arctic America: narrative of the Fifth Thule Expedition.**
Knud Rasmussen. New York; London: G. P. Putnam's Sons, 1927. 388p. 4 maps.

The Fifth Thule is one of the most significant scientific and ethnographic expeditions of the early 20th century in the Arctic. This book is an abridged translation of the Danish original, *Fra Gronland til Sillehavet*. Rasmussen and his colleagues travelled from Greenland across the Canadian Arctic to Western Alaska, starting in 1921 and finishing in 1924. The scientific results, authored by the various scientists involved, were published over a period of twenty years, but are too specialized for inclusion in a general bibliography such as this. Although Alaska was only one portion of this journey, a number of classic observations were made.

171 **Alaska bird trails: adventures of an expedition by dog sled to the delta of the Yukon River at Hooper Bay.**
Herbert Brandt. Cleveland, Ohio: Bird Research Foundation, 1943. 464p.

This is an account of the Hooper Bay Expedition of 1924, a co-operative study of birds by the United States Biological Survey and the Bird Research Foundation. Heavily illustrated with paintings, drawings and photographs, it is an account of the land and people on the 40-day, 850-mile, sled journey as well as the scientific work of the expedition.

172 **Alaska wilderness: exploring the Central Brooks Range.**
Robert Marshall, edited by George Marshall. Berkeley, California: University of California Press, 1970. 2nd ed. 173p. 6 maps.

Published posthumously in 1956 under the title *Arctic wilderness*, this is an account of the personal exploration and mapping of the Koyukuk drainage, conducted from 1929 to 1939 during a number of visits to the region. Much of this area is now a part of the Gates of the Arctic National Park, the creation of which was inspired in large part by Marshall. This classic of wilderness writing has had a powerful influence on the wilderness movement.

173 **Arctic daughter: a wilderness journey.**
Jean Aspen. Minneapolis, Minnesota: Bergamot Books, 1988. 205p.

The author and a companion paddled up an unnamed river in Alaska's Brooks Range to build a cabin and stay for four years. They start out ill-prepared and learned on the way, with the usual rite of self-discovery.

174 **Arctic night's entertainments: being the narrative of an Alaskan-Estonian digger August Masik as told to Isobel Wylie Hutchinson during the Arctic Night of 1933-34 near Martin Point, Alaska.**
August Masik, Isobel Wylie Hutchinson. London; Glasgow: Blackie & Son, 1935. 234p.

Masik was an arctic trader at the time Hutchinson met him at his wintering post off the Arctic coast of Alaska. His previous experiences included work as a sailor, aide to arctic explorers (especially Stefansson), dog musher, miner and trapper. He traded from Nome across to Siberia after the Russian Revolution and up the coast of Alaska.

175 **Arctic odyssey: the diary of Diamond Jenness.**
Edited and annotated by Stuart E. Jenness. Hull, Quebec: Canadian Museum of Civilisation, 1991. 859p. bibliog.

Destined to become one of Canada's most eminent anthropologists, Jenness started his northern career with the Canadian Arctic Expedition (1913-18). He was ultimately responsible for five volumes of the expedition's 14-volume report. These diaries cover the period 1913-16. The expedition started from Alaska. The ship *Karluk* became stuck in the ice and sank, but not before a party, including Jenness, had moved across the ice to shore. Only the first portion of the diaries deal with Alaska, but this experience formed the basis for his *Dawn in Arctic Alaska*. Appended material includes a list of people encountered or mentioned in the diaries, a list of Eskimo words in the diary, a list of items traded for artefacts, a description of Jenness's collections gathered for the National Museum of Canada, a list of singers of Copper Eskimo songs recorded by Jenness, and a list of his photographs with their subject matter. His original drawings are reproduced with the text.

176 **Cradle of the storms.**
Bernard R. Hubbard, SJ. London: George G. Harrap & Co., 1936. 267p.

The 'Glacier Priest' was a member of the geology faculty at the University of Santa Clara. He spent his summers photographing Alaska and much of his winters on the lecture circuit. This trip was to the Aleutians and the Alaska Peninsula, especially Katmai, to examine volcanoes. As with his other publications, this one is popularly written and illustrated with his photographs, and is designed as much for entertainment as it is to convey information.

177 **The cruise of the *Northern Light*: explorations and hunting the Alaskan and Siberian Arctic, in which the sea-scouts have a great adventure.**
Mrs John Borden (Cortney Letts de Espil). New York: Macmillan, 1928. 317p. maps.

This is the account of the Borden-Field Museum 1927 Arctic Expedition. It is essentially a yacht hunting trip, with the added task of collecting flora and fauna (especially bear, walrus and seal) for the Field Museum of Natural History in Chicago. They took along eight boy (sea) scouts.

178 **God's frozen children.**
Harold McCracken. Garden City, New York: Doubleday, Doran, 1930. 291p.

McCracken was a prolific western writer who often picked Alaskan themes. In this work he relates his own experience, written for a popular audience. His goal is to discover Aleut mummies, which he does after many adventures. Modesty concerning his own accomplishments is never allowed to get in the way of a good story.

179 **A guide to Alaska, last American frontier.**
Merle Colby. New York: Macmillan, 1939. 247p. 3 maps. bibliog. (American Guide Series).

Although no longer valuable for current information, this general guide to Alaska depicts the territory as it was on the eve of the Second World War. It is part of the Federal Writers Project conducted under the auspices of the Works Progress Administration, a 'New Deal' agency under the Depression-era administration of President Franklin Roosevelt.

180 **Journeys to the far North.**
Olaus J. Murie. Palo Alto, California: American West Publishing, 1973. 255p.

Murie was a biologist who conducted wildlife research in northern Canada and Alaska for 47 years. These travel accounts depict life on the trail – on foot, in poling boats and with dog teams. A number of ecological issues are raised concerning the Arctic.

181 **99 days on the Yukon: an account of what was seen and heard during 99 days on the Yukon River in the company of Charles A. Wolf, gentleman canoeist.**
Thomas McGuire. Anchorage: Alaska Northwest, 1977. 184p.

In this Yukon River account a younger man learns about the river and reflects upon various issues in the company of his older travelling companion, a retired military musician who has spent his retirement years trapping and travelling in Alaska, most often in his favourite canoe, exploring the rivers. McGuire describes the people he meets along the river, many of them old friends of Charlie Wolf.

182 **North to the rime-ringed sun: being the record of an Alaskan-Canadian journey made in 1933-34.**
Isobel Wylie Hutchison. London; Glasgow: Blackie & Son, 1934. 262p. map.

Hutchison travelled to Alaska to gather wildflowers for the Royal Herbarium of Kew. This popularly written account covers her journey up the Inside Passage, through Dawson and down the Yukon and then on to her Arctic travels. Her account is full of the memorable people that she met along the way to the Mackenzie Delta along Alaska's Arctic coast. She has written a separate book about one of them, August Masik (item no. 174). She travelled by various means, primarily dog-sled and made occasional use of aircraft.

183 **Reading the river: a voyage down the Yukon.**
John Hildebrand. Boston, Massachusetts: Houghton Mifflin Company, 1988. 243p. 3 maps. bibliog.

Hildebrand's solo canoe trip also serves as a voyage of self-discovery and reflection. He revisits the Alaska that he knew as a young college instructor during the height of the pipeline boom. There are vignettes of people he meets along the way during his voyage from Whitehorse in the Yukon Territory to the river's mouth on the Bering Sea. This book is one of the best of the genre.

184 **33 days hath September: a travel adventure cookbook for Alaska's Yukon River.**
Karen Cauble. Fairbanks, Alaska: Vanessapress, 1992. 100p.

This book is unusual in its combination of contents. It is a travel account by a social worker who takes the time from her career to sign up as a cook on a Yukon River tug boat. She describes life aboard the craft with the crew of seven men (whom she describes as the seven dwarfs). She also writes about the country, with its small wilderness villages, that they pass through. For each day's entry, she includes a menu of what she cooked and a recipe.

185 **Tracks across Alaska.**
Alastair Scott. New York; London: Atlantic Monthly Press; John Murray Limited, 1990. 247p. map.

A Scottish visitor comes to Manley Hot Springs, acquires a dog team, and then travels across the Interior to the Bering Sea. This is a well-written account of long-distance recreational mushing, and includes a description of the landscape, the people, and the dogs.

186 **The Valley of Ten Thousand Smokes.**
Robert F. Griggs. Washington, DC: National Geographic Society, 1922. 341p. 9 maps.

An intense eruption of Katmai on the Alaska Peninsula completely altered a 50-square-mile area and deeply affected the surrounding regions, including Kodiak Island. The National Geographic Society considered this one of the wonders of the world and expended a great deal of effort in documenting, exploring and photographing this new landscape of steaming fissures and craters. In part due to the publicity given to it by the Society, this region was established as the Katmai National Monument by President Woodrow Wilson.

187 **Winter watch.**
James Ramsey. Anchorage: Alaska Northwest Books, 1989. 144p.

This journal details log-cabin life from September to June in the northwestern Brooks Range north of the Arctic Circle.

Flora and Fauna

188 **Alaska mammals.**

Edited by Jim Rearden. Anchorage: Alaska Geographic Society, 1981. 184p. (*Alaska Geographic*, vol. 8, no. 2).

This is a popular, brief introduction to seventy-nine species of animals, both land and marine mammals. Each is accompanied by a photograph and a simple sketch-map showing the distribution of habitat.

189 **Alaska mushroom hunter's guide.**

Ben Guild, illustrated by Jack Van Hoesan. Anchorage: Alaska Northwest, 1977. 286p. bibliog.

Mushrooms in Alaska, as elsewhere, are considered great delicacies, but one can make a truly fatal error if they are not correctly identified. Guild also offers advice on how to prepare mushrooms for eating.

190 **Alaska trees and shrubs.**

Leslie A. Viereck, Elbert L. Little. Washington, DC: US Forest Service, 1972. 256p. map. bibliog. (Agriculture Handbook, no. 410).

This is the standard reference. A drawing and a small plant distribution map accompany each description. It was reprinted in paperback by the University of Alaska Press in 1986.

191 **Alaskan bird sketches of Olaus Murie.**

Compiled and edited by Margaret Murie. Anchorage: Alaska Northwest Publishing Company, 1979. 58p. map.

These water-colours and notes were done during the scientific field studies of a biologist active in Alaska during the 1920s and 30s. Locations range from the Aleutian Islands to the Arctic and the Interior.

192 **Alaska's farms and gardens.**
Edited by Robert A. Henning. Anchorage: Alaska Geographic, 1984. 137p. (*Alaska Geographic*, vol. 11, no. 2).

An overview and a general guide to what is, and what can be, raised in Alaska. Due to the length of the growing season, the hours of daylight in the summer, and climatic conditions, not everything can be grown. However, a number of specialized strains have been developed for Alaska, and lists of plants provide information on the varieties available, planting requirements, and the care necessary. There are also chapters on grain and livestock, which include dairy cattle, beef, poultry, swine, sheep, horses and reindeer.

193 **Alaska's saltwater fishes and other sea life.**
Doyne W. Kessler. Anchorage: Alaska Northwest, 1985. 385p. map. bibliog.

This is a field guide that identifies 375 species.

194 **Alaska wild berry guide and cookbook.**
Editors of *Alaska Magazine*. Anchorage: Alaska Northwest, 1982. 201p.

The first part of the book is a short field guide to edible berries, and includes photographs and drawings to aid in identification. Well over half of the book is devoted to the preparation, storage and use of berries in breads, desserts, beverages and as a condiment.

195 **Anderson's flora of Alaska and adjacent parts of Canada.**
Jacob Peter Anderson, Stanley L. Welch. Provo, Utah: Brigham Young University Press, 1974. 3rd ed. 724p. maps. bibliog.

Jacob Anderson collected plants extensively from the 1920s onward. He died in 1953, and the first edition was published in 1959. The current (third) edition was revised and enlarged by Welsh and it remains a frequently used reference.

196 **Animals of the Arctic.**
Bernard Stonehouse. New York: Holt, Rinehart & Winston, 1971. 172p. maps. bibliog.

Stonehouse's introduction to Arctic animals emphasizes the relationships that exist between climate (sometimes micro-climates adjacent to one another) and plants and animals. There is recognition of the variety of habitat within the Arctic, and the work covers birds, land animals and sea life. For the layman, this is a good place to begin.

197 **Birds of Alaska.**
Ira Gahrielson, Frederick C. Lincoln, illustrated by Olaus J. Murie, Edwin R. Kalmbach. Harrisburg, Pennsylvania: Stackpole, 1959. 922p. bibliog.

The authors started working on this substantial reference work in 1942. The lists and descriptions are preceded by a useful 30-page summary of the history of Alaskan ornithology. The list includes only those species that are supported by preserved specimens.

198 **The boreal ecosystem.**

James A. Larsen. New York: Academic Press, 1980. 500p. bibliog.

The boreal forests extend over much of Alaska and across Canada, but Eurasia has about two-thirds of the total area. Larsen treats a variety of subjects, including soil systems, climate, animal populations, cycles, vegetation and boreal communities, and differentiates a number of regional sub-systems. He broadly discusses the state of scientific research as it was in 1980.

199 **Brown bear summer: life among Alaska's giants.**

Thomas Bledsoe. New York: Truman Talley Books, 1987. 249p. bibliog.

Observations were made at the extraordinary McNeil River site on the Alaska Peninsula by a young biologist working with a Utah State University project from 1973 to 1980. As many as 66 bears have been observed here at one time.

200 **Circumpolar arctic flora.**

Nicholas Polunin. Oxford: Clarendon Press, 1959. 514p. map. bibliog.

Despite its age, this remains a valuable guide to the vascular plants of the Arctic. This book is based upon the author's field-work from 1930 to 1949. There are line-drawings for each of the species. An extensive glossary and an index are included.

201 **Field guide to Alaskan wildflowers: a roadside guide.**

Verna Pratt. Anchorage: Alaskakrafts, 1989. 136p.

This field guide is arranged by general appearance: blue and violet flowers, red plants, pink-flowered plants, etc. It includes information on miscellaneous plants and trees, a pictorial glossary, a guide to outstanding areas for finding flowers, and blooming-time charts.

202 **Flora of Alaska and neighbouring territories: a manual of the vascular plants.**

Eric Hultén. Stanford, California: Stanford University Press, 1968. 1,008p. maps. bibliog.

The authoritative reference for Alaska flora, this volume covers 1,974 taxa belonging to 1,559 species, with 1,735 separate range maps that show the distribution for all known Alaskan plants. It is the result of more than 40 years of work. Line-drawings and photographs of the plants accompany the text.

203 **Freshwater fishes of northwestern Canada and Alaska.**

J. D. McPhail, C. C. Lindsey. Ottawa: Fisheries Research Board of Canada, 1970. 381p. (Bulletin of the Fisheries Research Board of Canada, no. 173).

This is a generally accepted, standard reference work.

204 **Frozen fauna of the mammoth steppe: the story of Blue Babe.**
R. Dale Guthrie. Chicago, Illinois: University of Chicago Press, 1990. 232p.

The story of a 36,000-year-old frozen extinct steppe bison that was found in an Alaska gold-mine. Guthrie recreates the environment in which the beast lived, how it most probably died, and why it was so well preserved. He presents and then solves the many mysteries surrounding a full explanation of the find. The book is richly illustrated with drawings and photographs. Guthrie ends with an explanation of how this specimen, dubbed 'Blue Babe', was prepared for exhibition at the University of Alaska Museum.

205 **The grizzlies of Mount McKinley.**
Adolf Murie. Washington, DC: US Department of the Interior, National Park Service, 1981. 251p. 2 maps. bibliog. (Scientific Monograph Series, no. 14).

Murie's classic study of the ecology and behaviour of bears in Denali National Park is based upon observations made between 1922 and 1970. The manuscript was completed posthumously by the author's son, Dr. Jan O. Murie, after Adolf's death in 1974. The length of the study allowed bear families to be observed through several generations.

206 **A guide to the birds of Alaska.**
Robert H. Armstrong. Anchorage: Alaska Northwest, 1981. 309p.

This is a bird-watchers' guide to the identification of 386 species of birds in Alaska. Each species has a photograph and some brief notes on the bird's appearance and habitat.

207 **Illustrated keys to the fresh-water fishes of Alaska.**
James E. Morrow. Anchorage: Alaska Northwest Publishing Company, 1974. 78p.

A brief, simple, general field guide which includes sketches of the fishes.

208 **Intertidal bivalves: a guide to the common marine bivalves of Alaska.**
Nora R. Foster. Fairbanks, Alaska: University of Alaska Press, 1991. 152p. map. bibliog.

This guide includes sketches as well as notes on distribution and habitat. There is also practical information concerning the use of these animals for human consumption, including cautions concerning the occurrence of paralytic shellfish poisoning.

209 **Monarch of Deadman's Bay: the life and death of a Kodiak bear.**
Roger A. Caras. Boston: Little, Brown and Company, 1969. 185p.

Caras explains a bear's life-cycle within its Kodiak Island habitat, including a confrontation with a hunter.

210 The mosses of Arctic Alaska.

William Campbell Steere. Vaduz, Liechtenstein: J. Cramer, 1978. 508p. 48 maps. bibliog.

Steere's work is based on ten years of collecting. It is an annotated catalogue, with a detailed guide to the relevant literature up to the date of publication. Maps show range information, even if specimens are also found outside Arctic Alaska.

211 A naturalist in Alaska.

Adolf Murie, illustrated by Olaus J. Murie. New York: Devin-Adair Company, 1961. 302p.

Murie was a pioneer wildlife specialist whose contributions included scientific observations of wolf behaviour, primarily in Mt. McKinley National Park. This anecdotal account recalls his personal observations and experiences with a host of different species, primarily large mammals.

212 The nature of Southeast Alaska: a guide to plants, animals and habitats.

Rita O'Clair, Robert Armstrong, Richard Carstensen. Anchorage: Alaska Northwest Books, 1992. 254p. maps. bibliog.

A well-illustrated and lively general guide to mammals, fish, invertebrates, fungi, and plants. All are placed within a habitat with a particular landscape and history determined by glacial activity over thousands of years.

213 No room for bears: a wilderness writer's experiences with a threatened breed.

Frank Dufresne. New York: Holt, Rinehart & Winston, 1965. 252p.

Dufresne, a past director of the Alaska Game Commission, gives an anecdotal account of a variety of bear behaviours. He voices an early concern about conservation of the bear and its habitat.

214 Pacific salmon life histories.

Edited by C. Groot, L. Margolis. Vancouver, British Columbia: University of British Columbia Press, 1991. 564p.

This book presents the life-stages of all seven salmon species.

215 A photographic field guide to the mosses, lichens and ferns of Northwest North America.

Dale H. Vitt, Janet E. Marsh, Robin B. Bovey. Seattle, Washington; Edmonton, Alberta: University of Washington Press; Lone Pine Publishing, 1988. 296p. bibliog.

This field guide covers a wide variety of climatic and vegetation zones. Terms and processes are explained in a way readily understood by the layman. Each species is provided with a colour photograph and a range map. The introduction discusses the broad categories of ecological settings, and provides guidelines for the collection, study and photography of specimens.

216 **Plant lore of an Alaskan island.**
Frances Kelso Graham. Anchorage: Alaska Northwest Publishing, 1985. 194p. bibliog.

Graham's book is the result of a three-year effort by an adult education specialist and her students working at Ouzinkie on Spruce Island, near Kodiak. It is an illustrated catalogue of local plants along with advice on how to harvest and store them, information on their medicinal qualities and recipes for cooking with them. Much of this information would be applicable elsewhere, and this effort serves as a model for other regions to develop their own catalogues.

217 **Red salmon, brown bear: the story of an Alaska lake.**
Theodore J. Walker. New York: World Publishing, 1971. 256p. map.

An account, in diary format, of a scientist who spent a little over six months observing and photographing plant and animal communities on remote Lake Eva on Baranof Island in Southeast Alaska.

218 **Tanaina plantlore, Dena'ina k'et'una.**
Priscilla Russell Kari. Anchorage: National Park Service, Alaska Region, 1987. 2nd rev. ed. 205p. bibliog.

Kari presents an ethnobotany of the Dena'ina Indians of Southcentral Alaska. It shows how available plant species are used. Common English names, scientific names and the Athabascan names, including local variations, are provided. There are pictures of each plant. Of special interest are those plants which have been used in traditional Native medicine.

219 **Wild Alaska.**
Dale Brown and the editors of Time-Life Books. New York: Time-Life Books, 1972. 184p. maps. bibliog.

A general, illustrated treatment of selected animals and plants at various specific locations within Alaska such as the Katmai National Monument, Mt. McKinley (Denali) Park and the Arctic National Wildlife Range.

220 **The wild grizzlies of Alaska: a story of the grizzly and big brown bears of Alaska, their habits, manners and characteristics.**
John M. Holzworth. New York; London: G. P. Putnam's Sons, 1930. 417p. map.

An early advocate for the preservation of bears and their habitat at a time when many argued for their destruction, Holzworth illustrates his book with 84 pictures showing bear behaviour in numerous places in Alaska. He also includes some notes on mountain sheep and caribou. The author had earlier worked for the United States Biological Survey.

221 **Wild harmony: the cycle of life in the northern forest.**
William O. Pruitt, Jr., drawings by William D. Berry. Saskatoon, Saskatchewan: Western Producer Prairie Books, 1983. 179p.

A thoughtful brief description of the taiga ecosystem is presented in lay terms. The life-cycles of predators – lynx and wolves – is treated along with the prey – hares, caribou and moose. Man, especially traditional native hunters, is a part of the system.

222 **Wildflowers of the Yukon, Alaska and Northwestern Canada.**
John G. Trelawny. Victoria, British Columbia: Sono Nis Press, 1988. 214p. bibliog.

This illustrated guide for the layman includes a useful illustrated glossary explaining terms used in the text.

223 **Wildlife management and subsistence hunting in Alaska.**
Henry P. Huntington. Seattle, Washington: University of Washington Press, 1992. 177p. maps. bibliog.

Managing the game resources of the state has become a complex social and political issue, in addition to the questions of science involved. This is a study of northern Alaska, primarily subsistence hunting by Inupiat Eskimo.

224 **The wolves of Mount McKinley.**
Adolph Murie. Washington, DC: National Park Service, United States Department of the Interior, 1944. 238p. bibliog. (Fauna of the National Parks of the United States. Fauna Series, no. 5).

Murie was one of the first biologists to study the wolf systematically over a period of years. This book is less a scientific treatise and more a general description that is buttressed by examples from his research. Wolves are not the only topic; chapters are also devoted to Dall sheep, caribou, moose, grizzly bears, the red fox, and the golden eagle. In each case Murie relates the species to the common ecosystem in which they live and also to each other.

Prehistory and Archaeology

225 **Ancient men of the Arctic.**
J. Louis Giddings. New York: Alfred A. Knopf, 1967. 319p. 9 maps. bibliog.

In this classic of arctic archaeology Giddings pushed back the known dates for settlement in Alaska and established a chronological sequence for Eskimo settlement across the North American Arctic. This well-written narrative is not a technical treatise, but rather a story of discovery with constant references to events and people surrounding the archaeological 'digs'.

226 **Archeological excavations at Kukulik, St. Lawrence Island, Alaska.**
Otto William Geist, Froelich G. Rainey. Washington, DC: GPO, 1936. 391p. (Miscellaneous Publications of the University of Alaska, no. 2).

This work was a major undertaking of the fledgling Alaska Agricultural College and College of Mines (later University of Alaska) from 1926 until 1935. At first it was funded primarily by donated labour and the personal contributions of the president, Charles Bunnell. Later, some help to complete the work was acquired through the Public Works project administered through the Bureau of Indian Affairs. The appendices include short articles by leading experts on the geography, geology, birds, mammals, molluscs, and natural history specimens from the island.

227 **The archaeology of Cape Denbigh.**
J. L. Giddings. Providence, Rhode Island: Brown University Press, 1964. 331p. bibliog.

In this work, Giddings sees the Bering Strait region as a cultural centre that serves as a focal point for archaeology. A crucial phase is the Denbigh Flint complex (2900 BC), an interpretation based upon the excavations made during the 1948, 1949, 1950 and 1952 field seasons described in this book. Cape Denbigh is on the northen Bering Sea coast at Norton Bay. This classic of Alaska archaeology is accompanied by 73 full-page plates and numerous other illustrations showing the artefacts that were discovered.

228 **The archaeology of Cape Nome, Alaska.**
John R. Bockstoce. Philadelphia: University of Pennsylvania, 1979. 132p. maps. bibliog. (University Monograph, no. 38).

Bockstoce places his excavations in a general context with an introduction to the Bering Strait region, an area which is extremely rich in its succession of cultures and its archaeological resources.

229 **The archaeology of Cook Inlet, Alaska.**
Frederica de Laguna. Anchorage: Alaska Historical Society, 1975. 264p. maps. bibliog.

The author established the presence of earlier Eskimo cultures in this region, which was inhabited by Tanaina Athabascan Indians at the time of first contact with Europeans. First published in 1934 by the University of Pennsylvania Press, this study has remained a foundation for later archaeologists right up to the present day. Most of the author's work was done at a site on Yukon Island in Kachemak Bay during the 1930, 1931 and 1932 field seasons.

230 **Archaeology of St. Lawrence Island, Alaska.**
Henry B. Collins, Jr. Washington, DC: Smithsonian Institution, 1937. 431p. bibliog. (Smithsonian Miscellaneous Collections, 96, no. 1).

Collins's report is based on work done from 1928 to 1931, especially the 1930 season at which James A. Ford assisted, and 1932 when the work was carried out by Moreau B. Chambers. The author compares the Old Bering Sea culture, which is renowned for the exquisite ivory carvings that it left, to other ancient Eskimo cultures and to modern Eskimo. Otto Geist (q.v.) was conducting work on the St. Lawrence at about the same time. The text is accompanied by 84 full-page plates depicting the excavations and the artefacts that were discovered there.

231 **The archaeology of the Yakutat Bay area, Alaska.**
Frederica de Laguna, Francis A. Ridell, Donald F. McGeein, Kenneth S. Land, J. Arthur Freed. Washington, DC: GPO, 1964. 245p. maps. bibliog. (Bulletin of the Bureau of American Ethnology, no. 192).

This project is part of a study of the northern Tlingit and the long-term cultural exchange between Tlingits and Eskimo populations.

232 **The Arctic woodland culture of the Kobuk River.**
J. Louis Giddings. Philadelphia: University Museum, University of Pennsylvania, 1952. 143p. bibliog.

This work is based upon field-work conducted in 1940, 1941 and 1947. Giddings pioneered tree-ring research (dendrochronology) as a means of dating in archaeology. The Kobuk drains a part of the westward extension (Baird Mountains) of the Brooks Range and flows into the Bering Sea near Kotzebue at about the Arctic Circle. This forest culture, which comprises trees only at the lowest elevation, contrasts with, but is related to, the nearby marine mammal cultures.

233 **The Bering Land Bridge.**
Edited by David Hopkins. Stanford, California: Stanford University Press, 1967. 495p. maps. bibliog.

The concept that Bering Strait is one of the great migration routes of the world has continued to gain acknowledgement as scholars study the effect of rising and subsiding seas, which caused the appearance and later disappearance of the Bering Land Bridge. The land bridge allowed migration to take place easily from Asia to the Americas. This is a landmark study of 'Beringia' with chapters on geology and on the Quaternary era, including the migration of plant and animal species.

234 **The Campus Site: a prehistoric camp at Fairbanks, Alaska.**
Charles M. Mobley. Fairbanks, Alaska: University of Alaska Press, 1991. 104p. bibliog.

The Campus Site is on the hill where the University of Alaska is situated. Discovery of stone artefacts from 1933 onwards became the evidence for a new theory involving migration via the Bering Land Bridge for the peopling of the Americas in pre-Columbian times. This work, which is of interest to the layman and expert alike, traces the history and exploitation of this site (1930s, 1960s, 1971), analyses the artefacts found there, and places the site in context based upon current knowledge.

235 **Chugach prehistory: the archaeology of Prince William Sound, Alaska.**
Frederica de Laguna. Seattle, Washington: University of Washington Press, 1956. 289p. maps. bibliog. (University of Washington Publications in Anthropology, no. 13).

Prince William Sound is home to the southernmost Eskimo in Alaska: the Chugach. The author has also conducted research on the neighbouring regions occupied by Taniana Athabascans, Eyak, and Tlingit Indians.

236 **Eskimo prehistory.**
Hans-Georg Bandi, translated by Ann E. Keep. College, Alaska: University of Alaska Press, 1969. 226p. maps. bibliog.

This is an introductory text on the circumpolar Eskimo. It emphasizes archaeological research and prehistoric cultures. Although it covers all Eskimo regions, Alaska is especially well represented.

237 **Eskimo warfare in Northwest Alaska.**
Ernest S. Burch, Jr. *Anthropological Papers of the University of Alaska*, vol. 16, no. 2 (1974), p. 1-14.

This is a landmark study. It has often been assumed that there was no war among the Eskimo, and that all Eskimo groups are the same. Burch interviewed informants in 1969 and 1970 whose parents or grandparents had participated. He discusses causes, strategy, personnel, logistics, command, battle, and the aftermath of wars. Through the use of oral traditions and archaeological evidence, the author has been able to examine a phenomenon that had disappeared by the modern historical era, which in this region is remarkably recent.

238 **The Eskimos and Aleuts.**
Don E. Dumond. London: Thames & Hudson, 1987. rev. ed. 180p. maps. bibliog. (Ancient Peoples and Places Series).

Another general introduction, but one that asks questions such as why the Eskimo settled where they did in prehistoric times. The author considers the primary Eskimo–Aleut homeland to be in Alaska, where the majority of Eskimo still live. He interprets what the archaeological record really means in terms comprehensible to the interested layman. This work is much indebted to Bandi (q.v.) and Giddings (q.v.), but it also reflects a fresh approach.

239 **The ethnoarchaeology of Crow Village, Alaska.**
Wendell H. Oswalt, James W. VanStone. Washington, DC: GPO, 1967. 136p. maps. bibliog.

This publication is the result of an historical archaeological project, located in a recently abandoned village on the Kuskokwim River. The goal of the project was to further the reconstruction of riverine Eskimo ethnography.

240 **Ipiutak and the arctic whale hunting culture.**
Helge Larsen, Froelich Rainey. New York: American Museum of Natural History, 1948. 276p. bibliog. (Anthropological Papers of the American Museum of Natural History, no. 42).

Excavations were conducted in one of the largest and oldest settlements in the American Arctic, at Point Hope, during the 1939, 1940 and 1941 field seasons. The authors conclude that the Ipiutak is the oldest known Eskimo culture, dating back almost 2,000 years. They argue that it originated in the northern part of the Ural region, near the mouth of the river Ob. Assisted by another well-known archaeologist, J. L. Giddings, this was a cooperative effort of the American Museum of Natural History, the University of Alaska and the Danish National Museum. The appendices include notes and illustrations of the excavations of 72 houses, 162 burials, an analysis of a fragment of an iron engraving tool, and an analysis of dog skulls conducted by naturalist Olaus Murie.

241 **Koniag prehistory; archaeological investigations at late prehistoric sites on Kodiak Island, Alaska.**
Donald Woodforde Clark. Stuttgart, Germany: Verlag W. Kohlhammer, 1974. 271p. bibliog. (Tuebinger Monographien zur Urgeschichte, no. 1).

These investigations were completed during four seasons by a University of Wisconsin team. The team identified five distinct prehistoric phases, of which this is the most recent. Clark uses pottery dated from AD 1500 to AD 1800 to support his analysis of the origin and extent of Koniag culture, and its relationship to other regional cultures, such as the Katchemak tradition described by Frederica de Laguna (q.v.). Fifty full-page plates show details of the excavation sites and the artefacts recovered.

242 **The late prehistoric development of Alaska's Native people.**
Robert D. Shaw, Roger K. Harrit, Don E. Dumond. Anchorage: Alaska Anthropological Association, 1988. 450p. maps. bibliog. (Aurora Monograph Series, no. 4).

This is a compilation of the work of 21 contributors who provide an overview of Alaskan archaeology. A number of regions are covered. Subjects include the origins of ethnic groups, population structure, nutrition, art and linguistics.

243 **Onion Portage: an archaeological site on the Kobuk River, northwestern Alaska.**
Douglas D. Anderson. Fairbanks, Alaska: University of Alaska Press, 1988. 163p. bibliog. (Anthropological Papers of the University of Alaska, 11, no. 1-2).

Anderson explains technical terms and the results of his findings in an especially clear way for the lay reader. He includes photographs and descriptions of current subsistence activity there which helps place his excavations in context. The site is on the middle Kobuk river, about 210 kilometres upstream from its mouth near Kotzebue. The house sites that he explores date from 9570 to 950 years before present.

244 **The paleoecology of Beringia.**
David M. Hopkins, John V. Matthews, Charles E. Schweger, Steven B. Young. New York: Academic Press, 1982. 489p. bibliog.

These are the proceedings of a major symposium held by the Wenner-Gren Foundation for Anthropological Research at Burg Wartenstein, Austria, in 1979. These contributions further develop Hopkins's ground-breaking work on Beringia (see item no. 233) and represent a substantial body of research undertaken during the intervening decade.

245 **The prehistory of northern North America as seen from the Yukon.**
Frederica de Laguna. Menasha, Wisconsin: Memoirs of the Society for American Archaeology, 1947. 360p. maps. (Supplement to *American Antiquity*, vol. XII, no. 3, part 2, 1947).

This is a classic archaeological study. Research was conducted along the Yukon River in 1935. De Laguna expanded her work from a regional report to be titled 'Notes on the archaeology of the middle and lower Yukon' to the comparative analysis published here. Not only does she compare her findings with studies of adjacent Eskimo and Athabascan sites, but she places them in a theoretical construct, whose primary tenet is a prehistoric culture drift from Asia throughout North America, specifically the circumpolar Eskimo cultures and the Northwest Coast Indian cultures.

246 **The story of a Tlingit community: a problem in the relationship between archaeological, ethnological, and historical methods.**
Frederica de Laguna. Washington, DC: GPO, 1960. 254p. bibliog. (Smithsonian Institution. Bureau of American Ethnology. Bulletin 172).

The community is Angoon, in Southeast Alaska, where field-work was carried out in 1949 and 1950. The question is: how well do the explanations offered by archaeology, historical records, and contemporary ethnography mesh? A variety of oral traditions are also considered.

History

General

247 **Alaska: a bicentennial history.**
William Hunt. New York: Norton, 1976. 200p. map.

The Bicentennial States Series was designed to provide interpretative summations of each state's history. Hunt's extended essay revolves around the paradox of unique lifestyles that are ultimately controlled by economic and political decisions made far away, especially in Washington, DC. He makes his points with brief examples from the lives of those involved. There is a photographic essay by Yavonne Mozee depicting Alaska in the mid-1970s.

248 **Alaska: a history of the 49th state.**
Claus-M. Naske, Herman Slotnik. Norman, Oklahoma; London: University of Oklahoma Press, 1987. 2nd ed. 349p. maps. bibliog.

This is the most current modern history of Alaska. Naske's emphasis is on the political history of the American era. Appendices include lists of governors, judges, delegates to Congress and summary population statistics. His bibliography is in the form of an essay.

249 **Alaska and its history.**
Edited by Morgan B. Sherwood. Seattle, Washington: University of Washington Press, 1967. 457p. bibliog.

Sherwood's anthology contains 25 selections by specialists on Alaska. A wide range of issues are addressed by short extracts from previously published works by the best-known historians of Alaska, up to the date of publication. Russian America is well represented, as is the transfer of sovereignty from Russia to the United States.

250 **The Alaska boundary dispute: a critical reappraisal.**
Norman Penlington. Toronto: McGraw-Hill; Ryerson, 1972. 141p. maps.

The actual boundary between Alaska and Canada became a burning issue with the gold rush. The Anglo-Russian Treaty of 1825 was necessarily vague because of the lack of available surveys at the time. An international tribunal ultimately decided the demarcation line in 1903, largely in favour of the case made by the United States. This book examines Canada's part in the matter.

251 **Alaska's heritage.**
Joan M. Antonson, William S. Hanable. Anchorage: Alaska Historical Society for the Alaska Historical Commission, 1984-85. 2 vols. maps. bibliog.

This is a public school textbook, the fruit of many years' labour by the Historical Commission. It is extensively illustrated with selected historical photographs.

252 **Alaskan historical documents since 1867.**
Compiled by Ron Lautaret. Jefferson, North Carolina: McFarland & Co., 1989. 151p.

Each of the 37 selections is accompanied by notes. The themes include economic development, self-government for Alaska, and native issues. They range from the Treaty of Cession (1867) through the Territorial Organic Act (1912), the Constitution (1956), and end with the Alaska Native Claims Settlement Act (1971).

253 **Alaska's history: the people, land and events of the north country.**
Harry Ritter. Anchorage: Alaska Northwest, 1993. 143p. bibliog.

Written as a series of short essays, this general introductory history includes short biographies of important figures and brief discussions of important issues. This is an interesting introduction to a number of topics, but its organization makes it difficult to read as a connected narrative history.

254 **Alaska: promyshlennik and sourdough.**
Stuart R. Tompkins. Norman, Oklahoma: University of Oklahoma Press, 1945. 350p. maps. bibliog.

This general history devotes about equal space to the Russian and American eras up to the 1903 border dispute. A brief chapter is appended to discuss the then current events of the Second World War era.

255 **The Americanization of Alaska, 1867-1897.**
Ted C. Hinckley. Palo Alto, California: Pacific Books, 1972. 285p. bibliog.

Long the standard modern history of American Alaska before the gold rush, this book explains that at first Alaska was not even a territory. It was simply a possession until the Organic Act of 1884 created an elementary government without a legislature.

256 Arctic passage: the turbulent history of the land and people of the Bering Sea 1697-1975.

William R. Hunt. New York: Charles Scribner's Sons, 1975. 395p. map. bibliog.

A general account with an emphasis on personalities and human interest, well illustrated with historical photographs.

257 Black on a background of white: a chronicle of Afro-Americans' involvement in Alaska's last frontier.

Everett Louis Overstreet. Fairbanks, Alaska: Alaska Black Caucus, distributed by That New Publishing Company, 1988. 237p.

This is the first book-length, and to date only, history of Blacks in Alaska. It covers 1867 to 1987. There were a few Blacks in Alaska in the early years, but significant numbers came from the 1940s onward. This is written as a collective biography, with a number of brief life-histories.

258 Bush cop: the true story of an American Mountie during the early years of Alaska.

Joe Rychetnik. Pacific Grove, California: Boxwood Press, 1991. 440p. map.

Rychetnik's district covered an enormous area, from south of the mouth of the Yukon River on the Bering Sea to Barrow on the Arctic Ocean. He served during the transition from the Territorial Police to the Alaska State Troopers following statehood.

259 Distant justice: policing the Alaska frontier.

William R. Hunt. Norman, Oklahoma: University of Oklahoma Press, 1987. 375p. bibliog.

There were few legal institutions in early American Alaska, and almost no law enforcement personnel. Changes came with the gold rush, but there were also chances to profit from corruption. There were few jails and no prisons. Hunt likes a good story, and many colourful tales are retold here.

260 Frontier Alaska: a study in historical interpretation and opportunity.

Robert A. Frederick. Anchorage: Alaska Methodist University Press, 1968. 171p.

These proceedings are of a conference held to commemorate the Alaska Purchase Centennial in 1967. It brought together the relatively small number of active Alaska historians. This, and the resurrection of the dormant Alaska Historical Society, marked a revitalization of history and historical scholarship within Alaska. Included are contributions by Robert A. Frederick, Donald R. Ellegood, Don E. Dumond, James W. VanStone, Richard A. Pierce, Stuart Ramsay Tompkins, Ted C. Hinckley, Jeannette Paddock Nichols, George W. Rogers, William H. Wilson, and Rodman Wilson Paul.

261 **Give or take a century: an Eskimo chronicle.**
Joseph E. Senungetuk. San Francisco, California: Indian Historian Press, 1982. 2nd ed. 198p.

This was written by an Eskimo artist and art professor originally from the village of Wales. He presents an alternative viewpoint to the standard histories that had been produced before this work was first published in 1971. He first considers his culture and then the impact of foreigners who moved in among the native population. The changes have been profound. He relates the history of his own family to explain his points. The book is illustrated with Senungetuk's own art.

262 **History of Alaska, 1730-1885.**
Hubert H. Bancroft. San Francisco, California: A. L. Bancroft, 1886. 775p. map. bibliog. (Works, no. 33).

Bancroft operated a 'literary factory', producing a considerable number of books on the American West and Northwest. The work of many hands, his *Alaska* has remained a fixture in Alaskan history despite its growing age and increasingly obvious errors. In part this is because there has been no large-scale and widely accepted synthesis of Russian American era history to replace it. However, for almost any particular subject, there is something more recent and usually more accurate by current academic standards.

263 **Interpreting Alaska's history: an anthology.**
Edited by Mary Childers Mangusso, Stephen W. Haycox. Anchorage: Alaska Pacific University Press, 1989. 468p.

A selection of 26 previously published articles and papers covering topics from Russia's eastward expansion toward Alaska to political history, economics, the history of the tourist trade, and the issue of wilderness.

264 **The last frontier.**
Melody Webb. Albuquerque, New Mexico: University of New Mexico Press, 1985. 416p. 9 maps. bibliog.

Webb has written a history of the Yukon River valley, from the Russian era through to the pipeline. The Yukon valley was the principal route to the vast interior of Alaska. It was at the edge of both the Russian (Russian-American Company) and the English (Hudson's Bay Company) frontiers. It was explored by Americans during the Western Union Telegraph expedition of the 1860s and was at the centre of the gold rush. During the gold rush, a number of military outposts were established and trade along the river thrived. Towns were founded, only to disappear as gold mining moved on. Webb also considers missionary work along the river and its impact. Roads and trails, railways, and air transportation left their mark as well – if only because they offered alternatives to river travel.

265 **The story of Alaska.**
C. L. Andrews. Caldwell, Idaho: Caxton Printers, 1953. 332p. bibliog.

A popular general history written by someone who had spent a considerable amount of time as a federal employee and newsman in Alaska.

266 **A warm past: travels in Alaska history.**
Stephen Haycox. Anchorage: Press North, 1988. 157p. map.

A compilation of fifty essays which appeared as a column entitled 'Alaska Yesterday' in the *Anchorage Times*. There are many brief biographical sketches of various individuals and descriptions of events.

267 **The way old-timers tell it: oral sources of Alaska history.**
William Schneider. *Alaska History*, vol. 2, no. 2 (Fall 1987), p. 33-49.

This is an overview of the range and subject matter of oral histories that have been collected in Alaska. Oral history is especially important in Alaska where the written record is frequently not available. This is especially so in the case of Native history with its rich variety of oral traditions.

268 **We shall be remembered.**
Evangeline Atwood. Anchorage: Alaska Methodist University, 1966. 191p.

This is about the 1935 Matanuska agricultural colony, written in personal terms by someone living in nearby Anchorage at the time. It is not a scholarly work on the subject, like that of Orlando Miller (q.v.), but rather a story filled with personal anecdotes, most of them collected through personal interview.

Russian America (1741-1867)

269 **The Alaska purchase and Russian–American relations.**
Ronald J. Jensen. Seattle, Washington: University of Washington Press, 1975. 185p. bibliog.

The sale of Russian America was a long and complicated process, with conflicting opinions in both the Russian and American governments. It was further complicated by the American Civil War. Jensen reviews relations between the two countries during the negotiations, which actually began as early as 1854. He sees the issues in geopolitical terms and as a piece of political history. Some circumstances remain murky, such as the Russian financing of the lobbying effort with Congress and the administration.

270 **The Alaska treaty.**
David H. Miller. Kingston, Ontario: Limestone Press, 1981. 231p. bibliog. (Alaska History, no. 35).

Miller originally published his summary as volume 9 in the 'Treaties and other International Acts of the United States' issued by the Department of State in 1944. All matter of detail is concisely presented, including the negotiations, the detailed provisions of the treaty itself, the actual transfer instructions dealing with property, official correspondence, and the nature and state of the records of the Russian-American Company.

271 **Colonial Russian America: Kyrill T. Khlebnikov's reports, 1817-1832.**
Kyrill T. Khlebnikov, translated and edited by Basil Dmytryshyn, E. A. P. Crownhart-Vaughan. Portland, Oregon: Oregon Historical Society, 1976. 158p. bibliog. (North Pacific Studies, no. 2).

This material was originally written as reports to headquarters by the Office Manager of the Russian-American Company in Sitka. He was stationed there for 17 years and was very well informed. His manuscript was first published in Russia in 1861, more than 20 years after his death. It is a broad overview, with many specific examples. This is a rich source of facts concerning the life in and finances of this remote trading and administrative centre.

272 **Conflict on the Northwest Coast: American–Russian rivalry in the Pacific Northwest, 1790-1867.**
Howard I. Kushner. Westport, Connecticut: Greenwood Press, 1975. 277p. map. bibliog.

Kushner emphasizes competition and rivalry more than most other writers. The 'Boston Men' and the Hudson Bay Company did indeed compete for the Northwest fur trade, but there were also periods in which negotiated understandings worked to ease supply problems. The book's documentation is much stronger for the American than for the Russian records, which are rather neglected. This is a revision of a PhD thesis completed at Cornell in 1970.

273 **The destiny of Russian America, 1741-1867.**
A. I. Alekseev, translated by Marina Ramsay, edited by Richard A. Pierce. Kingston, Ontario; Fairbanks, Alaska: Limestone Press, 1990. 335p. (Alaska History, no. 34).

Alekseev is a prolific Russian specialist on Alaska and the Russian Far East. He has, among other things, produced several important biographies which are currently being translated for publication into English. One of the strengths of this general history is the attention spent on biographical sketches of key personnel.

274 **The end of Russian America: Captain P. N. Golovin's last report, 1862.**
Pavel Nikolaevich Golovin, translated by Basil Dmytryshyn, E. A. P. Crownhart-Vaughan. Portland, Oregon: Oregon Historical Society, 1979. 249p. 8 maps. bibliog. (North Pacific Studies).

Golovin and Sergei Kostlivtsov were sent to Alaska on a fact-finding mission during a period of intense internal debate concerning the future of Russia's commercial colony. This report, which was published upon his return, was extremely influential. It is a description of the value and commercial viability of the establishment, with various suggestions for improvements. There is extensive information on the number and condition of structures, the state of the Church, the ships, the educational facilities, the state of medical care, and relations with natives.

275 **Feeding the Russian fur trade: provisioning of the Okhotsk seaboard and the Kamchatka Peninsula, 1639-1856.**
James R. Gibson. Madison, Wisconsin; London: University of Wisconsin Press, 1969. 337p. 10 maps. bibliog.

The early exploration and trading voyages to Alaska were sent out from what is now the Russian Far East. Supplying this endeavour was no small feat, and governance from far-distant St. Petersburg was often ineffectual. This book should be read in conjunction with Gibson's *Imperial Russia in frontier America* (q.v.) for an understanding of the economic geography of the region before 1867.

276 **A history of the Russian-American Company.**
Petr Alexandrovich Tikhmenev, translated from the Russian edition of 1861-63 by Richard A. Pierce, Alton S. Donnelly. Seattle, Washington: University of Washington Press, 1978. 522p. 6 maps. Volume II (documents) published separately by the Limestone Press, Kingston, Ontario in 1979. 257p. (Materials for the Study of Alaska History, no. 13).

The major portion of the Russian-American Company archives that remained in Russia following the sale, was destroyed by accident in the 1870s. Many of these primary sources are known only through Tikhmenev's work. He was an employee of the firm and this work was made available just before the company charter was up for renewal in 1863. This is an encyclopaedic work that is indispensable for a study of the Russian era in Alaska.

277 **Imperial Russia in frontier America: the changing geography of supply of Russian America, 1784-1867.**
James R. Gibson. New York: Oxford University Press, 1976. 257p. 6 maps. bibliog.

The nature and extent of the Russian-American Company's occupation of Alaska is made clear through a study of how the effort was provisioned and supported economically. Gibson makes excellent use of Russian primary and secondary sources. He demonstrates that changing economic and natural conditions fundamentally altered the viability of the company and required radically new directions.

278 **The Khlebnikov archive: unpublished journal (1800-1837) and travel notes (1820, 1822, and 1824).**
K. T. Khlebnikov, translated by John Bisk, edited with introduction and notes by Leonid Shur. Fairbanks, Alaska: University of Alaska Press, 1990. 212p.

K. T. Khlebnikov was the Office Manager for the Russian American colonies, based in Sitka, at the time these journals were kept. Of greatest interest are the travel notes, which cover commercial voyages to California. There is some adventure, such as a major shipwreck, but of greatest importance is the information provided on commerce first with Spanish and then Mexican officials. There is also information on the Russian American agricultural colony of Fort Ross, located north of San Francisco, and on Russian sea-otter hunting crews, staffed primarily by Aleuts, who were active in California waters.

279 **Memorandum of Captain 2nd Rank Golovnin on the condition of the Aleuts in the settlements of the Russian-American Company and on its promyshlenniki.**
Vasilii Mikhailovich Golovnin, translated by Katherine L. Arndt. *Alaska History* vol. 1, no. 2 (1985), p. 59-71.

Golovnin made two trips to Alaska. His first eventful voyage in command of the *Diana* lasted from 1807 until 1814, including a spell in captivity in Japan. He was sent to the colonies again in 1817 with orders to investigate the treatment of natives. His voyage accounts were soon published, but his report on the condition of the Aleuts was published in Russian only much later, as a part of the controversy over the sale of Alaska in the 1860s and long after his death. His report substantiates most of the original accusations, which he notes the new Chief Manager, Hagemeister, was working to correct.

280 **Russia in North America: proceedings of the 2nd international conference on Russian America, Sitka, Alaska, August 19-22, 1987.**
Edited by Richard A. Pierce. Kingston, Ontario; Fairbanks, Alaska: Limestone Press, 1990. 527p. maps. bibliog.

The second conference proceedings involve some 40 contributors, and a number of new issues are explored that were not considered during the first conference (Starr [q.v]). Native versions of encounters between Russians and the indigenous population are presented, there is consideration of the role of the Orthodox Church in native cultural encounters, and there are a number of papers on the historical archaeology of Russian America.

281 **Russian America: the great Alaskan venture, 1741-1867.**
Hector Chevigny. New York: Viking Press, 1965. 274p. maps. bibliog.

Drawing on his earlier books on Rezanov (item no. 413) and Baranov (item no. 412), Chevigny writes a narrative account in broad outlines.

282 **Russia's American colony.**
Edited by Frederick S. Starr. Durham, North Carolina: Duke University Press, 1987. 430p. map. (A special study of the Kennan Institute for Advanced Russian Studies of the Woodrow Wilson International Center for Scholars).

These are fourteen published papers from a US–USSR conference held in Sitka, Alaska, in 1979 during a time when such meetings were very difficult to arrange because of the Cold War. The participants were published scholars whose topics include the Russian expansion to the North Pacific, the Russian-American Company, relations with native populations, cultural life in Russian America, US–Russian relations, and scholarly resources for the study of Russian America.

283 **Russian America: statistical and ethnographic information.**
Baron Ferdinand von Wrangell, translated from the German edition of 1839 by Mary Sadouski, edited by Richard A. Pierce. Kingston, Ontario: Limestone Press, 1980. 204p. map. (Materials for the Study of Alaska History, no. 15).

Wrangell, a Baltic German, was one of the most exacting Chief Managers of the Russian-American Company, serving from 1830 to 1835. He was an active explorer himself in an earlier part of his career and a co-founder of the Russian Geographical Society later. This is a descriptive survey of the colonies, with statistics. He surveys the native peoples, and includes material on Indians living in the vicinity of the company's California outpost at Fort Ross. There is additional material contributed by Petr Kostromitinov, a manager at Ross; an extract of Andrei Glazunov's expedition of 1834 in interior Alaska; material on the Aleuts by Ioann Veniaminov; and native vocabularies.

284 **The Russian American colonies, a documentary record.**
Translated and edited by Basil Dmytryshyn, E. A. P. Crownhardt-Vaughn, Thomas Vaughn. Portland, Oregon: Oregon Historical Society, 1989. 590p. maps. bibliog. (*To Siberia and Russian America: three centuries of Russian eastward expansion*, vol. 3).

This volume begins with the acts and decrees establishing the Russian-American Company. Other translated documents include naval officer journal entries, correspondence between officials of the Russian-American Company, official government reports on conditions in the colonies, and diplomatic exchanges. The book ends with document 91: the treaty ceding Alaska to the United States.

285 **Russian America: the forgotten frontier.**
Edited by Barbara S. Smith, Redmond J. Barnett. Tacoma, Washington: Washington State Historical Society; Anchorage Museum of History and Art, 1990. 255p.

This heavily illustrated introduction to Russian America was published in conjunction with an outstanding exhibition, 'Russian America: the forgotten frontier'. The exhibition brought together artefacts and manuscripts from both North America and a number of Russian repositories. Twenty-one individual chapters by leading authorities cover a wide range of topics including health care, architecture and art.

286 **The Russian American Company.**
Semen Bentsionovich Okun, translated by Carl Ginsburg. Cambridge, Massachusetts: Harvard University Press, 1951. 311p.

Okun's work first brought a number of important documents to the attention of scholars. Tikhmenev's history (see item no. 276) was available in English only much later. It remains a useful, if brief, account. It is written from a strongly Marxist standpoint.

287 **The Russian population in Alaska and California (late 18th century to 1867).**

Svetlana G. Fedorova, translated from the Russian edition of 1971 by Richard A. Pierce, Alton S. Donnelly. Kingston, Ontario: Limestone Press, 1973. 376p. maps. (Materials for the Study of Alaska History, no. 4).

This work begins with a survey of sources and then brings together information from many scattered records and reports, primarily housed in the central archives of St. Petersburg and Moscow. The primary subject is the Russian population in Russian America itself: how many, where they were, where they come from. At the time of sale, the company estimated that there remained 34 places in Alaska with Russian populations, but the totals were quite small. Fedorova also considers families, mixed marriages and the Creole population. She presents considerable detail on living conditions and the colonial economy.

288 **The wreck of the *Neva*.**

Vasilii Nikolaevich Berkh, V. M. Golovnin, Iakov Podoskin, translated by Antoinette Shalkop. Anchorage: Alaska Historical Society, 1979. 64p. maps. bibliog.

The British-built *Neva* was part of the first Russian circumnavigation in 1803-06. She returned in 1807 and remained in and near Alaska until she went down within sight of Sitka in 1813. It was a tremendous loss to the small colony. The designated replacement for the ageing Alexander Baranov, Chief Manager of the colony, was lost with the ship.

Whales, seals, fish and fur

289 **Arctic Alaska and Siberia: or eight months with the arctic whalesmen.**

Herbert L. Aldrich. Chicago; New York: Rand, McNally, 1899. 234p. map.

This is an account of a whaling voyage made in 1887, with various other brief accounts from whaling captains included under 'some typical experiences'. Aldrich moved around among nine different vessels in the whaling fleet. Much of his account concerns a description of the life of natives who were in direct contact with whaling ships and their crews in northern Siberia and Alaska north of Bering Strait. There are a number of early photographs of Arctic whaling.

290 **The Bering Sea fur seal dispute 1885-1911: a monograph on the maritime history of Alaska.**

G. O. Williams. Eugene, Oregon: Alaska Maritime Publications, 1984. 85p.

The fur seal dispute was an important international political issue, but it also had its practical side as the US squadron worked to capture pelagic sealers who were poaching the fur resource. This is the story of the revenue cutters and US and British cruisers who were engaged in suppressing the sealing schooners, or in protecting third-party interests. There was the potential for a major incident that would pit the British against the US Navy, but it all ended peacefully with the Pacific Fur Seal Convention of 1911. Williams includes photographs of sealing schooners, naval cruisers and revenue cutters.

291 **Big game in Alaska: a history of wildlife and people.**
Morgan B. Sherwood. New Haven, Connecticut: Yale University Press, 1981. 200p. bibliog. (Yale Western Americana Series, no. 33).

The end of an era of little game regulation for a small human population ended when relatively large numbers of new residents came north as a part of the military developments immediately preceding the Second World War. Major General Simon Bolivar Buckner, Jr., challenged in court the hunting restrictions placed on him as a non-resident. The necessity then to manage increased hunting pressure led to a continuing evolution of regulation. Sherwood uses the legal challenge of 1941 as a central dramatic event around which to organize an examination of the extent of knowledge of wildlife populations through time, the changes in hunting technology, the extent and nature of extant game refuges, attitudes toward wildlife (especially bears), native use of game resources, and the legal system in place to enforce game laws.

292 **A century of servitude: Pribilof Aleuts under U.S. rule.**
Dorothy Knee Jones. Lanham, Maryland: University Press of America, 1980. 190p. bibliog.

The Russians moved a number of Aleut natives to the Pribilof Islands to conduct a continuing seal harvest. After the purchase of Alaska by the United States, this practice continued, with the two Pribilof villages of Saint Paul and Saint George as parts of a special government reservation. Responsibility for its administration rested with the Secretary of the Treasury, but actual sealing was conducted through a lease to the Alaska Commercial Company. This book describes the lives and working conditions of Aleuts living under this system.

293 **The Etholén collection: the ethnographic Alaskan collection of Adolf Etholén and his contemporaries in the National Museum of Finland.**
Piro Varjola, with contributions by Julia P. Averkieva and Roza G. Liapunova. Helsinki: National Board of Antiquities of Finland, 1990.

This is a joint publication effort, involving the Soviet Academy of Sciences as well as the National Museum of Finland. There are many outstanding Alaska items in the collection, and they were made a part of a major exhibit that was held in Helsinki from 1988 to 1990 – it then moved to the United States. Finns were were quite active in Russian America, especially in the fleet and in administration. Etholén himself served for twenty years in Alaska, rising eventually to become the Chief Manager. The opening chapters of this catalogue detail the positions held by Finns in Alaska, which included other high officials (Hampus Furuhjelm, also Chief Manager), Lutheran clergymen, geologists, mining engineers, physicians, and substantial numbers of sea captains (by the 1850s, a majority of the Russian American vessels were commanded by Finns). The artefacts are depicted through excellent photographs.

The collection is especially rich in Aleut and Koniag hunting, whaling and sealing technology. Included are harpoons, throwing boards, hunting kayak models, and hunting clothing, including striking examples of Aleut hunting hats and waterproof kamleikas. The Indians of the Northwest Coast, Eskimo cultures, and Athabascan Indians are also represented.

294 **Furs along the Yukon: Hudson's Bay Company – Native trade in the Yukon river basin, 1830-1893.**

Kenneth Coates. *BC Studies*, vol. 55 (1982), p. 50-79.

As the Russian-American Company expanded its fur trade along the western coasts of Alaska and started up some of the major rivers, the Hudson's Bay Company was expanding overland and along the rivers from the east. This is a study of trade in the Yukon basin preceding the gold rush.

295 **Libby: the sketches, letters & journal of Libby Beaman, recorded in the Pribilof Islands, 1879-1880.**

Edited by Betty John. Tulsa, Oklahoma: Council Oak Books, 1987. 203p. map.

Libby Beaman accompanied her husband to the Pribilof sealing islands where he was to serve as a government agent. The sealing concession was administered by the Alaska Commercial Company. These letters were assembled by her granddaughter who has '. . . filled in some gaps by conjuring up memories . . .'. This book is of questionable value as an historical source document.

296 **The silver years of the Alaska canned salmon industry: an album of historical photos.**

Collected and edited by Laurence Freeborn. Edmonds, Washington: Alaska Geographic, 1976. 168p. (*Alaska Geographic*, vol. 3, no. 4).

During most of the Territorial days, taxes collected from the salmon industry provided more than half of the small government's revenues. Over-fishing with such techniques as the fish trap eventually led to the near collapse of the industry.

297 **Soft gold: the fur trade and cultural exchange on the Northwest Coast of America.**

Thomas Vaughan, Bill Holm. Portland, Oregon: Oregon Historical Society Press, 1982. 297p. bibliog.

This was published to accompany an elaborate and extensive exhibition of artefacts and documentary art. Among the hundreds of well-documented illustrations are a number of paintings and drawings of early observers in Alaskan waters, including artists and scientists. Of special interest are the drawings of Sigismund Bacstrom in the 1790s, Webber drawings made on Cook's third voyage, and those by Henry Humphrys and Georg von Langsdorff.

298 **Trails of an Alaska game warden.**

Ray Tremblay. Anchorage: Alaska Northwest, 1985. 176p.

Tremblay was a warden during the 1950s, 1960s and into the 1970s. The book is written as a series of short vignettes or adventures. Although it is not analytical, it provides a flavour of territorial and early statehood wildlife management and bush life.

299 **The vagabond fleet: a chronicle of the North Pacific sealing schooner trade.**
Peter Murray. Victoria, British Columbia: Sono Nis Press, 1988. 260p. map. bibliog.

Sealing created an international dispute between the United States, which had inherited the land-based harvest on the Pribilof Islands from the Russians, and Canadian sealing schooners which engaged in pelagic sealing. Sealing in the Pribilofs was conducted by the Alaska Commercial Company which was granted a monopoly by the American government. The dispute began in the 1870s and was finally resolved by an international agreement reached in 1911. The enforcement of US interests fell to the Revenue Cutter Service, which eventually began seizing foreign vessels. Murray chronicles the details of the sealing trade and the lives of people engaged in it.

300 **The whalers of Akutan: an account of modern whaling in the Aleutian Islands.**
Knut B. Birkeland. New Haven, Connecticut; London: Yale University Press, 1926. 171p.

This is an account of the commercial whale industry in the Aleutians as it existed in 1915. Birkeland travelled there as a representative of the Norwegians who owned a controlling interest the North Pacific Sea Products Company.

301 **Whales, ice and men: the history of whaling in the western Arctic.**
John R. Bockstoce. Seattle, Washington; London: University of Washington Press in association with the New Bedford Whaling Museum, 1986. 400p. 8 maps. bibliog.

The first whaling vessel arrived in Bering Strait in 1848 and the last commercial kill was made in 1921. At the height of activity, there were as many as 220 vessels in the fleet, and by 1890, the first ships began wintering at Herschel Island in the Arctic Ocean. Many ships were lost. The changes that were wrought in the natural resources of the region were profound, as were the effects on Eskimo natives. Bockstoce has spent his summers for decades in the region, working as an anthropologist, and participating as a member of an Eskimo whaling crew. This extensively researched volume is richly illustrated.

302 **A year with a whaler.**
Walter Noble Burns. New York: Outing Publishing Company, 1913. 250p.

The brig *Alexander* cruised the Bering and Chukchi Seas. The author sailed as a 'green hand.'

Gold rush

303 **Alaska's pre-Klondike mining: the men, the methods and the minerals.**

Billie Barnes Jensen. *Journal of the West*, vol. 6, no. 3 (July 1967), p. 417-32.

This is a brief survey of the history of mining, which really began in Alaska with the discovery of gold in 1880 on the Gastineau Channel by Joseph Juneau and Richard Harris at the location where the capital city of Juneau now stands. There were small gold rushes in the Yukon drainage area in the 1880s and eventually the 1896 Klondike strike.

304 **Alaskan gold mine: the story of No. 9 Above.**

Leland H. Carlson. Evanston, Illinois: Northwestern University Press, 1951. 108p. map. bibliog.

Number 9 Above was claimed by Scandinavian miners close to the Swedish Covenant Church mission in gold rush Nome. A massive legal dispute eventually erupted involving claim jumpers. The ensuing legal battle was in eleven courts for a total of eighteen years. It even reached the United States Supreme Court on four occasions. This history involves claim jumping, dishonest judges, reforming judges, immigrant claimants, Alaska native claimants, arbitration commissions, and a host of lawyers.

305 **The Blue Parka Man: Alaskan gold rush bandit.**

H. C. Landru. New York: Dodd, Mead, 1980. 169p. maps.

Bandits, of the old Wild West variety, were extremely rare during the gold rush. However, in 1905, there were a string of highway robberies by a man in a blue parka as miners from the creeks transported their gold from Cleary and Fairbanks Creek to the banks in town. Charles Hendrickson was eventually captured, escaped, and led the federal marshal on a long and protracted chase through gold camps and wilderness. There were yet more escapes and captures before the culprit was finally incarcerated at the Ft. Levenworth federal penitentiary.

306 **A crooked past: the history of a frontier mining camp, Fairbanks, Alaska.**

Terrence Cole. Fairbanks, Alaska: University of Alaska Press, 1991. 163p. maps. bibliog.

This was originally published by Alaska Northwest as *E. T. Barnette: the strange story of the man who founded Fairbanks*. Barnette was an entrepreneur of dubious character who established a trading post in 1901, just in time for the gold stampede to the Fairbanks District. His career in Fairbanks ended when his Washington–Alaska Bank failed in 1911. Cole provides a vivid picture of this boom town and the mining communities that grew up in the surrounding camps.

307 **Golden years: the decline of gold mining in Alaska.**
Terrence Cole. *Pacific Northwest Quarterly*, vol. 80, no. 2 (April 1989), p. 62-71.

This is a brief summary of what happened to the gold-mining industry in Alaska after it had peaked in 1906. While total production went down, the value of the gold itself rose as world prices rose. By the late 1930s dredges had, by and large, displaced the small placer operations of the early rush years. All mines were closed in 1942 as a part of the war effort because they were considered a non-essential industry.

308 **Journey to the Koyukuk: the photos of J. N. Wyman, 1898-1899.**
J. N. Wyman. Missoula, Montana: Pictorial Histories Publishing Company, 1988. 128p. map.

Wyman was part of the rush to the Koyukuk, one of the secondary gold rushes following the strike on the Klondike in the Yukon Territory.

309 **Klondike contraptions: inventions in transportation.**
Terrence Cole. *Northern Review*, no. 3/4 (June 1989), p. 118-34.

A demonstration of the inappropriate application of technology to poorly understood conditions.

310 **Klondike fever: life and death of the last great gold rush.**
Pierre Berton. New York: Alfred A. Knopf, 1956. 457p. bibliog.

Berton was born in Dawson and has since had a distinguished career as a Canadian journalist and author. The Klondike gold rush was intimately intertwined with Alaska. Most of the gold seekers came from or through US territory (Skagway, Dyea, the Yukon River, Circle City, Valdez) and many went on from there to Alaskan gold rushes (Nome, Fairbanks).

311 **Klondike women: true tales of the 1897-98 gold rush.**
Melanie J. Mayer. Athens, Ohio: Swallow Press; Ohio University Press, 1989. 267p. maps. bibliog.

Most of this book is about the experience of getting to the Klondike, especially life on the trails and the camps along the way. There are substantial chapters on the riverboat route up the Yukon from Alaska, the tidewater settlements of Dyea and Skagway and the Chilkoot trail. These anecdotal accounts quote widely from diaries and letters of women of diverse backgrounds.

312 **Lady sourdough.**
Ella Francis Fitz, as told to Jerome Odlum. New York: Macmillan, 1941. 319p.

Fitz was a stenographer who was deeply involved with the legal mining controversies in Nome in 1900. She also published a newspaper in Council City and was a mining entrepreneur in her own right.

313 **Mad rush for gold in the frozen North.**
Arthur Arnold Dietz. Los Angeles, California: Times-Mirror Press, 1914. 281p.

This is the tale of an attempt at one of the alternate routes to the Klondike over glaciers near Yakutat, Alaska. It took a winter longer than planned and left twelve of the party of eighteen New Yorkers dead. There is some question about the historical veracity of this account, but it does make interesting reading.

314 **Miners' justice: migration, law and order on the Alaska–Yukon frontier, 1873-1902.**
Thomas Stone. New York: Peter Lang Publishing, 1988. 308p.

Stone writes from the viewpoint of an anthropologist, not a lawyer or an historian. He studies the miners' meetings, which served as an ad hoc court of law to settle disputes, and contrasts the Canadian and the American legal systems that eventually replaced these meetings.

315 **Nome, city of the golden beaches.**
Terrence Cole. Anchorage: Alaska Geographic Society, 1984. 183p. (*Alaska Geographic*, vol. 11 no. 1).

This is a general history of Nome, the largest of the Alaskan gold-rush settlements. Cole continues beyond the colourful days of the rush itself to the period after the Second World War when Nome served as a major lend-lease facility for the transport of aircraft to the Soviet Union. Nome had many special difficulties in fitting American urban ways to the environment, especially the storms off the Bering Sea. This well-written account is extensively illustrated with historical photographs.

316 **North of 53: the wild days of the Alaska–Yukon mining frontier, 1870-1914.**
William R. Hunt. New York: Macmillan, 1974. 323p. 7 maps. bibliog.

Hunt covers the numerous gold strikes and events that followed from the 1870s through to 1914. He emphasizes the larger strikes on the Klondike and at Nome and Fairbanks. Hunt loves a good story, and the volume abounds with anecdotes. This would be a good place to start for an overview that provides the flavour of the times.

317 **Old Yukon: tales – trails – and trials.**
James Wickersham. St. Paul, Minnesota: West Publishing Company, 1938. 514p.

James Wickersham came to Alaska as a federal judge, first in Eagle, on circuit travels, and then in the new town of Fairbanks, which he named. He served from 1900 to 1908. He then became active in politics, serving a total of 14 years as Alaska's elected, but non-voting delegate to Congress. He travelled extensively on his circuit and vividly describes life and conditions on the trail, especially dog-sled travel. He also participated in an attempt to climb Mt. McKinley, heard a number of interesting cases, and describes social life in gold-rush Alaska.

318 **One man's gold rush: a Klondike album.**
Murray C. Morgan, photographs by Eric Hegg. Seattle, Washington; London: University of Washington Press, 1967. 213p. maps.

The 'one man' in this book is Eric Hegg, who became a leading photographer of the gold rush. Many of the most memorable, and frequently published, photographs of Dyea, Sheep Creek, the Chilkoot trail and the route to Dawson were by Hegg. He then established a studio in Skagway. When gold was discovered in Nome, Hegg went there, too. Many of the Hegg photographs have been lost, but 207 of those that still exist are reproduced in this volume.

319 **Sourdough sagas: the journals, memories, tales and recollections of the earliest Alaskan gold miners, 1883-1923.**
Herbert Heller. Cleveland, Ohio; New York: World Publishing Co., 1967. 217p.

This is a compilation of the experiences of a number of individuals who moved north during the gold-rush era. Many of the settlements that are described have disappeared, such as Chena, or are ghost towns, such as Flat. There are numerous details of everyday life, such as travel on the Valdez–Fairbanks trail in 1906 and the roadhouse life along the way.

320 **Through the Yukon and Alaska.**
T. A. Rickard. San Francisco: Mining and Scientific Press, 1909. 392p. maps. bibliog.

Rickard was a mining engineer who visited a number of mining districts in 1908, and wrote perceptively about conditions and the attitudes of the miners.

Transportation

321 **The Alaska Highway: papers of the 40th anniversary symposium.**
Edited by Kenneth Coates. Vancouver: University of British Columbia Press, 1985. 208p. maps.

These fourteen papers cover the planning, building, international relations, impact and post-war use of the highway. Authorized for construction in 1942, this military project had a profound effect upon Alberta, northern British Columbia and the Yukon Territory as well as the end of the road in Alaska, where the only land link with the remainder of North America terminates.

322 **Alaska railroad in pictures, 1914-1964.**
Bernardin LeMay Prince. Anchorage: K. Wray's Print Shop, 1964. 2 vols.

Brief explanations, reproduced documents such as railroad reports, old time-tables and, above all, photographs are the raw material of history presented here. The more than 1,000 photographs in this 1,092-page work are what make it most valuable. Many of these well-documented pictures are from private collections and are not otherwise available. There is no index or bibliography and there are no footnotes.

323 Alaska steam: a pictorial history of the Alaska Steamship Company.

Lucile McDonald in cooperation with the Puget Sound Maritime Historical Society. Anchorage: Alaska Geographic, 1984. 145p. bibliog. (*Alaska Geographic*, vol. 11, no. 4).

The Alaska Steamship Company was a dominant force in transportation to and from Alaska from 1894 to 1971. The gold-rush era placed special pressures upon shipping. The economics of shipping and the difficulties in servicing this route – with the seemingly inevitable shipwrecks – are treated here.

324 The copper spike.

Lone Janson. Anchorage: Alaska Northwest, 1975. 175p. bibliog.

The Copper River & Northwestern Railway was the winner in a fierce competition of up to fifty railroad concerns (only five actually started construction) to build a railroad from tide-water on Prince William Sound towards the interior. A railroad was eventually completed from Cordova to the copper mine at Kennecott. The Guggenheim and Morgan Alaska Syndicate supplied the funding. The politics of coal and oil (at nearby Katalla) were also involved. Towns prospered or died, depending upon how the railroad developed.

325 A dog puncher on the Yukon.

Arthur Treadwell Walden. Boston, Massachusetts: Houghton Mifflin, 1928. 289p.

This book is written in a fast-paced anecdotal style. Walden was involved with dog-team freighting during the gold rush. He also helped establish dog-racing in Alaska. He later was a chief dog-driver for Admiral Byrd in Antarctica and eventually retired to New England to breed sled dogs.

326 800 miles to Valdez: the building of the Alaska pipeline.

James P. Roscow. Englewood Cliffs, New Jersey: Prentice-Hall, 1977. 227p. map. bibliog.

The construction, use, and income from the Trans-Alaskan Pipeline has been the dominant factor in Alaska's government and economy since 1969. Most of Alaska's tax and royalty revenues come from Prudhoe Bay oil shipped through the line. This is a straightforward chronological account of the line's planning and construction.

327 Flying beats work: the story of Reeve Aleutian Airways.

Stan Cohen. Missoula, Montana: Pictorial Histories Publishing, 1988. 116p.

This is primarily a book of photographs, featuring the career of Bob Reeve and his airline.

328 The flying North.

Jean Potter. New York: Macmillan, 1947. 261p.

This is one of the first of many books about the history of bush aviation in Alaska. Most of the nine pilots featured here subsequently had individual biographies published.

329 Frank Barr, bush pilot in Alaska and the Yukon.

Dermot Cole. Edmonds, Washington: Alaska Northwest, 1986. 115p. maps. bibliog.

Barr was a 'bush pilot' active during the 1930s and 1940s. He operated a one-man company that flew all over the territory. He also was one of the 55 delegates to the Alaska Constitutional Convention. His company's slogan was 'If you feel you must get there in the worst way, fly with Barr'.

330 Glacier pilot: the story of Bob Reeve and the flyers who pushed back Alaska's air frontiers.

Beth Day. New York: Holt, Rinehart and Winston, 1957. 348p. maps.

Bob Reeve was one of the first commercial pilots in Alaska, operating out of Valdez for many years before the Second World War. Some of his flying involved taking off from wet mud flats at Valdez in the summer with skis so that he could land on snowy glaciers to supply mining operations. After the war, he was eventually able to turn his one-man operation into an airline serving the 'air route nobody wanted': the Aleutian chain.

331 Journeys down the line: building the Trans-Alaskan Pipeline.

Robert Douglas Mead. Garden City, New York: Doubleday, 1978. 609p. map. bibliog.

This is a partially autobiographical account of the construction of the pipeline. It is filled with public policy issues, living conditions, and the actual history of construction. Many elements beyond the author's own direct experience are covered, such as details of the labour agreements, the impact of the project on the native population of Alaska and the economic and social consequences of the resulting boom times. For a reliable account of what this recent era was like, this is the best available account. For the underlying historical significance of this project, see Peter Coates (item no. 344).

332 Lifeline to the Yukon: a history of Yukon River navigation.

Barry C. Anderson. Seattle, Washington: Superior, 1983. 152p. bibliog.

This is a general popular history of powered riverboats. It includes numerous historical photographs and a small section describing the fleet of the Yutana Barge Company, based in Nenana on the Tanana River, a tributary of the Yukon.

333 Mudhole Smith, Alaska flyer.

Lone E. Janson. Anchorage: Alaska Northwest, 1981. 143p.

Smith was a Midwestern barnstormer who moved to Alaska in 1937 to fly out of Cordova. He eventually accumulated 22,000 hours of Alaskan flying time by the time he retired.

334 **North to Alaska.**
Ken Coates. Fairbanks, Alaska: University of Alaska Press, 1992. 304p. map.

A history of the Alaska Highway from its construction during the Second World War through to its reconstruction and modernization to the 1990s. Publication of Coates's book coincided with the celebration of the fiftieth anniversary of the highway. Much of it is about the impact of the highway on the lives of people who live along it. The author spent part of his childhood in Whitehorse while his father worked as an engineer engaged in reconstruction of the highway. The highway remains the sole land link between Alaska and points farther south and east.

335 **Northern lights: tales of Alaska's lighthouses and their keepers.**
Shannon Lowry, photographs by Jeff Schultz. Harrisburg, Pennsylvania: Stackpole Books, 1992. 118p.

Lighthouses and their keepers performed a much-needed service before they were replaced by automated systems and electronic navigational aids. Lowry has interviewd a substantial number of surviving lighthouse men and has visited a number of lighthouse sites while researching this interesting brief account.

336 **On the 'White Pass' pay-roll.**
By the President of the White Pass & Yukon Route [S. H. Graves]. New York: Paladin Press, 1970. reprinted ed. 258p.

This is an anecdotal account, originally published in 1908, of the construction and early operation of this pioneer railway. It supplied the Yukon gold-fields through the coastal mountain range from tidewater at Skagway, Alaska, through Whitehorse, in the Yukon Territory. For a more analytical account see Minter (item no. 346).

337 **Paving Alaska's trails: the work of the Alaska Road Commission.**
Claus-M. Naske. Lanham, Maryland: University Press of America, 1986. 339p.

From 1905 until 1956, the Alaska Road Commission, led by army officers, was in charge of developing public roads and maintaining summer and winter trails. There was not much money, but there were problems of supply, equipment, permafrost, muskeg [swamp, bog] and other impediments. Naske appends a number of useful references, including the membership of the Board of Road Commissioners for Alaska, the laws governing road construction, and various official plans and survey reports. The book is illustrated with a number of historical photographs.

338 **Pioneer bush pilot: the story of Noel Wien.**
Ira Harkey. Seattle, Washington: University of Washington Press, 1974. 307p. map.

Noel Wien was one of the very first aviators in the Territory, arriving in 1924. He was the first to fly many routes that later became routine, including scheduled winter flying. He was famous for a very cautious approach to flying and maintenance and he kept himself in top physical condition, before polio slowed him down, so that he would be able to walk out through the Alaskan bush if he crashed. He founded an airline and remained an active flyer into the 1970s.

339 **Railroad in the clouds: the Alaska Railroad in the age of steam, 1914-1945.**
William H. Wilson. Boulder, Colorado: Pruett, 1977. 279p. 3 maps. bibliog.

This is the most professional of the several histories of the Alaska Railroad during its construction and early operational phases. It is extensively illustrated, especially with photographs of rolling stock. The railroad was also heavily involved with shipping, in the first instance because it relied upon steamships for passengers and freight to carry. Additionally, it unloaded freight in Nenana for transport on the Tanana and Yukon river systems. There is much useful information on the old Tanana Valley Railroad both before and after it was purchased by the Alaska Railroad.

340 **Rails north: the railroads of Alaska and the Yukon.**
Howard Clifford. Seattle, Washington: Superior, 1981. 200p. bibliog.

This is a survey of railroads in the region. Only two of the larger lines are still in operation. Each railroad description is extensively illustrated and a list of locomotives with number, manufacturer and type is included. There is a brief history of each machine; many served on multiple lines during their active years. Many of these roads were quite short, serving mines and other commercial interests.

341 **The sinking of the *Princess Sophia*: taking the North down with her.**
Ken Coates, Bill Morrison. Toronto: Oxford University Press, 1990; Fairbanks, Alaska: University of Alaska Press, 1991. 220p. maps. bibliog.

The *Princess Sophia* sank in Lynn Canal after leaving Skagway in October 1918. Not only were 353 people killed, but many prominent individuals were among them, especially from the Yukon Territory. The gold rush was already over and the North was in economic decline.

342 **Skystruck: adventures of an Alaskan pilot.**
Cliff Cernick. Edmonds, Washington: Alaska Northwest, 1989. 169p.

Herm Lerdahl was a pilot active during the 1930s and 1940s.

343 **Steamboats on the Chena: the founding and development of Fairbanks, Alaska.**
Basil Hedrick, Susan Savage. Fairbanks, Alaska: Epicenter Press, 1988. 115p. maps. bibliog.

Steamboating on the Yukon, Tanana and Chena rivers started in 1901. The story ends in 1923, when the completion of the Alaska Railroad to Fairbanks closed this era. There are a number of historical photographs of steamboats and their crews.

344 **The Trans-Alaska Pipeline controversy: technology, conservation, and the frontier.**
Peter A. Coates. Bethleham, Pennsylvania; London: Lehigh University Press; Associated University Press, 1991. 447p. maps. bibliog.

Originally a copiously documented dissertation, this is published as a book-length study of the place of the pipeline project in the history of the state. Coates describes the somewhat tortuous process of the pipeline's approval through the US Congress. He also describes the construction and considers its impact. As with many dissertations, this might better have been two or three books, but it remains the most detailed work on the subject.

345 **Wheels on ice: bicycling in Alaska 1898-1908.**
Edited by Terrence Cole. Anchorage: Alaska Northwest, 1985. 64p. bibliog.

Unlikely as it may seem, given the Alaska terrain, bicycles were an important means of transportation, and most useful for travelling on frozen rivers in the winter when one could not afford the luxury of a dog team. Some travelled as far as from Dawson to Nome, from Valdez to Fairbanks, and from Point Barrow to Nome. Cole has assembled five contemporary accounts of travel during the gold rush.

346 **The White Pass: gateway to the Klondike.**
Roy Minter. Fairbanks, Alaska: University of Alaska Press, 1987. 394p. maps. bibliog.

The White Pass route runs from Skagway at the head of Lynn Canal in Alaska to Whitehorse in the Yukon Territory. There, riverboats used to pick up freight and passengers going to and from the gold-fields. Construction began in 1898 on this 175-kilometre railroad through the coastal mountain range and it was completed in 1900.

Commerce and industry

347 **Extreme conditions: big oil and the transformation of Alaska.**
John Strohmeyer. New York: Simon and Schuster, 1993. 287p.

This book is more about the changes in Alaska brought on by a large dominant industry than about the oil industry or construction itself. The author has done an especially thorough job with state politics. Despite some sensationalism, the book is full of useful information.

348 **Fifty years below zero: a lifetime of adventure in the far North.**
Charles DeWitt Brower in collaboration with Philip J. Farrelly, Lyman Anson. New York: Dodd Mead, 1942. 2nd ed. 1954. numerous printings. 310p.

At the time the book was written, Charley Brower, known as the 'King of the Arctic', had spent 57 years on Alaska's North Slope, primarily in Barrow. He was involved with commercial whaling early on, and continued with trade after that era ended.

349 **Fifty years in Alaska.**
Carl J. Lomen. New York: David McKay, 1954. 302p.

The Lomens were pioneer businessmen with many interests in Nome. This autobiography concentrates on the reindeer industry established on the Seward Peninsula, which became embroiled in a major political battle that finally closed down the Lomen operation.

350 **Fort Yukon trader: three years in an Alaskan wilderness.**
C. Masten Beaver. New York: Exposition Press, 1955. 185p.

A man-and-wife team, totally new to Alaska, travelled to the settlement of Fort Yukon in 1943 to help run the Northern Commercial Company trading post. Their perspective on native life reflects the values of that era.

351 **The frontier in Alaska and the Matanuska colony.**
Orlando W. Miller. New Haven, Connecticut: Yale University Press, 1975. 329p. map. bibliog. (Yale Western Americana, no. 26).

This is the definitive history of the Roosevelt New Deal experiment to settle displaced farmers from Midwestern America to Alaska. Although small by outside standards, these 200 new farms had a profound effect upon Alaska. The expectations were much too high, and the colony would have no doubt disappeared had it not been for the military build-up of the Second World War with its need for local agricultural production. Miller examines the myths involved with a belief in the existence of wide-open spaces awaiting pioneers to produce a new prosperity.

352 **Recollections of the Yukon: memories from the years 1868-1885.**
François Xavier Mercier, translated and edited by Linda Finn Yarborough. Anchorage: Alaska Historical Society, 1986. 102p. maps. bibliog.

This is one of the very few first-person accounts of life on the Yukon before the gold rush of the 1890s. Mercier was a Canadian trader who worked for several companies in various locations along the Yukon during his time there. This account was translated from the original French-language manuscript housed in the Oregon Province Archives of the Society of Jesus at Gonzaga University. It is organized into topical chapters, including a list of all known traders on the Yukon in 1868, the first white woman in the district, early prospectors, biographical sketches of several Catholic priests, a Koutcha-Kutchin chief, and several explorers. Mercier also has a list of all of the villages which he knew existed at the time, from Fort Saint Michael near the mouth of the Yukon to Fort Reliance, and he includes an estimate of the distances between them.

Politics and government

353 **Alaska: a history of its administration, exploitation, and industrial development during its first half century under the rule of the United States.**

Jeanette Paddock Nichols. New York: Arthur H. Clark, 1924. 456p. bibliog.

This is a classic of Alaska history. Alaska is cast as a victim of exploitation by the federal government and outside interests, a theme taken up by numerous later historians and politicians.

354 **A history of the United States Forest Service in Alaska.**

Lawrence Rakestraw. Anchorage: Alaska Historical Commission and the Alaska Region, United States Forest Service, Department of Agriculture, 1981. 221p. 6 maps. bibliog.

National forests were established in Alaska as the result of the national conservation movement and the involvement of President Theodore Roosevelt and forester Gifford Pinchot. The Afognak, Tongass and Chugach National Forests cover the majority of wooded coastal areas in Alaska. From the gold rush onwards, the timber industry and its regulation have posed political and economic issues involving government, outside interests, and the politics of Washington, DC. This has also been true of mining and fishing. Rakestraw's account is a succinct history of the timber industry and its technology as well as a history of an agency.

355 **Land of the midnight sun: a history of the Yukon.**

Kenneth S. Coates, William R. Morrison. Edmonton, Alberta: Hurtig Publishers, 1988. 326p. maps. bibliog.

There are many parallels between Yukon history and Alaska history, often in reaction to the same influences such as cycles in the gold-mining industry. Special attention is paid to economic history and the impact of development upon the lives of Yukon natives. The thesis is that Yukon residents have not had control over their own destiny. More than anything else, this is a political history that mirrors (for the Yukon) the basic philosophical and historical approach to politics so powerfully presented earlier (for Alaska) by Ernest Gruening (item no. 357).

356 **Reaching for a star: the final campaign for Alaska statehood.**

Gerald E. Bowkett. Fairbanks, Alaska: Epicenter Press, 1989. 162p.

A constitutional convention was held in 1955, not only to develop a framework for Alaskan statehood, but also to help build political pressure in both Alaska and Washington, DC. Statehood was finally granted in 1959.

357 **The state of Alaska.**

Ernest Gruening. New York: Random House, 1968. rev. ed. 661p. 2 maps.

The first edition of this book was published in 1954, and was designed to show the neglect Alaska had received at the hands of the federal government and to urge statehood for Alaska – it was actually granted in 1959. Some of the author's chapter titles tell his story: 'the era of total neglect (1867-1884)', 'the era of flagrant neglect (1884-1898)', 'the era of mild but unenlightened interest (1898-1912)', 'the era of indifference and unconcern (1912-1933)', 'the era of growing awareness (1933-1954)'. Gruening had served as Governor of the Territory (1939-53) and later became one of Alaska's first two senators.

358 **Tarnished expansion: the Alaska scandal, the press and Congress, 1867-1871.**
Paul Sothe Holbo. Knoxville, Tennessee: University of Tennessee Press, 1983. 145p.

This is a study of the politics of the Alaska purchase with an emphasis on the corruption involved.

Education

359 **A century of service, 1858-1958. A history of the Sisters of Saint Ann and their contribution to education in British Columbia, the Yukon and Alaska.**
Sister Mary Margaret Down. Victoria, British Columbia: The Sisters of Saint Ann, 1966. 195p.

The Catholic Order of the Sisters of Saint Ann arrived in Victoria, BC in 1858. They established Saint Ann's School in Juneau in 1886 and the Indian Mission School in Holy Cross on the Yukon in 1888.

360 **The College Hill chronicles: how the University of Alaska came of age.**
Neil Davis. Fairbanks, Alaska: University of Alaska Foundation, 1993. 627p.

Davis grew up in Fairbanks, attended the University of Alaska and spent his scientific career there. His book centres on the creation and early history of the University's renowned Geophysical Institute and the tenure of the second President of the University of Alaska, Terris Moore. The author is always aware of the political circumstances governing the university's development and he includes material about the workings of the territorial legislature, business interests and the role of national government. For example, the Geophysical Institute was created by an act of Congress which took 12 years of effort to effect. How could a university be supported when the territory had almost no taxing powers?

361 The cornerstone on College Hill: an illustrated history of the University of Alaska Fairbanks.

Terrence Cole. Fairbanks, Alaska: University of Alaska Press, 1994. 394p. bibliog.

A lively style and extensive illustrations place this well-researched history a cut above the usual official institutional account. Cole situates his story within the context of the unique economic and political setting of the interior of Alaska during the territorial era. There are a number of colourful personalities, such as the self-taught archaeologist Otto Geist, and their biographies are intertwined with the history of the Alaska Agricultural College and School of Mines, which became the University of Alaska in 1935.

362 Education in Alaska's past: conference proceedings, Valdez Alaska.

Edited by Gary C. Stein. Anchorage: Alaska Historical Society, 1983. 210p.

Three of these fourteen papers concern the first Alaska Commissioner of Education, the Presbyterian minister Sheldon Jackson. One is about education in Russian America; the remainder relate the experiences of individual educators. Most are autobiographical.

363 Education in Russian America.

J. Lincoln Starr. Juneau: Alaska State Library, 1972. 61p. bibliog. (Alaska State Library Historical Monographs, no. 2).

Russian colonial educational institutions included missionary schools, several secular schools for practical occupations and even a seminary. Information on personnel, curriculum and numbers of students are provided where that information is available. Research is based upon the Russian Orthodox Church records at the Library of Congress, which have since been indexed and microfilmed. Many of the Russian-language sources listed in the bibliography have since been translated into English.

364 Education in the territories and outlying possessions of the United States.

Charles F. Reid. New York: Bureau of Publications, Teachers College, Columbia University, 1941. 593p. bibliog.

A substantial part of this book, pages 9-144, is devoted to Alaska. The dual system of education, the small proportion of school-age children in the total white population, and issues of native education are examined. According to the last census (1930) used for this book, natives made up 85.8 per cent of the entire population in the arctic region, 59.2 per cent in central Alaska, 44.7 per cent on the Alaska Peninsula and along the Aleutians, and 31.0 per cent in south-eastern Alaska. There is considerable information on numbers of students, the organization of education, and educational budgets.

365 **Farthest north college president: Charles E. Bunnell and the early history of the University of Alaska.**
William R. Cashen. Fairbanks, Alaska: University of Alaska Press, 1972. 387p.

This biography of the founding president of the university was written by a member of the faculty, who had himself been a student at the University during the 1930s. Bunnell had previously been a school teacher on Kodiak Island and a federal judge in Fairbanks. Never adequately funded, Bunnell kept the institution together by force of personality for nearly thirty years.

366 **Historical status of elementary schools in rural Alaskan communities, 1867-1980.**
Carol Barnhardt. Fairbanks, Alaska: Center for Cross-Cultural Studies, University of Alaska, 1985. 63p. map. bibliog.

This is a well-organized reference to all known schools, by community. Dates of operation and the agency administrating them are listed. There is a short introduction which gives a brief overview of the history of schools in Alaska.

367 **Juneau stories of teaching on the Last Frontier.**
Compiled by the Juneau Retired Teachers' Association. Juneau: Juneau-Douglas City Museum, City and Borough of Juneau, 1993. 190p.

There has been tremendous change in Alaska's schools following statehood and the Alaska oil boom and the experiences of these teachers reflect that.

368 **Life in Alaska: the reminiscences of a Kansas woman, 1916-19.**
May Wynne Lamb, edited by Dorothy Wynne Zimmerman. Lincoln, Nebraska: University of Nebraska Press, 1988. 177p. map.

Lamb was a school teacher in the Eskimo community of Akiak on the Kuskokwim River, 1916-19. She was also involved with other government duties and healthcare delivery.

369 **North to Alaska's shining river.**
Hazel Dunaway Berto. Indianapolis, Indiana; Bobbs-Merrill, 1959. 244p.

This is an autobiographical account of a Bureau of Indian Affairs teaching couple who were stationed on Norton Sound from 1925 to 1928. It deals to some extent with living conditions and public health issues, especially tuberculosis among the Eskimo. It should be used with care as some portions appear to have been fictionalized.

370 **North country challenge.**
Ernest N. Patty. New York: David McKay, 1969. 272p.

Ernest Patty came to the fledgling Alaska Agricultural College and School of Mines in 1922 to teach mining. He later had a highly successful career managing various mining interests in Alaska and the Yukon Territory before being asked to return to the University as its third president in 1953.

371 **Our schools: a history of elementary and secondary public education in the Fairbanks area.**
Fairbanks, Alaska: Fairbanks North Star Borough School District, 1989. 78p.

This is the result of a 1989 silver anniversary district-wide project. It involved students in researching the history of each of the more than thirty schools.

372 **Tisha: the story of a young teacher in the Alaskan wilderness.**
Anne Purdy. Toronto; New York: St. Martin's Press, 1976. 358p.

This is the story of a school teacher who arrived in the rural mining community of Chicken just after the height of the gold rush. She continued teaching throughout the 1920s and 1930s.

Medical and social history

373 **Alaska hooch: the history of alcohol in early Alaska.**
Thayne I. Anderson. Fairbanks, Alaska: Che-Noo Press, 1988. 272p. bibliog.

This is a consideration of the role of alcohol in the early exploration of Alaska by Europeans, trade with Alaska Natives, and the governmental regulations which were imposed over a period of time. Anderson has researched alcohol use among the Northwest Coast Indians and among the Russians who came to Alaska. He considers the relationship between alcohol and violence, and provides a number of historical examples. He considers how it has affected public health, and considers the regulatory climate in Alaska, especially the role of the US Army, the courts, the missionaries, and government officials. His story ends with a consideration of the prohibition era in Alaska.

374 **An army doctor's wife on the frontier: letters from Alaska and the far west, 1874-1878.**
Emily Fitzgerald, edited by Abe Laufe. Pittsburgh, Pennsylvania: University of Pittsburgh Press, 1962. 352p.

Fitzgerald was in Sitka, 1874-75, accompanying her husband, an army surgeon. In these letters to her mother, she relates the daily life of raising a small family in what she saw as a very remote place.

375 **Chills and fever: health and disease in the early history of Alaska.**
Robert Fortuine. Fairbanks, Alaska: University of Alaska Press, 1989. 393p. maps. bibliog.

A retired Public Health Service physician, Fortuine continues to teach and write. He is especially concerned with the Alaskan native population, and has done extensive and innovative research on the pre-contact and early exploration eras. The introduction of alcohol, tobacco and a variety of infectious diseases is chronicled, as is the influence of traders, whalers and missionaries. He evaluates the importance and validity of various sources such as oral traditions and eye-witness accounts. He makes extensive use of archaeology, anthropology, history and associated disciplines.

376 **Doctor Hap.**

Clara Heinz Burke, Adele Comandini. New York: Coward-McCann, 1961. 319p.

This is a biography of Dr. Crafton Burke, an Episcopal medical missionary. It is written from the point of view of his wife, and tells as much about her experiences as about his.

377 **Dog team doctor.**

Eva Greenslit Anderson. Caldwell, Idaho: Caxton Printers, 1940. 298p.

Dr. Joseph Herman Romig arrived in 1896 as a Moravian medical missionary on the Kuskokwim River. He subsequently moved to Anchorage and became a US Commissioner of Health.

378 **Eskimo medicine man.**

Otto George. Portland, Oregon: Oregon Historical Society, 1979. 278p. map.

These are the memoirs of a US Indian Service physician who worked and lived with his family in western and northern Alaska during the 1930s.

379 **The race to Nome.**

Kenneth A. Ungermann. New York: Harper & Row, 1963. 117p. map.

The annual 1,000-mile Iditarod sled dog race takes place in memory of a diphtheria serum run in 1925 at the height of a deadly epidemic in Nome. This is an account of the original event.

380 **The treatment of the mentally ill in Alaska, 1884-1912.**

Thomas G. Smith. *Pacific Northwest Quarterly*, vol. 65, no. 1 (Jan. 1974), p. 17-28. bibliog.

This is a concise statement of the issues involved during the period that the Territory of Alaska functioned under the 1884 Organic Act. There were no hospitals that could treat the mentally ill in Alaska and the US government was extremely reluctant to bear the expense of transporting the mentally ill out of the area. Smith compares Alaska to other territories of that era, such as Arizona.

381 **Tuberculosis in western Alaska 1900-1950.**

N. E. Flanders. *Polar Record*, vol. 23, no. 145 (Jan. 1987), p. 383-96. maps. bibliog.

Tuberculosis was at one time the leading cause of death among the native population of Alaska. It came under control only after concentrated efforts made during the 1950s and 1960s. Flanders examines the primary effects of this disease on the population, provides some detailed statistical information, and then examines the short-term and long-term effects upon society.

War and the military

382 **The Alaska highway in World War II: the U.S. army of occupation in Canada's Northwest.**
Ken S. Coates, William R. Morrison. Norman, Oklahoma; London: University of Oklahoma Press, 1992. 309p. map. bibliog.

The construction of the highway strongly impacted north-western Canada as well as Alaska. There were 40,000 US military and civilian workers injected into a sparsely populated region, constituting a 'friendly invasion'. Military authorities were not always sensitive to the needs of local residents. This work is extensively researched and includes many personal interviews with participants.

383 **Aleutian echoes.**
Charles C. Bradley. Fairbanks, Alaska: University of Alaska Press, 1994. 275p.

Bradley participated in a top-secret training mission in the Aleutians to prepare for a planned invasion of the Kuril Islands, but it was rendered unnecessary when the Japanese surrendered. During the training mission, which lasted 18 months, his unit tested all matter of survival and cold-weather equipment. Bradley finds that there are humorous aspects to his experience.

384 **Aleutian warriors: a history of the 11th Air Force and Fleet Air Wing 4.**
John Haile Cloe. Anchorage; Missoula, Montana: Anchorage Chapter, Air Force Association; Pictorial Histories, 1990. 344p. maps.

This is an extensively illustrated history of the Second World War air campaign in the Aleutian Islands.

385 **Armed forces on a northern frontier: the military in Alaska's history 1867-1987.**
Jonathan Nielson. Westport, Connecticut: Greenwood Press, 1988. 298p. bibliog.

This is the most comprehensive of the military histories of the state. The army has been responsible for much of the exploration of Alaska's interior: it established a presence during the gold rush, fought the only land engagement of the Second World War on American soil (in Alaska), and became a major economic force in the territory during the Cold War.

386 **Castner's Cutthroats: saga of the Alaska Scouts.**
Jim Rearden. Prescott, Arizona: Wolfe Publishing Company, 1990. 319p.

This is well-reseached historical fiction about the Alaska Scouts of the Second World War. The Scouts included many Alaskan natives and this unit assisted in the Aleutian campaign under Colonel Lawrence V. Castner. The author interviewed former members of the platoon over a period of forty years. The book includes a number of historical photographs.

387 **Cobras over the tundra.**
Everett Long, Ivan Negenblya. Fairbanks, Alaska: Artika, 1992. 115p.

This book is in both Russian and English. It is a collaborative effort by a freelance aviation writer from Fairbanks and a former member of the Aeroflot Civil Aviation Detachment in Yakutsk. It concerns the lend-lease ferry of 7,926 aircraft from the United States through Fairbanks and Nome to the Soviet Union during the Second World War. The most common plane that was flown over was the P-39 Aircobra, hence the book title.

388 **The forgotten war: a pictorial history of World War II in Alaska and northwestern Canada.**
Stan Cohen. Missoula, Montana: Pictorial Histories Publishing, 1988. 254p. maps. bibliog.

This pictorial history reproduces over five hundred photographs, maps, diagrams and drawings.

389 **Guys on ice.**
Lyman R. Ellswort. New York: David McKay, 1952. 277p.

This book is about the experiences of a small contingent of US soldiers stationed on the Pribilof Islands during the Second World War.

390 **Historical aspects of the building of the Washington–Alaska Military Cable and Telegraph System, with special emphasis on the Eagle–Valdez and Goodpaster telegraph lines, 1902-1903.**
William A. Quirk. [Washington, DC]: Bureau of Land Management, US Department of the Interior, 1974. 28p. bibliog.

WAMCATS, the Washington–Alaska Military Cable and Telegraph System, was Alaska's first direct communications link with the rest of the United States. Before the telegraph line, written communications could take up to a year, from one navigational season to the next, although the use of dog-team mail routes could sometimes shorten the time to a matter of months. The first segment of the line was built to Canada from Fort Egbert at Eagle. The message was then carried overland to Skagway and shipped south, shortening the transmission time to 5 days. The system was eventually expanded across Alaska to Nome and Valdez, and underwater cables were laid to Seattle in 1904.

391 **History of U.S. naval operations in World War II, volume VII, Aleutians, Gilberts, Marshalls.**
Samuel Elliot Morison. Boston, Massachusetts: Little, Brown, 1951.

The Aleutian campaign is but a small part of this 15-volume study. It occupies only pages 1 to 66 of this volume. However, this is an excellent and concise narrative account.

392 **Journal of an Aleutian year.**
Ethel Ross Oliver. Seattle, Washington: University of Washington Press, 1988. 248p. maps.

The Japanese launched an air attack against Dutch Harbor and invaded the Aleutian islands of Attu and Kiska. A number of native Aleuts were captured by the Japanese. The village of Atka was hastily evacuated by the United States and the villagers spent the war in camps in Southeast Alaska. Ethel Oliver was a teacher assigned to Atka for the first year that the population returned to their destroyed village, and she kept a journal of this crucial time of relocation and rebuilding. An appendix lists the persons on Attu during the Japanese invasion, their wartime experience, and their residence and age in June 1947. Many had died in Japan.

393 **The opening of Alaska.**
William L. Mitchell, edited by Lyman L. Woodman. Anchorage: Cook Inlet Historical Society, 1982. 111p. map. bibliog.

Billy Mitchell in later life became well known for his uncompromising advocacy of 'air power' for the US military, which eventually ended in a court martial in the 1920s. Long before that, however, he was assigned, at 21 the youngest lieutenant in the army, to direct construction of a portion of the Washington–Alaska Military Cable and Telegraph System (WAMCATS). This is the edited version of a manuscript report that he wrote around 1935, which is now deposited at the Library of Congress. It describes conditions and construction along the Yukon, Tanana and Goodpaster rivers.

394 **The thousand mile war: World War II in Alaska and the Aleutians.**
Brian Garfield. Garden City, New York: Doubleday, 1969. 351p. maps. bibliog.

This is the most widely read and popular account of the Aleutian campaign of the Second World War. It has been frequently reprinted.

395 **Top cover for America: the Air Force in Alaska, 1920-1983.**
John Haile Cloe with Michael F. Monagan. Missoula, Montana: Pictorial Histories Publishing Company, 1984. 258p. 27 maps.

The period covered starts with the Black Wolf Squadron's flight to Alaska in 1920 and continues through the Second World War Aleutian Campaign to the Cold War defence systems. It is copiously illustrated, but lacks an index.

396 **Track of the *Bear*.**
William Bixby. New York: David McKay, 1965. 309p. bibliog.

The *Bear* had an extraordinary career in polar waters and elsewhere that lasted 89 years. She was in Alaskan service for 41 of those years, starting in 1886. She later served Admiral Byrd in the Antarctic. While with the Revenue Cutter Service, she made voyages north for the annual Bering Sea patrol, often in difficult ice and fog conditions. She was involved with the enforcement of sealing and whaling regulations in an era of intense international controversy, with US–Native relations, with numerous humanitarian missions, and with the events of the gold rush.

Biographies and autobiographies

397 **Aghvook, white Eskimo: Otto Geist and Alaska archaeology.**
Charles J. Keim, foreword by Olaus J. Murie. College, Alaska: University of Alaska Press, 1969. 313p.

Otto Geist arrived in Alaska as a recent emigrant from Germany. He became a self-taught archaeologist, working closely with Charles Bunnell, president of the University of Alaska. He was instrumental in organizing and working on a number of important sites, the best known at Kukulik on St. Lawrence Island (see item no. 226). Over the years he collected assiduously for the University of Alaska museum, both in natural history and human prehistory. He had an excellent working relationship with miners, who would inform him when they uncovered mammoth remains and other items of interest during their operations. The author emphasizes the positive aspects, and does not provide a critical review of Geist's career.

398 **Alaskan apostle: the life story of Sheldon Jackson.**
J. Arthur Lazell. New York: Harper & Brothers, 1960. 218p. maps.

Sheldon Jackson was one of the most influential men in Alaska during the late 1880s, 1890s and early years of the twentieth century. He was not only a successful Presbyterian missionary, but also the United States Commissioner of Education for Alaska and he had close political ties in Washington, DC. However, the author goes too far when he states that Jackson alone '. . . was responsible for saving the Alaskan Eskimo from extinction and for the founding of Alaska's school system'.

399 **Alaska broker.**
Edward M. Boyd. Portland, Oregon: Binford & Mort, 1988. 356p.

This is the autobiography of an Anchorage real-estate agent and multi-millionaire.

400 **Alaska pioneer and west coast town builder, William Sumner Dodge.**
Ted C. Hinckley. *Alaska History*, vol. 1, no. 1 (Fall 1984), p. 1-26.

Dodge came north immediately following the purchase of Alaska as a Treasury Special Agent and became mayor of Sitka in a failed attempt to boost the urban development of Alaska through private speculation. It is a good demonstration of the very real limits of economic activity in the late 1860s and 1870s.

401 **Alaskan John G. Brady, missionary, businessman, judge, and governor, 1878-1918.**
Ted C. Hinckley. Columbus, Ohio: Published for Miami University by the Ohio State University Press, 1982. 398p. bibliog.

Missionaries in Alaska held political influence in Washington, and the Presbyterians more than any other denomination. Judges and the territorial governor were all appointed by the President in Washington. The Presbyterian Brady was governor through the early years of the gold rush. He left the governorship under a cloud due to his questionable business decisions. Hinckley explains the policy issues that touched upon Brady's public career during this formative period in Alaska's history.

402 **Back to the Smoky Sea.**
Nutchuk, Alden Hatch, illustrated by Nutchuk. New York: Messner, 1946. 225p.

This is the continuation of *Son of the Smoky Sea* (q.v.), an autobiographical account of Simeon Oliver, an accomplished concert musician who grew up in the Aleutians.

403 **Baranov, chief manager of the Russian colonies in America.**
Kyrill T. Khlebnikov, translated from the Russian edition of 1835 by Colin Bearne, edited by Richard Pierce. Kingston, Ontario: Limestone Press, 1973. 140p. (Materials for the Study of Alaska History, no. 3).

This biography of the first Chief Manager of the Russian American Colonies, Alexander Baranov, was written by his younger contemporary, the Office Manager, who came to help put financial matters in order when Baranov retired at an advanced age. Baranov's tour took place at a turbulent time, and Khlebnikov frequently quotes Baranov's own letters and reports to describe events.

404 **Barrett Willoughby: Alaska's forgotten lady.**
Nancy Warren Ferrell. Fairbanks, Alaska: University of Alaska Press, 1994. 188p.

Willoughby spent her career writing novels set in Alaska (see items 644, 649). Unlike other popular novelists writing after the gold rush, she actually spent about twenty years living in the North. Her novels sold well during the 1920s and 1930s, and several were made into films. Willoughby's books are no longer in print and her style seemed outmoded by the 1950s, but she is perhaps the most widely read writer of Alaskan romances of her day.

405 **Biographical sketches of authors on Russian America and Alaska.**
Henry W. Elliott, transcription and bibliography by John W. Carnahan. Anchorage: Historical and Fine Arts Museum, Municipality of Anchorage. 52p. bibliog.

Elliott himself was a long-term specialist on Alaska, especially on issues involving the Pribilof fur seal industry. These sixty sketches were completed during the early part of this century in manuscript form for James Wickersham who was preparing his own bibliography (see item no. 407). Carnahan has included works by and about Elliott in the bibliography.

406 **Breaking trail: Hudson Stuck of Texas and Alaska.**

David M. Dean. Athens, Ohio: Ohio University Press, 1988. 344p. maps. bibliog.

Hudson Stuck was an Episcopal missionary actively serving an extensive region in interior Alaska between 1904 and 1920. Stuck was a keen observer with strong opinions concerning native issues. He wrote classic descriptions of travel and travel conditions in Alaska's interior and arctic coast. A number of Stuck's publications are included in this bibliography (see items 163, 167, 169).

407 **Frontier politics: Alaska's James Wickersham.**

Evangeline Atwood. Portland, Oregon: Binford & Mort, 1979. 449p.

This is the only full-length biography of Alaska's most important pre-World War II political figure, a judge and non-voting delegate to Congress, active in Alaska from 1900 to the 1930s. The work is neither critical nor analytical, but it chronicles the many facets of Wickersham's judicial work in newly established judicial districts, his influence upon public policy, his national and territorial politics, his book collecting and bibliographical endeavours, and his private ventures.

408 **The great Russian navigator, A. I. Chirikov.**

Vasilii Divin, translated and annotated by Raymond H. Fisher. Fairbanks, Alaska: University of Alaska Press, 1993. 319p. bibliog. (Rasmuson Library Historical Translation Series, no. 6).

Chirikov was the second in command during the Bering expedition which discovered Alaska in 1741. In most accounts, the Russian, Chirikov, has not received the same level of attention as has the Dane, Bering. Divin set out to rectify this during the early years of the Cold War. While some of the rhetoric seems overly strident and doctrinaire in today's world, this remains the only full-length biography of Chirikov. Raymond Fisher has extensively and critically annotated Divin's work.

409 **Johnny's girl: a daughter's memoir of growing up in Alaska's underworld.**

Kim Rich. New York: William Morrow, 1993. 302p.

Rich's father was a gambler and involved with other illegal activities. He was eventually murdered in 1973 by other criminals. It was an extremely difficult home-life for a small child. Her mother developed severe mental problems and died at 37 of cancer. The daughter lived alone with her father from when she was 9 years old until she was 14. This is a powerful book.

410 **Kusiq: an Eskimo life history from the arctic coast of Alaska.**
Waldo Bodfish, compiled and edited by William Schneider, in collaboration with Kisauta Okakok, James Nageak. Fairbanks, Alaska: University of Alaska Press, 1991. 330p. maps. bibliog. (Oral Biography Series, no. 2).

Kusiq grew up in a traditional Eskimo society which was heavily impacted by the whaling industry, Western education, and the newly introduced reindeer. During his life, he lived at various places along the Arctic Coast and learned to be a reindeer herder, a skilled trapper, hunter, and Eskimo whaler. In later years he became well known for his extensive knowledge of the Eskimo way of life and was of great help to several generations of researchers including Helge Larson, Otto Geist and those that followed. The appendices include a number of aids for understanding the text, including guides to pronunciation, a glossary of personal names mentioned in the text, and a table of genealogical relations.

411 **The life I've been living.**
Moses Cruikshank, recorded and compiled by William Schneider. Fairbanks, Alaska: University of Alaska Press, 1986. 132p. (Oral Biography Series, no. 1).

Moses Cruikshank has had an extraordinarily rich and varied life that has touched upon many aspects of several distinct historical periods in interior Alaska. In this sensitive and carefully crafted oral history, Schneider assembles Cruikshank's experiences and observations on the legacy of the gold stampeders; the development of the trapping economy; the development of the mission school system and mission travel by dog-sled; steamboat travel; railroad construction; the development and changes in Fairbanks, Nenana and elsewhere wrought by government projects and the Second World War; rural development work; and land claims and other public affairs issues.

412 **Lord of Alaska: Baranov and the Russian adventure.**
Hector Chevigny. Portland, Oregon: Binford and Mort, 1951. 2nd ed. 320p. map. bibliog.

This is a well-executed popular account of the first Chief Manager of the Russian American Colonies, published before the wealth of new documentation that has come to light during the past several decades. Baranov was one of the most colourful and intriguing of the cast of characters associated with the Russian era in Alaska, and this account does him justice.

413 **Lost empire: the life and adventures of Nikolai Petrovich Rezanov.**
Hector Chevigny. New York: Macmillan, 1937. 356p.

Court Chamberlain Rezanov was close to Imperial circles, under Catherine the Great, Paul I, and Alexander I. He was the son-in-law of Gregorii Shelikhov, the founder of the Russian-American Company. He had great ambitions for Russian expansion and sailed on Russia's first circumnavigation on a mission to Japan and Russian America. He also visited Spanish California. This account, written for a popular audience, moves quickly.

414 **My life of high adventure.**
Grant H. Pearson with Philip Newill. Englewood Cliffs, New Jersey: Prentice-Hall, 1962. 234p.

Pearson came to Alaska in 1925, worked at various jobs, primarily in mining, and then became a ranger at Mount McKinley National Park in 1926. He worked in other parks as well, but spent most of his time at McKinley and became the Park Superintendent. After retirement, he was elected to the Alaska legislature. His career spanned many developments in the history of conservation, and he was intimately involved with much of the history of the climbing of Mount McKinley.

415 **My way was north: an Alaskan autobiography.**
Frank Dufresne. New York: Holt, Rinehart and Winston, 1966. 247p.

This autobiography is of a man who acquired many talents during his stay in Alaska. He arrived in 1920 and soon began working for the US Biological Survey on the Seward Peninsula. He later moved to Fairbanks, and eventually on to Washington, DC, when the story ends. The book is mostly about life in Alaska during the 1920s and 1930s.

416 **O rugged land of gold.**
Martha Martin. Fairbanks, Alaska: Vanessapress, 1989. reprinted ed. 226p.

This is the autobiographical account, using a pen-name, of Helen Bolyan's life on and around the Cobol Mine on Chichagof Island. Details are significantly altered to make the story flow better. Events prevent her husband from returning from a trip and she is left pregnant and alone on an island full of bears.

417 **On the edge of nowhere.**
James Huntington. New York: Crown Publishers, 1966. 183p.

These are the personal adventures of the son of an Athabascan mother and a trapping and gold-mining father who came to Alaska during the gold rush. The extended Huntington family is highly respected and well known in Alaska.

418 **Russian America: a biographical dictionary.**
Richard A. Pierce. Kingston, Ontario; Fairbanks, Alaska: Limestone Press, 1990. 555p. (Alaska History, no. 33).

An invaluable tool for the study of Russian America, and the product of decades of work with the sources. Pierce has assembled brief biographies of 675 individuals who were active in Alaska, or had significant influence over Alaskan events. Any number of mysteries have been solved and errors common to the literature corrected. A number of portraits have been appended. Names are in alphabetical order, but there is no index. In order to find sea captains, or naval officers, or merchants, or any other class of individual, one must look through the entire book unless a name or list of names is already at hand.

419 **Sadie Brower Neakok, an Inupiaq woman.**
Margaret B. Blackman. Seattle, Washington: University of Washington Press, 1989. 274p. bibliog.

Neakok served as the first bilingual Eskimo magistrate in Barrow, starting in 1960. This life history covers many aspects of Eskimo culture and its relationship to twentieth-century economic and social influences.

420 **Shadows on the Koyukuk: an Alaska native's life along the river.**
Sidney Huntington. Anchorage: Alaska Northwest, 1933. 235p.

This is another story of the respected Huntington family. The author's brother James published his autobiographical account in 1966 (see item no. 417). Huntington writes of the Koyukon Athabascan country and relates stories from the region as well as his own experiences. He served for almost twenty years on the Alaska Game Board and has been an active supporter of local education.

421 **Six Alaskan native women leaders: pre-statehood.**
Michael J. Oleksa. Juneau: Alaska Department of Education, 1991. 60p.

These biographies are of Belle Herbert, Della Keats, Maggie Lind, Elizabeth W. Peratrovich, Anfesia Shapsnikoff and Sophia Vlasoff.

422 **Son of the smoky sea.**
Nutchuk, Alden Hatch, illustrated by Nutchuck. New York: Messner, 1941. 245p.

This is the autobiography of Nutchuk (Simeon Oliver), the orphaned son of a Norwegian trapper and an Eskimo mother on the Alaska Peninsula. He grew up at the Jesse Lee Home at Unalaska, an orphanage. He was able to go 'outside' to college at Northwestern for several years and then entered a career as a concert musician. The sequel is titled *Back to the Smoky Sea* (q.v.).

423 **This old house: the story of Clara Rust.**
Jo Anne Wold. Anchorage: Alaska Northwest, 1976. 262p.

This is the account of a young girl who arrived in 1908, and later married and raised a family in Fairbanks. It is based upon Rust's journals and upon conversations with Jo Anne Wold. The house changed along with the circumstances of the family.

424 **Two in the far North.**
Margaret E. Murie, illustrated by Olaus J. Murie. New York: Alfred A. Knopf, 1962. 438p. Issued with additional text and illustrations by the Alaska Northwest Publishing Company, 1978.

Margaret Murie grew up in Fairbanks and was the first woman graduate of the University of Alaska (then Alaska Agricultural College and School of Mines). She married biologist Olaus J. Murie and travelled with him on several of his Alaska expeditions. These memoirs describe her childhood in Fairbanks and their travel to such places as the Koyukuk country and the Old Crow River.

425 **Where else but Alaska.**
Sara Machetanz. New York: Charles Scribner's Sons, 1954. 214p.

This was one of the best selling of its genre – the autobiographical homesteading account. Fred Machetanz made films for a lecture circuit and is one of Alaska's best-known artists.

426 **Wolf Smeller (Zhoh Gwatsan): a biography of John Fredson, native Alaskan.**
Clara Childs Mackenzie. Anchorage: Alaska Pacific University Press, 1985. 201p. map. bibliog.

As a boy Fredson worked with Hudson Stuck, participated in the first successful climb of Mount Denali and then attended school in the 'lower 48'. He returned to work with the Episcopal hospital in Fort Yukon, the Northern Commercial Company, and as a teacher in Chandalar. He had considerable political influence and was instrumental in creating the Venetie Reservation.

Select regional and local histories

427 **Anchorage: a pictorial history.**
Claus-M. Naske, L. J. Rowinski. Norfolk, Virginia: Donning, 1981. 179p. map. bibliog.

Anchorage started as a railroad construction camp run by the Alaska Engineering Commission. It became Alaska's largest city after the Second World War with more than half of the state's entire population. A pictorial history is especially important because the physical appearance of Anchorage has continued to change rapidly over the years, and little is left of the Anchorage of even 20 or 30 years ago.

428 **The cheechakoes.**
Wayne Short. New York: Random House, 1964. 244p.

The Short family settled in a remote area of Southeast Alaska immediately after the Second World War. Cheechako is a slang term for someone inexperienced and lacking in the skills needed to survive, especially in the bush.

429 **Fairbanks: a pictorial history.**
Claus-M. Naske, L. J. Rowinski. Norfolk, Virginia: Donning, 1981. 197p.

This superficial popular history is extensively illustrated. The short bibliography does not always include books mentioned in the text and captions, and the brief index is haphazard and misses most of the people identified in captioned photographs.

430 **Fortunes from the earth: a history of the base and industrial minerals of Southeast Alaska.**
Patricia Roppel. Manhattan, Kansas: Sunflower University Press, 1991. 139p. maps.

Gold mining in Alaska has received most of the press, but there is an extensive history of mining for other minerals as well such as copper, nickel, zinc, antimony, uranium, tungsten and molybdenum. There was also some coal mining and there were rock quarries. Roppell surveys all of the known mines, and provides a brief history with carefully identified photographs whenever such information is available.

431 **Historic McCarthy, the town that copper built.**
M. J. Kirchhoff. Juneau: Alaska Cedar Press, 1993. 137p. bibliog.

The Kennecott copper mine, and the railroad that supplied it from the coastal town of Cordova, was one of the major industrial developments in Alaska during the early twentieth century. McCarthy developed as a small supply and recreation centre near the mine, and was also involved in supporting nearby gold-mining efforts. When the copper mine closed down, so did most of McCarthy. The town's remnants are now within Wrangel-St. Elias National Park and it has become a tourist attraction.

432 **Historic settlement patterns in the Nushagak River region, Alaska.**
James W. VanStone. Chicago, Illinois: Field Museum of Natural History, 1971. 149p. maps. bibliog. (*Fieldiana: Anthropology*, no. 61).

This is a detailed study of 64 village sites, based upon five seasons of fieldwork. VanStone finds changing settlement patterns during the 19th and early 20th centuries.

433 **A history of mining on the Kenai Peninsula.**
Mary Barry. Anchorage: Alaska Northwest, 1973. 214p. maps. bibliog.

There was some mining activity during the Russian American era, most notably coal mining at Port Graham in 1855. There was also some coal mining during the American era, but gold prospecting started in earnest in the 1880s with an influx of new miners during the 1890s in such communities as Hope and Sunrise City. Commercial petroleum production began at the Swanson field in the late 1950s with off-shore discoveries in 1962.

434 **Images from the inside passage: an Alaskan portrait by Winter & Pond.**
Victoria Wyatt. Seattle, Washington: University of Washington Press, 1989. 144p. map. bibliog.

A selection of historical photographs from the studios of Winter & Pond. The collection is now located at the Alaska Historical Library in Juneau. The photographs were taken between 1893 and 1910; the subjects are primarily Tlingit and Haida Indians.

435 **Independence mine and the Willow Creek mining district.**
Kathryn Koutsky Cohen, edited by Karen L. Lew. Anchorage: Office of History and Archaeology, Department of Natural Resources, State of Alaska, 1982. 169p. maps. bibliog.

The Independence Mine is located at a high elevation near a mountain pass. The Willow Creek District was in operation from 1916 until 1951. Independence mine was like a small, isolated town, with its own small school and other facilities. The Independence Mine State Historical Park was created in 1980 and historic preservation work was begun on the remaining structures. A wealth of historical photographs and site drawings document the technology of mining and life at the mine.

436 **Interior Alaska: a journey through time.**
Robert M. Thorson (et al.). Anchorage: Alaska Geographic Society, 1986. 256p. bibliog.

Geological history, natural history, early man through archaeological study and recent ethnohistory are the subjects covered in this collection of essays by five contributors.

437 **Kijk: an historic Tanaina Indian settlement.**
James W. VanStone, J. B. Townsend. Chicago, Illinois: Field Museum of Natural History, 1970. 202p. bibliog. (*Fieldiana: Anthropology*, no. 59).

This is a work of historical archaeology (1966 season) that included the gathering of ethnographical information about the Athabascan-speaking Tanaina Indians. It is a clearly written account that can be read with profit by the layman and specialist alike.

438 **Nushagak: an historic trading center in Southwestern Alaska.**
James W. VanStone. Chicago, Illinois: Field Museum of Natural History, 1972. 93p. map. bibliog. (*Fieldiana: Anthropology*, no. 62).

This is another of VanStone's series (q.v.) of studies of Southwest Alaska. This study involved five field seasons, culminating in an archaeological dig in 1969. In this case, the village had been occupied by Yupik-speaking Eskimos. Alexsandrovski Redoubt was established in the vicinity in 1818, and the first Russian Orthodox chapel was built there in 1832. There are a number of supporting photographs.

439 **Once upon the Kenai: stories from the people.**
Jetret S. Petersen, director and co-ordinator. Kenai, Alaska: Kenai Historical Society, 1984. 468p.

The Kenai Historical Society attempted to interview anyone who was a pre-1963 resident in the west central region of the Kenai Peninsula. There were over 400 responses, and the completed personal stories and brief biographies are listed chronologically, many with photographs. There are also short pieces on various organizations and churches.

440 The roots of Ticasuk: an Eskimo woman's family story.
Ticasuk (Emily Ivanoff Brown). Anchorage: Alaska Northwest, 1981. 107p. map.

The first edition was published in 1974 under the title *Grandfather of Unalakleet*. The author writes 'I wish that my descendants may know who their people are. To this end I attended the University of Alaska to learn enough of the humanities, social sciences, folklore and mythology that I might properly preserve in writing the culture of my people.'

441 Salmon from Kodiak: a history of the salmon fishery of Kodiak Island, Alaska.
Patricia Roppel. Anchorage: Alaska Historical Commission, 1986. 355p.

Salmon had been a subsistence resource since time immemorial. The first attempts at commercial use were by the Russian-American Company selling salted fish. Large-scale commercial exploitation began with the first salmon cannery in 1882. Roppel details the history of commercial operations in this regional study, especially the continued competition for a limited resource.

442 Southeast Alaska: a pictorial history.
Patricia Roppel. Norfolk, Virginia: Donning, 1983. 206p. bibliog.

Copiously illustrated with carefully selected black-and-white historical photographs, this book really begins with the gold strike at Juneau in 1880. The Russian years are passed over lightly.

443 The story of Sitka.
C. L. Andrews. Seattle, Washington: Lowman & Hartford, 1922. 108p. map.

Most of the book concerns Sitka as the chief factory of the Russian-American Company. The accompanying map reproduces a survey of the Sitka townsite made at the time of transfer, with labels for 34 of the 129 numbered locations within the Russian, but not the native portion of town.

444 They don't speak Russian in Sitka: a new look at the history of southern Alaska.
David Wharton. Menlo Park, California: Markgraf Publications Group, 1991. 217p. bibliog.

This is a collection of brief histories of the seven largest towns in Southeast Alaska: Sitka, Wrangell, Juneau, Haines, Ketchikan, Skagway and Petersburg. They are written in an informal and rambling style.

445 Up the Koyukuk.
Bill Sherwonit, Terrence Cole, Tishu Ulen, Shirly English, Walter Johnson. Anchorage: Alaska Geographic, 1983. 147p. map. (*Alaska Geographic*, vol. 10, no. 4).

The Koyukuk was explored by Lt. Henry T. Allen in 1885 and became one of the oldest mining districts in Alaska, with large numbers of miners peaking in 1899.

A chapter entitled 'Tishu's World' describes life in the Eskimo/White settlement of Wiseman from 1905, when she was born, up through the 1920s and 1930s. Today, the community is no longer isolated and the small number of local residents can drive along the pipeline haul road to Fairbanks.

446 **The way it was: of people, places and things in pioneer interior Alaska.**

Jo Anne Wold. Anchorage: Alaska Northwest, 1988. 165p.

This is a series of 32 vignettes. Most are the experiences of settlers and their children. Some deal with business establishments now long gone. Others are scenes from Wold's own childhood.

447 **Wrangell and the gold of the Cassiar: a tale of fur and gold in Alaska.**

Clarence Leroy Andrews. Seattle, Washington: L. Tinker, 1937. 60p. map.

Wrangell was an early Russian trading establishment (Fort Dionysius, later Fort Stikine) that was located at the site of an existing native village. It was not continuously used by the Russians, and the Hudson's Bay Company operated a trading post for a time under a special agreement with them, starting in 1840. After the transfer of Alaska to the United States, there was an army post there, which was abandoned in 1871. The nearby Stikine River gold rush occurred in the 1870s and brought renewed life to the town.

Native Population

448 **The Alaskan Eskimos.**
Wendell H. Oswalt. San Francisco, California: Chandler Publishing Company, 1967. 297p. map. bibliog.

At the time of first contact with Europeans, Oswalt estimates that of the 48,000 Eskimos in the world, 26,000 lived in Alaska – more than in Canada, Greenland and Siberia combined. He is careful to differentiate between the customs and living conditions of Alaskan Eskimos and those who lived farther east and whose culture is better known to the general lay public. He argues that there are 21 'tribes', not counting the Saint Lawrence Islanders, who are Siberian Yupik. The area covered extends some 800 miles, east to west, and 1,000 miles, north to south.

449 **Alaska native culture and history.**
Edited by Yoshidobu Kotani, William B. Workman. Osaka, Japan: National Museum of Ethnology, 1980. 321p. maps. bibliog. (Senri Ethnological Studies, no. 4).

These are well-edited papers based upon presentations made at the Second International Symposium of the National Museum of Ethnology in Osaka, Japan, in August 1978. The subject matter includes studies of subsistence systems, prehistory, palaeoecology, acculturation, native languages, whaling and traditional societies. There is also an assessment of the extent and nature of Japanese anthropological research on Alaska topics.

450 **Alaska native land claims.**
Robert D. Arnold. Anchorage: Alaska Native Foundation, 1978. 2nd ed. 367p.

A broad introduction to the topic of native land claims, necessary for an understanding of the Alaska Land Claims Settlement Act of 1971 which has profoundly affected all of Alaska. The book first briefly describes the nature and antiquity of native settlement in Alaska, treats the general history of US Indian policy, the arrival of non-natives in Alaska, the changing legal status through the years, the events leading to the legislation of 1971, the provisions of the act itself, and the complex problems of implementation. The act designates regional and village native corporations as the vehicles to manage the money and land settlements. Although much has happened since 1978, this remains one of the best introductions.

451 **Alaska natives in a century of change.**
Michael J. Levin. *Anthropological Papers of the University of Alaska*, vol. 23, no. 1-2 (1991). 217p. bibliog.

This is a landmark historical demography, using US census data from 1880 to 1980. Levin analyses social and economic changes.

452 **Alaska's native people.**
Edited by Lael Morgan. Anchorage: Alaska Geographic Society, 1979. 304p. maps. bibliog. (*Alaska Geographic*, vol. 6).

Morgan gives us a richly illustrated general overview of the diverse native populations of Alaska: Inupiat, Yupik, Aleut, Koniag, Chugach, Athabascan, Eyak, Tlingit, Haida and Tsimshian peoples. Although the text is necessarily quite brief for such a broad coverage, it is well researched and carefully presented for a popular readership.

453 **Alaska natives: a survey of their sociological and educational status.**
Hobson Dewey Anderson. Stanford, California: Stanford University Press, 1935. 472p.

Anderson's important early study of Western Alaska (principally Yupik and Aleut populations) was funded by the Carnegie Foundation.

454 **The Aleutian and Commander Islands and their inhabitants.**
Ales Hrdlicka. Philadelphia, Pennsylvania: Wistar Institute of Anatomy and Biology, 1945. 630p. maps. bibliog.

This is an account of an anthropologist/archaeologist's expeditions in 1936, 1937 and 1938. He attempts to provide comprehensive coverage through the inclusion of numerous quotations from earlier authorities on the region, varying from one sentence to several paragraphs in length. His greatest interest is in Aleutian mummies. His own discoveries are presented in the form of a diary or journal, accompanied by photographs.

455 **Aleuts: survivors of the Bering Sea land bridge.**
William S. Laughlin. New York: Holt, Rinehart and Winston, 1980. 150p. maps. bibliog.

Written as a case-study text for advanced undergraduates in anthropology, this work covers many aspects of Aleut life, history and the archaeological record.

456 **And the land provides: Alaskan natives in a year of transition.**
Lael Morgan. Garden City, New York: Anchor Press, 1974. 325p.

Morgan, a journalist with prior Alaskan experience, spent a foundation-funded year documenting Alaskan native life following the passage of the Alaska Native Claims Settlement Act of 1971. She starts with the inland Eskimo at Anaktuvuk Pass, and then continues with chapters which examine life in each representative area: the coastal Eskimo town of Point Hope with its whaling tradition, the Athabascan town of Galena, Aleut Atka, Bethel on the Kuskokwim, the Tlingit Indian village of Angoon. She finishes with a chapter on subsistence living. The book is written throughout in the first person, with personal interaction with the residents that Morgan encounters.

457 **Arctic village.**
Robert Marshall, preface by Terrence Cole. Fairbanks, Alaska: University of Alaska Press, 1991. reprinted ed. 399p. maps.

Marshall was a forester, a high official in the Roosevelt administration, and a leading conservationist and founder of the Wilderness Society. This classic study of the community of Wiseman on the upper Koyukuk drainage was conducted in 1930 and 1931. It depicts every aspect of life in what Marshall thought was one of the most happy civilizations on earth, far from modern industry and bustle. Marshall employed statistics and other contemporary sociological tools to augment his detailed narrative of a lifestyle among the miners and interior Eskimos which was soon to disappear.

458 **Athapaskan adaptations: hunters and fishermen of the subarctic forests.**
James VanStone. Chicago, Illinois: Aldine, 1974. 145p. maps. bibliog. (Worlds of Man: Studies in Cultural Ecology).

This book is concerned with adaptive strategies that allow a culture to survive in a difficult environment. The intended readership level is college undergraduate or beginning graduate student. This is a sound work on the ethnography of the northern Athabascans and it is based upon many years of fieldwork and curatorial experience.

459 **Atka: an ethnohistory of the western Aleutians.**
Lydia T. Black. Kingston, Ontario: Limestone Press, 1984. 219p. map. bibliog. (Alaska History, no. 24).

A closely argued revision of widely held views of the ethnography of the Aleuts, especially those in the Atka district. Black makes extensive use of primary documents that have seldom been consulted in the past. She has created a number of helpful compilations and translated others from Russian sources including an historical table of Russian voyages, the number of Russian fur-hunting vessels in the North Pacific by year, the sea otter catch size, and a table of the Russian companies that were active. Other translated documents include an 'Extract from the travel journal of the Navigator Vasil'ev'.

460 **Bashful no longer: an Alaskan Eskimo ethnohistory, 1778-1988.**
Wendell H. Oswalt. Norman, Oklahoma: University of Oklahoma Press, 1980. 270p. maps. bibliog.

This study is of the Kuskokwim Eskimo. Oswalt uses Russian-American Company records, explorers' journals, missionary records and newspapers, as well as other sources, including especially personal contacts and oral histories. His thesis is that the nature of the Yupik response to outside cultural influence has changed through time. He also traces differences in the history of sub-regions within this extensive area.

461 **The Cama-i book: kayaks, dogsleds, bear hunting, bush pilots, smoked fish, mukluks, and other traditions of Southwestern Alaska.**
Edited by Ann Vick. Garden City, New York: Anchor Press/Doubleday, 1983. 411p. map.

Done in the tradition of the 'Fox Fire' books which depict folkways and traditions, this material was gathered by high-school students from eight communities in the Kodiak–Bristol Bay region of Alaska. This is a selection from the 4,000 pages published in the villages, starting in 1974.

462 **The Chandalar Kutchin.**
Robert Addison McKennan. Montreal: Arctic Institute of North America, 1965. 165p. maps. bibliog. (Arctic Institute of North America Technical Paper, no. 17).

The Chandalar Kutchin Athabascans were still relatively isolated when McKennan travelled there in 1933 to study them. Their territory centres on the East Fork of the Chandalar River. He describes the aboriginal culture and significant changes that resulted from contacts with whites.

463 **The Chugach Eskimo.**
Kaj Birket-Smith. Copenhagen: Nationalmuseets Publikations Fond, 1953. 261p. map. bibliog. (Nationalmuseets Skrifter. Etnografisk Raekke, no. VI).

This ethnology is based upon fieldwork in Prince William Sound in 1933, conducted by Birket-Smith, representing the Danish National Museum and Frederica de Laguna representing the University of Pennsylvania Museum. The archaeological part of their work had been previously published by de Laguna (q.v.).

464 **Contributions to the ethnography of the Kutchin.**
Cornelius Osgood. New Haven, Connecticut: Human Relations Area Files Press, 1970. reprinted ed. 189p. bibliog.

The Kutchin Athabascans live along the Peal River and the Mackenzie flats in Canada; and on the Porcupine River, Black River, and Yukon flats in Alaska. Osgood conducted his fieldwork in 1932 and the study was first published by Yale University Press in 1936.

465 **Crossroads of continents: cultures of Siberia and Alaska.**
Edited by William W. Fitzhugh, Aron Crowell. Washington, DC: Smithsonian Institution Press, 1988. 360p. maps. bibliog.

Published to accompany an exhibition mounted jointly by the Smithsonian and the USSR Academy of Sciences, this is a magnificently illustrated volume (458 figures and illustrations). The subject of the exhibition is Beringia: lands on both sides of Bering Strait defined broadly enough to include the Even, Chukchi and Korak cultures in Siberia and the Aleut, Eskimo, Athabascan and Tlingit cultures in Alaska.

466 **E. W. Nelson's notes on the Indians of the Yukon and Innoko rivers, Alaska.**
Edited by James W. VanStone. Chicago, Illinois: Field Museum of Natural History, 1978. 80p. map. bibliog. (*Fieldiana: Anthropology*, no. 71).

VanStone has edited the manuscript notes that were made by Nelson of a trip made in 1880. VanStone's introduction is a 15-page summation of the history of exploration of this region.

467 **The Eskimo about Bering Strait.**
Edward William Nelson, introduction to the 1983 edition by William W. Fitzhugh. Washington, DC: Smithsonian Institution Press, 1983. 518p. maps. bibliog. (18th Annual Report of the Bureau of American Ethnology for the Years 1896-1897).

Richly illustrated with 107 leaves of plates, this remains the foundation of all subsequent work on the Bering Sea region. It is based upon natural history and ethnological fieldwork conducted between 1877 and 1881 while Nelson was based at his field station at St. Michael. His official duties were those of weather observer. He made a number of short journeys, and one long one of 1,200-miles, to remote regions to collect, observe, draw and photograph. The original edition was published in 1899. Nelson collected and shipped a prodigious number of natural history and ethnographic specimens to Washington.

468 **Eskimo essays: Yup'ik lives and how we see them.**
Ann Fienup-Riordan. New Brunswick, New Jersey: Rutgers University Press, 1990. 269p. maps. bibliog.

The author is concerned with western observations and the relationship of these observations to Yupik Eskimo life. In these thoughtful essays, she covers Yupik cosmology, the impact of missionaries, Hollywood depictions of Eskimo life, legal concepts and the Yupik relationship to nature.

469 **The Eskimos of Bering Strait, 1650-1898.**
Dorothy Jean Ray. Seattle, Washington: University of Washington Press, 1975. 305p. map. bibliog.

The Bering Strait area includes the Seward Peninsula, King Island, and the adjacent coast and islands. This book is a history that begins with the state of knowledge in 1650, and then brings the account up through the various early explorers active in the region: James Cook, Ivan Kobelev, Joseph Billings, Otto von Kotzebue, Adolf Etolin, Vasilii Khromchenko, Gleb Shishmarev and Frederick Beechey. The author chronicles the mutual contact and acculturation that took place in more recent times up to the time of the gold rush. This includes the various voyages in search of John Franklin, the whaling ships, the introduction of domestic reindeer, and the establishment of US missionary and Bureau of Education schools.

470 **Eskimos of Northwest Alaska in the early nineteenth century, based on the Beechey and Belcher collections and records compiled during the voyage of H. M. S. *Blossom* to Northwest Alaska in 1826 and 1827.**
John R. Bockstoce. Oxford: Pitt Rivers Museum, 1977. 139p. bibliog. (Monograph Series, no. 1).

These two collections are rich in the details of Eskimo life that they illustrate. There are reproductions of numerous drawings and paintings as well as photographs of artefacts. The visual record is well integrated with the explanatory text.

471 **Eskimos of the Nushagak River: an ethnographic history.**
James W. VanStone. Seattle, Washington: University of Washington Press, 1967. 192p. 4 maps. bibliog.

This is an account of discovery and change, but it is also an attempt to reconstruct what the population was like in past eras: where people lived, their yearly cycles, how patterns differed from that which was in place in the 1960s. This study is based upon historical records and extensive field interviews. Especially important as an agent of change were the trading establishments and the salmon-fishing industry, with its canneries that were first established in the 1880s at the mouth of Nushagak Bay.

472 **The ethnography of the Tanaina.**
Cornelius Osgood. New Haven, Connecticut: Yale University Press, 1937. 229p. maps. bibliog. (Yale University Publications in Anthropology, no. 16).

This study of the Tanaina Athabascans of Cook Inlet is based upon fieldwork conducted in 1931 and 1932. The author stayed for brief periods in Seldovia, Iliamna, Eklutna, Tyonek, Susitna and Kenai. He describes material culture, social culture and mythology. Osgood attempts to describe the culture as it would have been just before contact, in the late 18th century.

473 **Ethnohistory in the Arctic: the Bering Strait Eskimo.**
Dorothy Jean Ray, edited by Richard A. Pierce. Kingston, Ontario: Limestone Press, 1983. 274p. maps. bibliog.

A compilation of previously published articles and new translations that complement Ray's earlier books on ethnography (see item no. 469) and Eskimo art (see items 696, 697). The diverse subject matter includes accounts of the little-known Vasil'ev-Shishmarev expedition of 1819-22, the introduction of firearms into the region long before the whalers arrived, the legend of the settlement of lost Russians at Kheuvoren; the trading settlement of Saint Michael in the 19th century; the Omilak silver mine; reindeer herding; a picture writing system from Buckland, Alaska; land tenure among the Eskimo; subsistence patterns; and Eskimo place-names.

474 **Ethnohistory in southwestern Alaska and the southern Yukon: method and content. Part two, the Aleut social system, 1750 to 1810, from early historical sources.**

Edited by Margaret Lantis. Lexington, Kentucky: University Press of Kentucky, 1970. 311p. bibliog.

These two works are published together, but have different formats. The first part is a compilation of articles on the methodology of ethnohistory among native populations of Alaska and the Yukon Territory. These articles include issues of cultural patterning, Tanaina ethnohistory and oral traditions among Natives of the first whites that were encountered in Northwestern America. The second part, pages 139 to 295, is exclusively concerned with the Aleut population.

475 **Ethnology and anthropology of the Aleut.**

Waldemar Jochelson. Washington, DC: Carnegie Institution of Washington, 1933. 91p. (Publication no. 432).

Jochelson was in the Aleutians conducting ethnographic research in 1909 and 1910. The archaeological portion was published in 1925. After a brief history, he presents a view of the life of the Aleuts, including the fur-seal harvests on the Pribilof Islands. There are 27 illustrations, primarily photographs.

476 **The Eyak Indians of the Copper River Delta, Alaska.**

Kaj Birket-Smith, Frederica de Laguna. Copenhagen: Levin & Munksgaard, 1938. 591p. maps. bibliog.

The material for this work was gathered in 1933 as a part of an archaeological expedition to Prince William Sound funded by the Danish National Museum. It is the major ethnography for the Eyak population.

477 **Final Report.**

Alaska Natives Commission. Anchorage: Joint Federal–State Commission on Politics and Programs Affecting Alaska Natives, 1994. 4 vols.

This study was mandated by the US Congress in 1990, and work began in 1992. The report brings together demographic information and a set of issues centred on a loss of social and cultural integrity. The study identifies a number of root causes for these maladies including periods of disease and famine in the past, missionary activity, educational systems that attacked native language and culture, and a loss of self-reliance as the world economy came to previously isolated areas. The report argues that the solutions must come from within the native community itself. Subsistence hunting and fishing, and local control are seen as key elements.

478 Forest Eskimos: an ethnographic sketch of Kobuk River people of the 1880's.
J. Louis Giddings. Philadelphia, Pennsylvania: University Museum, 1956. 61p. (*Bulletin* of the University Museum, vol. 20, no. 2).

Giddings interviewed three elderly natives during the 1940, 1941 and 1947 archaeological field seasons. He takes his readers through the round of a year's activity. It involves frequent moves in order to follow game.

479 The fourth world: the heritage of the Arctic and its destruction.
Sam Hall. New York: Knopf, 1987. 240p. maps. bibliog.

This is a review of the history of technological change that has impacted on Eskimo culture throughout the Arctic, including Alaska. Its treatment of the issues is shallow and over-generalized. It should be used with caution.

480 The Han Indians: a compilation of ethnographic and historical data on the Alaska–Yukon boundary area.
Cornelius Osgood. New Haven, Connecticut: Department of Anthropology, Yale University, 1971. 173p. map. bibliog. (Yale University Publications in Anthropology, no. 74).

The Han Athabascans live in the area most heavily impacted by the Klondike gold rush: the upper Yukon above Circle to Dawson, and along the Klondike and Fortymile rivers. Unlike some of Osgood's other studies on Athabascan ethnology (q.v.), this is more of an assessment based on historical observations by others, and less a study relying upon direct interviews with the population being studied. Osgood analyses the cultural changes taking place in various periods: before 1847, 1847-97, 1897-1947, and after 1947.

481 Handbook of the North American Indians: vol. 5: Arctic.
Volume editor David Dumas. Washington, DC: Smithsonian Institution, 1984. 829p. maps. bibliog.

A summary of knowledge as of 1984, primarily concerning the circumpolar Eskimos. In addition to general topics covering the entire region, there is a substantial section on Alaska (Western Arctic), pages 80-358, with contributions from 21 acknowledged experts.

482 Handbook of North American Indians: vol. 6: subarctic.
Edited by June Helm. Washington, DC: Smithsonian Institution, 1981. 837p. maps. bibliog.

The subarctic Indian territories within Alaska include the Ingalik, Koyukon, Kolchan, Tanaina, Kutchin, Tanana, Ahtna and Han.

483 **Handbook of North American Indians: vol. 7: Northwest Coast.**
Edited by Wayne Suttles, series editor William C. Sturevant.
Washington, DC: Smithsonian Institution, 1990. 770p. maps. bibliog.

A monumental compilation of the work of 59 authors. The area covered goes from northern California, north through Oregon, Washington, British Columbia and through the Alaska panhandle. It is the most authoritative single source available.

484 **A history of Alaskan Athapaskans, including a description of Athapaskan culture and a historical narrative, 1785-1971.**
William E. Simeone. Anchorage: Alaska Historical Commission, [1982]. maps. bibliog.

This book is based upon secondary works and is designed for a popular readership. It is organized chronologically and by major subgroupings: Taniana, Ahtna, Koyukon. It is illustrated with a number of historical photographs.

485 **Hunters of the northern forest: designs for survival among the Alaskan Kutchin.**
Richard K. Nelson. Chicago, Illinois: University of Chicago Press, 1986. 2nd ed. 303p. maps. bibliog.

Nelson's study of the Chalkyitsik region is a detailed description of subsistence hunting and fishing techniques, and of the setting in which they occur.

486 **Hunters of the northern ice.**
Richard Nelson. Chicago, Illinois: University of Chicago Press, 1969. 429p. maps. bibliog.

The fieldwork for this study of adaptive strategies was conducted during the winter of 1964-65 and the summer of 1966 in northern Alaska, especially the Eskimo settlement of Wainwright on the Chukchi Sea. Nelson describes the characteristics of sea ice and how hunters survive on it through storms and weather changes. The animal resources and hunting techniques are described for fish, birds, and marine mammals including whales, walrus and seals.

487 **Indians of the Northwest coast.**
Philip Drucker. New York; Toronto; London: published for the American Museum of Natural History by McGraw-Hill, 1955. 209p. bibliog. (Anthropological Handbook, no. 10).

This general introduction to the entire region includes Southeast Alaska and the coast south through British Columbia, Washington and Oregon. Drucker gives a well-balanced account of the common elements and the substantial diversity.

488 **Ingalik material culture.**
Cornelius Osgood. New Haven, Connecticut: Human Relations Area Files Press, 1970. reprinted ed. 500p. maps. bibliog. (Yale University Publications in Anthropology, no. 22).

Originally published in 1940, before his *Social culture* (see item no. 489), this volume is now a classic of Alaskan anthropology. It is especially useful for its description of traditional hunting and fishing technology and the implements used and tools of every sort. Many descriptions are accompanied by simple drawings.

489 **Ingalik social culture.**
Cornelius Osgood. New Haven, Connecticut: Yale University Press, 1958. 289p. maps. (Yale University Publications in Anthropology, no. 53).

Most of the research for this work was completed by the late 1930s. The Ingalik are an Athabascan-speaking people who live in western Alaska, around the lower Yukon and Kuskokwim and adjacent to large Eskimo populations. Osgood treats all aspects of this culture, which remained relatively free from disruptive outside influences until rather late. His account is especially rich in its treatment of traditional ceremonies.

490 **Inua: spirit world of the Bering Sea Eskimo.**
Edited by William W. Fitzhugh, Susan A. Kaplan. Washington, DC: Smithsonian Institution Press, 1982. 294p. maps. bibliog.

This was prepared in conjunction with an exhibit of the Edward William Nelson Bering Sea Eskimo ethnology collection of the National Museum of Natural History.

491 **The Inupiat and Arctic Alaska: an ethnography of development.**
Norman A. Chance. Fort Worth, Texas: Holt, Rinehart and Winston, 1990. 241p. bibliog. (Case Studies in Cultural Anthropology).

The research for this book was conducted between 1958 and 1989, and was centred in the community of Kaktovik during a period of rapid development and change that resulted from statehood, oil development, the Alaska Native Claims Settlement Act and the creation of powerful regional native corporations. However, change in a variety of forms had been occurring for a period of about 150 years, even before this. Chance makes sense of this complex situation in a format that is designed to be read by the interested layman or student.

492 **Koyukuk River culture.**
Annette McFadyen Clark. Ottawa: National Museums of Canada, 1974. 282p. maps. bibliog. (Mercury Series. Canadian Ethnology Service Paper, no. 18).

Clark's study is of an area populated by both Indian and Eskimo groups: the Koyukuk Koyukon Athabascans, the Kobuk Eskimos and the Nunamiut Eskimos. They share many aspects of material culture. Euro-American contact began indirectly as early as 1646 through trade networks, and trading posts were established within the region by 1838.

493 **The Kuskowagmiut: riverine Eskimos.**
Wendell H. Oswalt. In: *This land was theirs: a study of North American Indians.* New York: John Wiley & Sons, 1978, 3rd ed., p. 103-43. bibliog.

Oswalt emphasizes the differences between this population, which traditionally relied upon salmon, and the better-known Arctic Coastal Eskimo who rely upon marine mammals. This is a good, brief introduction to a complex culture, based upon his extensive study of the Napaskiak.

494 **Make prayers to the raven: a Koyukon view of the northern forest.**
Richard K. Nelson. Chicago, Illinois: University of Chicago Press, 1983. 292p. bibliog.

Ethnographer Nelson has created an especially sensitive portrait of life on a major tributary of the lower Yukon in northwestern interior Alaska. He has based his study of this northern Athabascan people on 16 months in the settlements of Huslia and Hughes over a period of about 10 years. This work is especially strong in its explanation of subsistence living and the spiritual aspects of that life. His organizational structure is based upon plant and animal species and their relationship with the Koyukon: spruce trees; berries; insects; fish; birds; small mammals such as snowshoe hare, squirrels, marmots, porcupines, muskrat and beaver; predatory mammals such as weasels, mink, marten, otter, wolverine, lynx, foxes and wolves; and the large mammals which include moose, caribou, black bear, brown bear and dogs.

495 **Moonlight at midday.**
Sally Carrighar. New York: Knopf, 1958. 392p. map.

Most of the book concerns the settlements of Nome and Unalakleet and the impact of outside civilization on the life of Eskimos. It is written more from a journalistic than a scientific point of view.

496 **Napaskiak: an Alaskan Eskimo community.**
Wendell H. Oswalt. Tucson, Arizona: University of Arizona Press, 1963. 178p. maps. bibliog.

A southwestern Alaska Eskimo village is depicted in the year 1956. It includes the activities of daily life, the physical environment, and contacts with the outside world at different times in the past.

497 **The Native Brotherhoods: modern intertribal organizations of the Northwest Coast.**
Philip Drucker. Washington, DC: Smithsonian Institution, 1958. 184p. bibliog. (Bureau of American Ethnology, no. 168).

The fieldwork for this study was conducted between 1952 and 1954. The Alaska Native Brotherhood was founded in Sitka in 1912. Almost all of the early membership were active members of the Presbyterian Church in Southeast Alaska. An 'Alaska Native Sisterhood' was founded a few years later. The organization became active politically and published an official journal, the *Alaska Fisherman*. Long-term issues included citizenship and educational rights of natives. The Alaskan movement's early leadership was exercised by William Paul, a Tlingit lawyer, and the Brotherhood became the leading advocate for native issues in Southeast Alaska.

498 **Native peoples and languages of Alaska.**
Compiled by Michael E. Krauss. Fairbanks, Alaska: Alaska Native Language Center, University of Alaska, 1974.

This wall map shows the distribution and relationships of native languages. It includes a table of language groups and an inset depicting the circumpolar range of Eskimo-Aleut. It has been frequently republished in a reduced size in books, and is often used in classrooms to graphically illustrate the complex relationship of Alaska's language groups.

499 **Native peoples of Alaska.**
Steve Langdon. Anchorage: Greatland Graphics, 1989. 80p. maps. bibliog.

This overview of Alaska's indigenous peoples includes culture, ceremonies, hunting methods, social organization and demographics.

500 **The Nelson Island Eskimo: social structure and ritual distribution.**
Ann Fienup-Riordan. Anchorage: Alaska Pacific University Press, 1983. 419p. maps. bibliog.

The definitive ethnography to date for this coastal Yupik Eskimo population. The fieldwork was completed from 1976 to 1978. It is illustrated with the sensitive photography of James Barker. Fienup-Riordan writes in an engaging style that helps display the vigorous culture that she describes.

501 **The north Alaskan Eskimo: a study in ecology and society.**
Robert F. Spencer. Washington, DC: Smithsonian Institution Press, 1969. reprinted ed. 490p. maps. bibliog. (Bureau of American Ethnology Bulletin, no. 171).

One of the standard ethnographies, based upon fieldwork conducted in 1952 and 1953. Spencer notes both the similarities and the substantial differences among the populations in this area which covers seventy thousand square miles. He also looks at changing settlement patterns.

502 **Notes on the islands of the Unalaska District.**
Ivan Veniaminov, translated by Lydia T. Black, R. H. Geoghegan, edited by Richard A. Pierce. Kingston, Ontario: Elmer Rasmuson Library Translation Program; Limestone Press, 1984. 511p. (Alaska History, no. 27).

This encyclopaedic text on the Aleutian Islands was compiled during Veniaminov's ten-year tenure as an Orthodox priest at Unalaska during the 1820s and 1830s. He learned the Aleut language and devised a writing system for it. He observed everything, including natural history and ethnography. He was a skilled craftsman, building chapels, furniture and even clocks and organs. He was later sent to Sitka where he founded a theological seminary and where he wrote a briefer set of observations on the Tlingit Indians (Koloshi), which is also included with this translation. He later rose to the highest possible rank in the Russian Orthodox Church, as Innokentii, Metropolitan of Moscow. He has more recently been named a saint by the Church. The book includes a short biography of Veniaminov by Richard Pierce, and Lydia Black has included a number of helpful explanatory footnotes.

503 **Pride and pain.**
Leslie Barber. *Alaska*, vol. 53, no. 5 (May 1987) p. 34-41.

The international World Eskimo–Indian Olympics held every year in Fairbanks uses traditional games of native athletic skill.

504 **The real people and the children of thunder: the Yup'ik Eskimo encounter with Moravian missionaries John and Edith Kilbuck.**
Ann Fienup-Riordan. Norman, Oklahoma: University of Oklahoma Press, 1991. 420p.

An anthropologist with a specialized knowledge of this population writes about the meeting of two cultures. It concerns the complex relationships that developed when a missionary couple, John and Edith Kilbuck, confronted Eskimo culture in the Central Yupik region of the Kuskokwim River. The Kilbucks founded the settlement of Bethel in 1885; it has since become a regional centre.

505 **Russian administration of Alaska and the status of the Alaskan natives.**
Vladimir Gsovski. Washington, DC: Library of Congress, 1950. 99p. bibliog.

Russian America functioned under several different legal regimes, depending upon the time and the company charter operable at the time. The author distinguishes four distinct periods: before the first charter (1741-99); the First Charter (1799-1818); the Second (1821) and Third (1844) Charters; and a transition period from the expiration of the Third Charter to the sale (1862-67). There were as many as four legal distinctions for Alaska natives: those of mixed race (called Creoles); the Aleuts and other dependent tribes; semi-independent groups under some control by the company such as the Kenais and Chugach; and the independent tribes not under the direct jurisdiction or obligation of the company.

506 **Tatl'awht/aenn Nenn': the headwaters peoples country.**
Translated by Kate John, James Kari, edited by James Kari. Fairbanks, Alaska: Alaska Native Language Center, University of Alaska Fairbanks, 1986. 219p. maps. bibliog.

These are narratives of the Upper Ahtna Athabascans told by Katie John, Fred John Sr., Adam Sanford, Huston Sanford, Jack John Justin and Nicholas A. Brown. These tales from the Copper River region focus on historical events. There is a complex system of mountain passes in this area, and this population possessed considerable military importance in prehistoric and early historic times.

507 **The Tlingit Indians: results of a trip to the Northwest Coast of America and the Bering Straits.**
Aurel Krause, translated from the German edition of 1885 by Erna Gunther. Seattle, Washington: University of Washington Press, 1956. 310p. bibliog.

The brothers Aurel and Arthur Krause were sent to the Northwest Coast by the Geographical Society of Bremen in 1881 and 1882. After their return to Germany, Aurel wrote a general ethnography of the Tlingit that remained the standard study for nearly 100 years, and it remains essential reading today. It contains detailed illustrations based upon drawings made during their journey. For more details on their travels, see the translation of their travel journals (item no. 164).

508 **The Tlingit Indians.**
George Thornton Emmons, edited with additions by Frederica de Laguna and a biography by Jean Low. Seattle, Washington: University of Washington Press, 1992. 488p. maps. bibliog. (Anthropological Papers of the American Museum of Natural History, no. 70).

Emmons spent the 1880s and 1890s with the navy in Alaska. He subsequently continued to collect substantial numbers of artefacts for museums. He left unedited manuscripts that have been carefully edited after many years of labour by Professor de Laguna.

509 **Tlingit Indians of Alaska.**
Archimandrite Anatolii Kamenskii, translated, with an introduction and supplementary material by Sergei Kan. Fairbanks, Alaska: University of Alaska Press, 1985. 166p. bibliog. (Rasmuson Library Historical Translation Series, no. 2).

Anthropologist Sergei Kan has extensively annotated the translation of an extremely scarce work published in Odessa in 1906. Kamenskii became the parish priest in Sitka in 1895, where he became active in strengthening Orthodox educational institutions and worked with a growing number of Orthodox Tlingit Indians. He was in competition with a vigorous Presbyterian missionary effort. This conflict is illustrated by supplementary materials included in the book. Kamenskii's ethnographic descriptions are coloured by his religious calling. He was an advocate of a traditional subsistence life. In his view not every Tlingit should become a carpenter or merchant. This is an important description of the Tlingits during a particular period of transition.

510 **The Tlingit: an introduction to their culture and history.**
Wallace M. Olson. Auke Bay, Alaska: Heritage Research, 1991. 81p. bibliog.

Distilled and condensed, this slim volume is designed to introduce Tlingit society and language to outsiders. Olson, an anthropologist, explains the Tlingit clan system, their material culture and recorded history.

511 **Tracks in the wildland: a portrait of Koyukon and Nunamiut subsistence.**

Richard K. Nelson, Kathleen H. Mautner, G. Ray Bane. Fairbanks, Alaska: Anthropology and Historic Preservation Cooperative Park Studies Unit, University of Alaska, Fairbanks, 1982. 465p.

This study provides details of subsistence practice by Koyukon Athabascan Indians and Nunamiut Eskimos along the Koyukuk River valley near or within the present Gates of the Arctic National Park. Trapping and hunting techniques, equipment, and food preparation are described within a traditional Native cultural context.

512 **Under Mount Saint Elias: the history and culture of the Yakutat Tlingit.**

Frederica de Laguna. Washington, DC: Smithsonian Institution, 1972. 3 vols. maps. bibliog. (Smithsonian Contributions to Anthropology, no. 7).

This monumental ethnography is based upon fieldwork conducted in 1949, 1952, 1953 and 1954. Extensive and careful use is made of earlier observations made during the 18th and 19th centuries by Russian, Spanish, and French explorers and by traders. There are extensive descriptions of the land and ecology of the region, and all aspects of life including myths, legends, songs, hunting, fishing, housing, the social world, the spiritual world, and recreation. The book is illustrated with 218 full-page plates and it includes the works and musical transcriptions of songs.

513 **The villagers: Athabaskan Indian life along the Yukon River.**

Claire Fejes. New York: Random House, 1981. 204p. bibliog.

Fejes, a well-known artist, visited a series of villages on a late summer river barge journey in 1974. She combines this experience with other visits through the years to provide portraits of people and villages along the Tanana and Yukon rivers, through words and drawings. Included are the communities of Old and New Minto, Tanana, Galena, Nulato, Kaltag, Grayling, Anvik, Holy Cross, Nenana, Beaver, Fort Yukon, Circle City, and Eagle.

514 **The wake of the unseen object: among the native cultures of bush Alaska.**

Tom Kizzia. New York: Henry Holt and Company, 1991. 275p. map.

This book is based upon very short visits to about fifteen of the state's 200 or so native villages. It is well written and offers a number of insights, but it relies primarily upon chance interviews, rather than on rigorous research methodology. It is best seen as a personal travelogue, and not as a scholarly assessment.

515 **The wolf and the raven.**

Viola E. Garfield, Linn A. Forrest. Seattle, Washington: University of Washington Press, 1961. 148p. bibliog.

This book was written to explain the totem poles preserved by native carvers working for the Civilian Conservation Corps in Saxman Totem Park, Ketchikan Totem Park, Mud Bight Village, and Klawok Totem Park. There is a photograph for each of the nearly seventy totems whose legends are explained.

516 The Yup'ik Eskimos as described in the travel journals and ethnographic accounts of John and Edith Kilbuck who served with the Alaska mission of the Moravian Church, 1886-1900.

Edited by Ann Fienup-Riordan. Kingston, Ontario: Limestone Press, 1988. 527p. bibliog. (Alaska History, no. 31).

These observations by a missionary couple have been carefully arranged and extensively annotated by the editor, an anthropologist who has a specialized knowledge of the Yupik Eskimo. John Kilbuck was the son of a Mohican and Delaware Indian couple who had moved to Kansas and who were members of the Moravian New Westfield Mission near Ottawa. John married the daughter of one of his former teachers. They founded the Moravian mission at Bethel, Alaska, in 1885. They had an immense influence over the development of this region. This account is rich in their perceptions of the people they lived among, as well as an account in some detail of the missionaries themselves.

517 The Yupik of Western Alaska and Russian impact.

Lydia T. Black. *Etudes/Innuit Studies*, vol. 8 (supplementary issue), (1984), p. 21-43.

Black examines the continuing influence of Russian culture on the Yupik. The Russian Orthodox Church, now staffed with a native clergy, has had profound influence, but there are other factors such as the impact of long-distance trade, which pre-dates the first direct contacts of the late 18th century. A variety of daily-use items were introduced such as metal traps, new methods of dog breeding, and household utensils. There are a considerable number of Russian loan words still in use in Yupik today.

Languages

518 Ahtna Athabaskan dictionary.

Compiled by James M. Kari. Fairbanks, Alaska: Alaska Native Language Center, University of Alaska Fairbanks, 1990. 702p. bibliog.

The Athabascan language family consists of 35 languages in North and South America. One of those, the Ahtna, numbers about 1,200 people and their region is the Copper River area of Southcentral Alaska. More than eighty native speakers contributed words, with a core of thirteen speakers who were the main source in a project which lasted from 1973 until 1989. The Ahtna writing system used here was established in 1973. The dictionary is preceded by a description of the language, sound system, orthography and phonetics.

519 Alaska Native languages: past, present and future.

Michael E. Krauss. Fairbanks, Alaska: Alaska Native Language Center, University of Alaska, 1980. 110p. bibliog.

Frequently reprinted, this is a comprehensive overview of the state of Alaska native languages. There were early translations of religious texts by various missionaries, but by the turn of the century the use of Native language in the schools was increasingly forbidden. The last of the Aleut religious schools, which taught both written Aleut and Russian, was forcibly closed in 1912. Krauss summarizes the research on Alaska native languages and discusses the rebirth of interest after 1960, especially in bilingual education.

520 Aleut dictionary, unangam tunudgusii: an unabridged lexicon of the Aleutian Pribilof, and Commander Islands Aleut language.

Compiled by Knut Bergsland. Fairbanks, Alaska: Alaska Native Language Center, University of Alaska Fairbanks, 1994. 739p. maps. bibliog.

This dictionary is of the highest scholarly standard. Bergsland treats the history and grammar of the language in detail in the introduction. Useful appendices include Aleut calendars, Aleut kinship terms, ancient Aleut personal names, baidarka terminology, place-names with maps, and loan words. There is an English index to Aleut words. Bergland has made use of all known fieldwork and scholarship on the Aleut language, covering more than two centuries of observations. [A baidarka (or bidarka) is a type of kayak; see item no. 641.]

521 **The Aleut language, the elements of Aleut grammar with a dictionary in two parts containing basic vocabularies of Aleut and English.**

Compiled by Richard Henry Geoghegan, edited by Fredericka I. Martin. Washington, DC: Department of the Interior, 1944. 169p.

This is a translation of Ivan Veniaminov's Russian-language Aleut grammar and his dictionary of the Aleut-Fox language published in 1834. Additions and annotations to the original were made by Geoghegan before his death in 1943.

522 **Beginning Tlingit.**

Nora Dauenhauer, Richard Dauenhauer. Juneau: Sealaska Tlingit Reader Inc., 1976. 280p.

Tlingit is a difficult language. The authors point out that there are more than 36 sounds that are not found in English. They provide advice about the best way to learn and teach the language.

523 **A conversational dictionary of Kodiak Alutiiq.**

Compiled by Jeff Leer. Fairbanks, Alaska: Alaska Native Language Center, University of Alaska, 1978. 119p.

This short dictionary is the result of a workshop held in Kodiak. The Koniag Alutiiq language is spoken on parts of the Alaska Peninsula as well as Kodiak and Afognak islands. The other major dialect is Chugach Alutiiq, which is spoken on parts of the Kenai Peninsula and Prince William Sound.

524 **Deg Xinag: Ingalik noun dictionary.**

James M. Kari. Fairbanks, Alaska: Alaska Native Language Center, 1978. 106p.

This Athabascan language is spoken by about 120 people on the Yukon (Anvik, Shageluk, and Holy Cross) and on the Kuskokwim (Stoney River).

525 **Dena'ina noun dictionary.**

Compiled by James M. Kari. Fairbanks, Alaska: Alaska Native Language Center, 1977. 355p. bibliog.

The Dena'ina (Tanaina) Athabascan Indians live in the Cook Inlet Basin. This dictionary contains 5,500 words grouped into thirty subject areas. This work is the result of gathering efforts involving language workshops with the participation of over seventy native speakers. Four major dialect areas are delineated: Outer (Cook) Inlet, Inner (Cook) Inlet, Iliamna and Inland. At the time of compilation there were about 200 native speakers of the language.

526 **Dictionary of Alaskan English.**
Russell Tabbert. Juneau: Denali Press, 1991. 294p. bibliog.

This is an historical approach to general Alaskan usage, arranged by semantic category. This is the only scholarly work of this kind on Alaska's variations on standard English.

527 **A dictionary of the St. Lawrence Island/Siberian Yupik Eskimo language.**
Compiled by Linda Womkon Badten, Vera Oovi Kaneshiro, Marie Oovi, edited by Steven A. Jacobson. Fairbanks, Alaska: Alaska Native Language Center, University of Alaska, 1987. 2nd prelim. ed. 410p.

This dictionary project, utilizing prior material as well, was started in 1976. It contains about 6,000 bases and 250 post bases. No loan-words from English or Russian are included.

528 **Dinjii zhuhginjik navwan tr'iltsaii, Gwich'n junior dictionary.**
Katherine Peter. Anchorage: National Bilingual Materials Development Center, 1979. 148p.

This small dictionary is designed to aid students in bilingual classes. This Athabascan language is spoken in the villages of Birch Creek, Arctic Village, Chalkyitsik, Circle, Fort Yukon and Venetie.

529 **English–Tlingit dictionary: nouns.**
Henry Davis. Sitka, Alaska: Sheldon Jackson College, 1976. 117p.

This work builds upon the earlier work by Constance Naish and Gillian Story (see item no. 534) which developed a standardized writing system for the Tlingit language.

530 **Haida dictionary.**
Compiled by Erma Lawrence. Fairbanks, Alaska: Society for the Preservation of Haida Language and Literature with the Alaska Native Language Center, University of Alaska, 1977. 464p.

There are a number of works that were published in the Haida language by 1900, but after 1910 all publications ceased. This was due to the suppression of native languages in schools. Starting anew, this work utilizes a new design devised in 1972 for a modern writing system.

531 **How to speak Alaskan.**
Edited by Mike Doogan, illustrated by Jamie Smith. Fairbanks, Alaska: Epicenter Press, 1993. 64p.

Written as humour and not as a serious guidebook, this is primarily about terms in general usage that a visitor might find unfamiliar. Terms include slang words or terms derived from native traditions that describe geographical, natural, and social phenomena such as 'cheekchako' or 'Kashim'. Doogan is a columnist for the *Anchorage Daily News* and Smith is a cartoonist. For a scholarly treatment of Alaskan terminology see Tabbert (item no. 526).

532 **Inupiallu tannillu uqalunisa ilavich–Inupiaq: abridged Inupiaq and English dictionary.**
Compiled by Edna Ahgeak Maclean. Barrow, Alaska: North Slope Borough Inupiat Language Commission with the Alaska Native Language Center of the University of Alaska, 1981. 168p.

The Inupiaq language programme began in the North Slope Borough School District in 1970, and at the University of Alaska in 1971. This dictionary is designed to support that continuing effort.

533 **Inupiat Eskimo dictionary.**
Donald H. Webster, Wilfried Zibell. Fairbanks, Alaska: Summer Institute of Linguistics, 1970. 210p. map.

This dictionary is organized by general subject area, with an index of English terms at the end.

534 **Tlingit verb dictionary.**
Compiled by Gillian L. Story, Constance M. Naish. College, Alaska: Alaska Native Language Center, University of Alaska, 1973. 329p.

This dictionary is based upon the central dialect of Tlingit spoken in Juneau, Sitka, Hoonah and Angoon. It expands upon an earlier work (1963) on nouns only.

535 **Yupik Eskimo dictionary.**
Compiled by Steven A. Jacobson. Fairbanks, Alaska: Alaska Native Language Center, University of Alaska, 1984. 757p. maps. bibliog.

Central Yupik, in its several dialects, is spoken in south-western Alaska. Yupik word-lists go back more than 200 years, but this project was started in 1961. The modern orthography in use is described in the introduction. Major dialectical differences in words are noted in the definitions. An English–Yupik index is appended. Appendix 10 is a list of loan-words in the language – about 190 from Russian with fewer from English, Aleut, Inupiaq, Chukchi, Koryak, Athabascan, Lappish and even three from Filippino (introduced by cannery workers on Bristol Bay at the turn of the last century).

Religion

536 Alaska missionary spirituality.

Edited by Michael Oleksa. New York: Paulist Press, 1987. 406p. map. bibliog.

These are letters, diaries, sermons and reports of Russian Orthodox missionaries written during the eighteenth and nineteenth centuries. It includes an appendix listing Aleut and Creole churchmen.

537 The Alaskan missions of the Episcopal Church: a brief sketch, historical and descriptive.

Hudson Stuck. New York: Domestic and Foreign Missionary Society, 1920. 179p.

This brief history of missions was written by the active and articulate Archdeacon Stuck. The Church was established on parts of the Yukon River and at Anvik on the coast by the time the gold rush brought a new wave of people. Stuck himself remained most interested in serving the natives, but the Church also became active in several new towns, especially Cordova. Several hospitals were established, the most notable at Fort Yukon.

538 The apostle of Alaska: the story of William Duncan of Metlakatla.

John William Arctander. New York: Revell, 1909. 375p. map.

William Duncan arrived in Old Metlakatla in British Columbia in 1857. Breaking with his superiors in the Church of England, he then established a new settlement at New Metlakatla in Alaska, moving his Tsimshian Indian parishioners with him. He strove to establish a model Christian community with various industrial endeavours, chiefly a salmon-canning operation, a sawmill, and a store. Duncan became embroiled in a number of controversies and eventually lost control of his colony. Arctander presents only Duncan's side of these issues.

539 **Archives of the Russian Orthodox Church in Alaska.**
Antoinette Shalkop. In: *Arctica 1978: 7th Northern libraries colloquy 19-23 September 1978*, edited by Sylvie Devers. Paris: Editions du Centre National de la Recherche Scientifique, 1982, p. 287-91. bibliog.

Shalkop prepared the finding aid for the microfilm edition of one of the most important sources for the study of the history of Russian America: the Alaska Church Archives (Russian Orthodox), held by the Library of Congress. This presentation is an assessment of the nature and importance of the collection.

540 **Baptist expansion in the last frontier: celebrating 40 years of Southern Baptist missions, 1946-1986.**
Anchorage: Alaska Baptist Convention, 1986. [210]p.

An unpaginated compilation in which each church association and institution has its own section. This work is useful in the detail it provides for individual congregations.

541 **Baptist history of the north Pacific coast, with special reference to western Washington, British Columbia, and Alaska.**
John Clapp Baker. Philadelphia, Pennsylvania: American Baptist Publication Society, 1912. 472p.

Baptist activity started on Kodiak and Afognak islands through teachers appointed as part of the partition plan promoted by Sheldon Jackson in his position of Commissioner of Education for Alaska. By 1899, there were ten members at the Wood Island Baptist Church. Along with the gold rush, they became active in Skagway as well. There are only ten pages devoted to Alaska, with some scattered references elsewhere. The book does not have an index.

542 **The Catholic Church in Alaska.**
Mary G. Balcom. Chicago, Illinois: Adams Press, 1970. 150p. map. bibliog.

Balcom's work is a brief narrative history, sprinkled with anecdotes.

543 **Charles John Seghers, pioneer in Alaska.**
Antoinette Bosco. New York: P. J. Kennedy, 1960. 190p.

Archbishop Seghers was murdered by one of his travelling companions in 1886 while journeying along the Yukon after a career in the Pacific Northwest and Alaska. This is written as a popular, uncritical, narrative account.

544 **Covenant Church in Alaska.**
L. Arden Almquist. Chicago, Illinois: Covenant Press, 1962. 159p. bibliog.

The Swedish Covenant work in Alaska began in 1887 with a mission to the Eskimo in Unalakleet. Although generally well researched, the book is cast in the form of a study guide and there is no index.

545 **Dayspring on the Kuskokwim.**
Anna Buxbaum Schwalbe. Bethlehem, Pennsylvania: Moravian Press, 1951. 264p.

The Moravian mission was first established in Bethel in 1885. There is a lot of useful detail, for example who served and when, but the book was written in part as a recruiting device for young missionaries and only positive aspects of the history are told.

546 **The Devil and Mr. Duncan: a history of the two Metlakatlas.**
Peter Murray. Victoria, British Columbia: Sono Nis Press, 1985. 341p. map. bibliog.

Murray draws upon archival resources that were not available to Arctander (q.v.) and other contemporaneous accounts. During, and even after, his lifetime Duncan was a centre of controversy. This was due not only to his own career, but also because of issues surrounding the impact of missionaries and especially his model of a native community, something that many saw as an attempt to create a native Christian utopia first at Old Metlakatla, British Columbia and then at New Metlakatla on Annette Island, Alaska. Murrary includes extensive information on business, economics, and the government of that time in so far as it affected Duncan's work.

547 **Father Tom of the Arctic.**
Louis L. Renner. Portland, Oregon: Binford and Mort Publishing, 1985. 163p. map. bibliog.

This is a biography of Thomas Patrick Cunningham, a Jesuit active in Holy Cross, Nome, Little Diomede, King Island, Kotzebue and Barrow from 1930 to 1959.

548 **Francis A. Barnum, S.J.: Pioneer Alaskan missionary and linguist.**
Louis L. Renner. *Alaska History*, vol. 1, no. 2 (1985), p. 19-41.

Barnum was active during the 1890s among the Central Yupik in Western Alaska. He produced the first Jesuit dictionary of that language.

549 **From Humboldt to Kodiak 1886-1895: recollections of a frontier childhood and the founding of the first American school and the Baptist mission at Kodiak, Alaska.**
Fred Roscoe, edited by Stanley N. Roscoe. Kingston, Ontario; Fairbanks, Alaska: Limestone Press, 1992. 211p. maps. (Alaska History, no. 40).

Frank Roscoe's recollections, written late in life, are of the work of his parents, Ida and Ernest Roscoe. The book is in the form of a series of short anecdotes. The Kodiak mission and orphanage was established on Woody Island, at the site of the old Russian American ice facility.

550 A gathering of saints in Alaska: an informational chronicle of the Church of Jesus Christ of Latter-day Saints in the State of Alaska.
Edited by Pat Jasper, Beverly M. Blasongame. Salt Lake City, Utah: Hiller Industries, 1983. 306p.

The Mormon Church first became active at the time of the gold rush, but real growth came only during and after the Second World War. This compilation lists all major Church officials up to the date of the publication.

551 Hall Young of Alaska: 'the mushing parson'.
S. Hall Young. New York: Fleming H. Revel, 1927. 448p.

Young was a Presbyterian missionary who arrived in Alaska well before the gold rush and then stayed for fifty years. He was initially involved in a training school venture in Wrangell. He travelled extensively with John Muir, whose writings did much to make the world aware of Alaska's natural attractions. He was present for the rush at Dawson, in Nome and in Fairbanks. He was also active in the newly prosperous copper-shipping port of Cordova.

552 Have gospel tent, will travel: the Methodist Church in Alaska since 1886.
Bea Shepard, Claudia Kelsey. Anchorage: Conference Council on Ministries, Alaska Missionary Conference of the United Methodist Church, 1986. 418p. maps. bibliog.

An illustrated account, this Methodist history touches upon the early division of missionary labour in Alaska, co-ordinated by the Presbyterian Sheldon Jackson. There was substantial co-operation among many of the Protestant churches during the gold-rush era. This is a well-organized and polished presentation.

553 The history of the Alaska Moravian Church, 1885-1985: harmonious to dwell.
James W. Henkelman, Kurt H. Vitt. Bethel, Alaska: Moravian Seminary & Archives, 1985. 418p. maps. bibliog.

The authors place the history of this church within the general context of both the history of the Moravian Church with its European roots, and the region into which they first moved in Alaska – the Kuskokwim river drainage centred at Bethel. This is a work of considerable scholarship.

554 A history of the Orthodox Church in Alaska (1794-1917).
Gregory Afonsky. Kodiak, Alaska: St. Herman's Theological Seminary, 1977. 105p. maps. bibliog.

Bishop Gregory (Afonsky) has written a brief historical overview of Alaska's oldest organized Christian church. Several short chronologies are included.

555 I have planted thee in this land; the story of the first 25 years of Southern Baptist Missions in Alaska.
Naomi Ruth Hunke. Anchorage: Alaska Baptist Convention, 1971. 334p. bibliog.

Arranged as a series of anecdotes and brief personal accounts, this history is designed to introduce non-Alaskan Baptists to the state and its missionary work. It is a lengthy account, and includes numerous small photographs of the 1964 Anchorage earthquake and the 1967 Fairbanks flood.

556 The journals of Iakov Netsvetov: the Atkha years, 1828-1844.
Translated with an introduction and supplementary historical and ethnographic material by Lydia Black. Kingston, Ontario: Limestone Press, 1980. 340p. (Alaska History, no. 16).

Netsvetov was the first native Alaskan Orthodox priest. He and his brothers received part of their education in Russia. He worked closely with Ivan Veniaminov in the development of a writing system for the Aleut language and as the parish priest for the Atka District, he built a school which prospered. The appendices include organizational charts, official records related to Netsvetov's career, a list of geographical terms used at the time, an extensive glossary, a list of vessels which serviced the Atkha District, and genealogical tables for the Netsvetov family.

557 The journals of Iakov Netsvetov: the Yukon years, 1845-1863.
Translated by Lydia Black. Kingston, Ontario: Limestone Press, 1984. 513p. bibliog. (Alaska History, no. 26).

After his successful service in the Atkha District (see above), Netsvetov was selected to serve in the newly developing Orthodox effort on the lower Yukon River. He served there for 18 years, learning a new language. Professor Black includes useful information on Russian, Yupik and Koyukon settlements and biographical details about Netsvetov's associates.

558 The Lutheran Church in Alaska: brief histories of the Lutheran churches in Alaska in chronological order of their founding.
Edited by J. L. Maakestad. Anchorage: [n.p.], 1978. 2nd ed. 57p.

Although there was a Lutheran church in Sitka during the Russian American era, the American Lutheran Church first became active in Alaska in 1894, on the Seward Peninsula. Each active church in Alaska has a brief listing and a historical sketch.

559 Marsden of Alaska, a modern Indian, minister, missionary, musician, engineer, pilot, boat builder, and church builder.
William G. Beattie. New York: Vantage Press, 1955. 246p.

Marsden, a Tsimshian Indian, was a member of William Duncan's congregation and was part of the move to New Metlakatla. He attended the Sitka mission school and then college and a seminary in Ohio. He was involved with the break between Duncan and the Church and the difficulties between Duncan and many residents of Metlakatla. Beattie personally knew both men.

560 The martyrdom of Brother Hooker: conflict and conversion on the Kuskokwim.

Ann Fienup-Riordan. *Alaska History*, vol. 3, no. 1 (Spring 1988), p. 1-26.

The article explores the cultural and religious tensions brought on by the activities of Moravian missionaries working among Yupik Eskimos who still practised traditional religion during the late 1880s and early 1890s. The continued presence of Russian Orthodoxy further complicated matters.

561 Memoirs of a Yukon priest.

Segundo Llorente. Washington, DC: Georgetown University Press, 1990. 223p. map.

This is the autobiography of a Spanish priest who completed his studies in the United States and then worked in Alaska from 1935 to 1975. He became a US citizen in 1956 and served two terms in the newly formed House of Representatives in Juneau following statehood. He is somewhat blunt in his assessment of the people that he met, and his account includes numerous brief sketches of both lay and religious figures who are little chronicled elsewhere.

562 Orthodoxy and Native Americans: the Alaskan mission.

Barbara S. Smith. Syosset, New York: Historical Society of the Orthodox Church in America, 1980. 37p. bibliog. (Orthodox Church in America Department of History and Archives, Historical Society Occasional Papers, no. 1).

The Orthodox Church in Alaska is today primarily a Native church. Barbara Smith's work with the collection and description of Alaska church records, recovered from old church buildings (see item no. 565) is the basis for her re-evaluation in this extended essay of the relationship between the Russian Orthodox Church and Alaska Natives. Up to this point, relatively little was known of the activities of the Church between the sale of Alaska in 1867 and the present.

563 Pioneer missionary to the Bering Strait Eskimos: Bellarmine Lafortune, S.J.

Louis L. Renner in collaboration with Dorothy Jean Ray. Portland, Oregon: Binford and Mort Publishing for the Alaska Historical Commission, 1979. 207p. map. bibliog.

Lafortune served in the Bering Strait area from 1903 until 1947. This is an account of the Catholic Eskimo missionary activity of which he was a part. Some of the more memorable events included the founding of orphanages, the health battles (especially the influenza epidemic of 1918) and work with the King Islanders. Lafortune was especially concerned with the preservation of the Eskimo way of life and their hunting culture.

564 **The Russian Orthodox religious mission in America, 1794-1837, with materials concerning the life and works of the monk German, and ethnographic notes by the hieromonk Gedeon.**
Translated by Colin Bearne, edited by Richard A. Pierce. Kingston, Ontario: Limestone Press, 1978. 186p. (Materials for the Study of Alaska History, no. 11).

The Orthodox Church followed the earlier movement of merchants into Alaskan waters. These letters and accounts of the first set of missionaries from the Valaam Monastery near St. Petersburg were first published in a Russian edition of 1894. Their early work was centred on Kodiak.

565 **Russian Orthodoxy in Alaska: a history, inventory, and analysis of the Church archives in Alaska with an annotated bibliography.**
Barbara S. Smith. Anchorage: Alaska Historical Commission, 1980. 171p. bibliog.

During the 1970s there was a major project to gather in the old documents and rare books that remained in the various Russian Orthodox church buildings, many no longer in use, scattered throughout the state. The richest finds were made in the Yukon River mission district. Through a co-operative effort involving the University of Alaska Anchorage and the Church, these recent finds have been described by Smith. She puts these records in context, with information on other resources, and analysis of the records, pictures of the churches and settlements, a chronology, and an excellent annotated bibliography.

566 **Salvation! comes to the last frontier.**
Evan W. Dowling. Juneau: Rainforest Publishing, 1986. 56p. map.

A brief chronicle of the Salvation Army's first 88 years in Alaska.

567 **Symbolic immortality: the Tlingit potlatch of the nineteenth century.**
Sergei Kan. Washington, DC: Smithsonian Institution, 1989. 390p. bibliog.

This is a study of mortuary customs and the memorial potlach written in a clear prose, and avoiding technical jargon.

568 **Tomorrow is growing old: stories of the Quakers in Alaska.**
Arthur O. Roberts. Newberg, Oregon: Barclay Press, 1978. 567p.

The Quakers built their first congregations in Southeast and Northwest Alaska. Consequently, membership included many Eskimo, and much of this history concerns the meeting of the two cultures during the gold-rush era and the following years. Eskimo Quakers have been deeply involved with ecological, land claims, and wildlife conservation/subsistence issues. This book has been extensively researched.

569 **The voice of Alaska: a missioner's memories.**
[Sister Mary Joseph Calasanctuis], translated from the French.
Lachin, Quebec: Sisters of St. Ann Press, 1935. 340p. map.

This account was written in Flemish by a nun originally from Belgium and the first edition was published in French. Sister Mary Joseph was one of the founders of the Holy Cross Mission on the Yukon.

Health, Welfare and Society

570 **Alaska Medicine.**
Anchorage: Alaska Medical Association and the American Society for Circumpolar Health, 1959- . quarterly.

This journal publishes articles of the social aspects of medical issues in addition to technical materials related to health issues in the north. Historical articles and notes frequently treat the history of medicine in Alaska, including the Russian American era.

571 **Alaska Review of Social and Economic Conditions.**
Anchorage: Institute of Social and Economic Research, University of Alaska, 1964- . quarterly.

Each issue is generally devoted to a particular topic such as prices and the cost of living, state school enrolment projections, oil and gas regulation, or issues concerning agricultural development.

572 **Crime reported in Alaska.**
Juneau: Uniform Crime Reporting, Department of Public Safety, 1982- . annual.

Gathered in various other formats since statehood, this agency has had the responsibility for collecting statistics from all law enforcement agencies in the state since 1982.

573 **What happened to Fairbanks?: the effects of the trans-Alaska oil pipeline on the community of Fairbanks, Alaska.**
Mim Dixon. Boulder, Colorado: Westview Press, 1978. 337p. bibliog.

Fairbanks was heavily impacted by the pipeline construction period, when a tremendous boom (relative to the small community's pre-pipeline economy) brought in hordes of outside job-seekers, massive amounts of new money, and rapid construction of non-conventional housing and commercial structures. Fairbanks is seen as a model for learning about such booms with many lessons of what to avoid and an evaluation of the unexpected impacts of this kind of development. Dixon, an anthropologist, worked in the local Fairbanks North Star Borough Impact Information Center, and became its director at the height of the pipeline boom.

Politics

574 **Alaska pipeline: the politics of oil and Native land claims.**
Mary Clay Berry. Bloomington, Indiana: Indiana University Press, 1975. 302p. bibliog.

This book went to press before the completion of the pipeline, but it gives an excellent overview of the political compromise that occurred with the passage of the Alaska Native Claims Settlement Act and the enabling legislation to construct the Trans-Alaska Pipeline. In addition to the question of Native land claims, this was the first major test of new environmental legislation and regulation in the United States.

575 **Alaska state government and politics.**
Edited by Gerald A. McBeath, Thomas A. Morehouse. Fairbanks, Alaska: University of Alaska Press, 1987. 357p.

Each of the thirteen chapters is written by an expert in the field. Topics include a brief discussion of the statehood movement; a description of Alaska's constitution; Alaska's political culture; federalism in Alaska; Alaska's elections; Alaska's political parties; interest groups in Alaska; public opinion, the press and Alaska politics; the legislature as an institution; the institution of governor; Alaska's administrative system; and courts in Alaska. As time passes, books on current politics such as this become increasingly dated, but it remains the single best description of the state's political system.

576 **The battle for Alaska statehood.**
Ernest Gruening. College, Alaska: University of Alaska Press in cooperation with the Alaska Purchase Centennial Commission and distributed by the University of Washington Press, 1967. 112p.

This is much shorter than Senator Gruening's other works on the statehood issue (see item no. 357.). It serves as a summary, but it is invaluable also in carefully acknowledging everyone who had any role whatsoever in the statehood movement, including people involved with congressional hearings in Alaska. In addition, it includes the many details of the advancement of statehood through Congress.

577 Edward Lewis Bob Bartlett of Alaska: a life in politics.
Claus-M. Naske. Fairbanks, Alaska: University of Alaska Press, 1979. 287p.

Bob Bartlett was one of the first two senators from the new state of Alaska. Before that he had been a non-voting delegate to Congress for over a decade and had served in the appointed position of Secretary of Alaska. He was originally a miner in interior Alaska, and in political life he devoted his political career to gaining statehood for Alaska.

578 Etok: a story of Eskimo power.
Hugh Gregory Gallagher. New York: Putnam, 1974. 259p.

This is the biography of an Eskimo political activist, Charles Edwardsen, Jr., who was important in the struggle for Native rights during the debate on the Trans-Alaska Pipeline and the period leading up to the Alaska Native Claims Settlement Act.

579 An interpretative history of Alaskan statehood.
Claus-M. Naske. Lanham, Maryland: University Press of America, 1985. rev. ed. 309p. bibliog.

A revision of Naske's dissertation was published in 1973, and this is a further revision of that. This remains the standard work on the statehood movement and the events leading to the granting of statehood to Alaska in 1959.

580 Letters to Howard: an interpretation of the Alaska Native land claims.
Frederick Seagayuk Bigjim, James Ito-Adler. Anchorage: Alaska Methodist University Press, 1974. 115p.

These letters were written to Howard Rock, editor of the *Tundra Times*, by two graduate students at Harvard, one an Eskimo and the other a former Peace Corps volunteer. They use the names Naugga Ciunerput and Wally Morton from a fictitious village in rural Alaska. They use this vehicle to analyse and critique the Alaska Native Claims Settlement Act.

581 Many battles: the autobiography of Ernest Gruening.
Ernest Gruening. New York: Liveright, 1973. 564p.

This is the autobiography of one of Alaska's most important politicians. Gruening completed medical school, but took up a career in journalism instead. He eventually became an expert on Latin America and was picked in 1934 to head President Roosevelt's new Division of Territories and Island Possessions in the Department of Interior, which included jurisdiction over Alaska. He was then appointed Governor of Alaska in 1938 and remained in that post for 13 years. He later became one of Alaska's first senators following statehood. He was a strong national advocate of making birth control widely available, and was an early and strong opponent of the Vietnam war.

582 **Village journey: the report of the Alaska Native Review Commission.**

Thomas R. Berger. New York: Hill and Wang, 1985. 203p.

Berger, a well-known Canadian jurist, headed a number of important commissions in Canada, including the Mackenzie Valley Pipeline Inquiry, before being selected for this Alaska study sponsored by the Inuit Circumpolar Conference and the World Council of Indigenous Peoples. This book reports the results of hearings in 62 villages and towns regarding native views on the results of the Alaska Native Claims Settlement Act (ANCSA) of 1971. Main topics include cultural identity and relationship to the land, the reality of the regional and village corporations under ANCSA, subsistence lifestyles and the native sovereignty movement.

Constitution and Legal System

583 Alaska local government encyclopedia.

Compiled by Carl Smith. Juneau: Dena Aka Corporation for the State of Alaska, 1979. 2nd ed. 375p.

This handbook was originally designed to aid local government officials in exercising their obligations of government. However, it is a most useful source for general information about borough, city and other local governments in Alaska. A glossary of key terms in local government usage is included.

584 Alaska Natives and American laws.

David S. Case. Fairbanks, Alaska: University of Alaska Press, 1984. rev. ed. 586p.

The first edition was originally entitled 'The special relationship of Alaska natives to the federal government'. Chapter eight, 'Traditional Alaska native societies' was written by an anthropologist, Ann D. Shinkwin. Case provides an excellent summary of the history of native legal status under the United States. While much of this system applies, Alaska generally lacks the reservation system in place in the 'lower 48' and the Alaska Native Claims Settlement Act further differentiates the Alaska legal environment.

585 Alaska statutes.

Alaska Legislative Council. Charlottesville, Virgina: Michie Co., 1962- . annual.

This compilation is annotated and indexed.

586 Alaska's constitutional convention.

Victor Fischer. Fairbanks, Alaska: University of Alaska Press, 1975. 277p.

The author was a member of the constitutional convention held in Fairbanks in 1955-56. The constitution was written (and approved by voters) two years before

Congress voted for statehood. Fischer covers the organization and administration of the convention; explains the process of deliberation and writing; and deals with the many issues and controversies addressed by the body. The constitution itself is reproduced as 'Appendix A'.

587 **Alaska's urban and rural governments.**
Thomas A. Morehouse, Gerald A. McBeath, Linda Leask. Lanham, Maryland: University Press of America, 1984. 261p.

In many particulars, the government of Alaska is unlike that of other US states. Although it has municipalities and has developed a borough form of local government, much like a typical US county, most of the land lies outside their boundaries as a part of the 'unorganised borough'. This book is becoming dated because of changes since publication, but it is still the best single guide to the constitutional provisions governing state and local government, state policies related to borough government, how local government is financed, differences between rural and urban governance, and the North Slope Borough as a special and very important case.

588 **A citizen's guide to the Constitution of the State of Alaska.**
Gordon S. Harrison. Anchorage: Institute of Social and Economic Research, University of Alaska, 1982. 134p.

A succinct explanation of the provisions of the Constitution.

589 **The tribal status of Alaska Natives.**
E. Smith, M. Kancewik. *University of Colorado Law Review*, vol. 61, no. 3 (1990), p. 455-516.

The issue of 'native sovereignty' hinges in part on the legal issues surrounding the separate status of Alaska under the Alaska Native Claims Settlement Act.

Economy, Industry and Trade

Economy

590 **Agricultural development in Alaska.**

Carol E. Lewis, Roger W. Pearson, Wayne C. Thomas. *Polar Record*, vol. 23, no. 147 (Sept. 1987), p. 673-82. map. bibliog.

The authors identify four periods of agricultural activity in Alaska over the past 200 years: the Russian and early US period; federal intervention, 1898 to World War II; commercial expansion, 1946 to 1967; and a new era for agriculture. Despite substantial state subsidies following the Prudhoe Bay oil discovery, only marginal success has been possible.

591 **Alaska business and industry: an illustrated history.**

Robert R. Richards, pictorial research by Renee Blahuta. [n.p.]: Windsor Publications, in cooperation with the Alaska State Chamber of Commerce, 1989. 318p. bibliog.

The last 112 pages of this sponsored history are a 'partners in progress' segment with single- and multiple-page spreads describing the sponsoring firms and organizations. Many entries contain useful information about the history of firms that is not readily available elsewhere.

592 **Alaska Business Monthly.**

Anchorage: Alaska Business Publishing Co., 1983- . monthly.

In this magazine, business firms are profiled, Alaska economic trends are examined, and information is presented which will be of use in Alaska about general national and international developments.

593 **Alaska Economic Trends.**
Juneau: Alaska Department of Labor, Research and Analysis Section, 1968- . monthly.

This monthly deals with a variety of economic issues. It usually features one or two themes in each issue, such as an analysis of the technical jobs in Alaska or the role of one of state's towns in a regional economy.

594 **Alaska in transition: the Southeast region.**
George W. Rogers. Baltimore, Maryland: published for Resources for the Future, by The Johns Hopkins Press, 1960. 384p.

This work is very much out of date for those seeking current information, but it is a useful synthesis of long-term issues by the dean of Alaska's economists.

595 **The Alaska Journal of Commerce.**
Anchorage: AJCH, Inc., 1977- . weekly.

This journal consists of two sections: the first is in a newspaper format, reporting on developments of interest to the business community; the second is titled the *Alaska Journal of Record* which contains official notices for Anchorage municipal government, public hearings that are scheduled, public notices of all types, and legal notices. There are also other supplements included from time to time, such as the *Alaska Oil & Gas Reporter*.

596 **Alaska's forest resources.**
Edited by Penny Rennick. Anchorage: Alaska Geographic, 1985. 193p. maps. (*Alaska Geographic*, vol. 12, no. 2).

A general historical treatment of the forest industry. It begins with an introduction to the variety of forest environments and the species growing in Alaska. There have been traditional uses of the forests by natives, and the Russians used wood for construction and the manufacture of charcoal. River boats originally required vast amounts of wood for fuel, and for a time it was also used for the generation of electricity. Most of the coastal timber is in national forests and involves long-term sales to large corporations. The role of fire in forest management is also explained.

597 **Contemporary Alaskan native economies.**
Edited by Steven J. Langdon. Lanham, Maryland: University Press of America, 1986. 183p. maps.

These are contributions by twelve experts in the field, covering subsistence economic activities and commercial endeavours. Subsistence is treated in general as well as regionally and most areas have developed a hybrid economy which mixes subsistence with a variety of endeavours generating cash, such as commercial fishing.

598 **Eskimos, reindeer and the land.**

Richard O. Stern, Edward L. Arobio, Larry L. Naylor, Wayne C. Thomas. Fairbanks, Alaska: Agricultural Experiment Station, School of Agriculture and Land Resources Management, University of Alaska, 1980. 205p. maps. bibliog. (Bulletin no. 59).

A study of the socio-economic and cultural aspects of reindeer herding in northwestern Alaska. It includes a history of the industry on and near the Seward Peninsula and a description of reindeer biology and ecology. Reindeer were introduced into this area in the 1890s and they have been a matter of controversy and study since then. This is a general introduction to the nature and importance of the industry.

599 **Flag over the North: the story of the Northern Commercial Company.**

L. D. Kitchener. Seattle, Washington: Superior, 1954. 349p.

The Alaska Commercial Company took over the seal-hunting monopoly on the Pribilof Islands and eventually established a chain of stores throughout Alaska before, during, and after the gold rush. In many cases these were in the same locations and even used the same buildings as the old Russian-American Company operations. The firm also operated a fleet of company riverboats and operated mail and stage lines. The firm became the largest retail outlet in Fairbanks following the gold rush there and they provided power to the new settlement through wood-fired steam electric generators.

600 **The future of Alaska: economic consequences of statehood.**

George W. Rogers. Baltimore, Maryland: published for Resources for the Future, by The Johns Hopkins Press, 1962. 311p.

Rogers wrote this just after Alaska's statehood in 1959 and before the 1964 earthquake or the Prudhoe Bay oil field spawned the Trans-Alaska Pipeline. The Alaska Native Claims Settlement Act lay in the future. Even so, this is a thoughtful and well-researched analysis of what the future might hold. Despite its age, it retains its value as a glimpse of what the state was like at the very beginning of statehood.

601 **Mr. Alaska: the Chuck West story: forty years of Alaska tourism, 1945-1985.**

Charles B. West. Seattle, Washington: Westee, 1985. 153p.

The autobiography of an entrepreneur who developed a tourist industry in Alaska following the Second World War. It included the operation of cruise ships, transport with bush planes, the construction of hotels, and establishing tourist bus operations. His Westours firm was eventually purchased by Holland-American Cruises.

602 **Outpost agriculture: the case of Alaska.**

Karl E. Francis. *Geographical Review*, no. 57 (October 1967), p. 496-505.

Alaska agriculture has always functioned to supplement the bulk of food items shipped from outside. Francis argues that as the economy of Alaska draws closer to that of the remainder of the United States, agriculture's function will continue to diminish. Remote northern areas of Canada display similar developments.

603 **Subsistence economies in Alaska: productivity, geography, and development impacts.**
Robert J. Wolf, Robert J. Walker. *Arctic Anthropology*, vol. 24, no. 2, p. 56-81. maps. bibliog.

This study is based upon a state-wide sample of the harvests of wild game in 98 communities during the 1980s. Wolf and Walker, who both work for the Division of Subsistence, Alaska Department of Fisheries, find that wild resources make substantial contributions to local economies, that vary in part based on proximity to the state's road system. There are substantial regional variations which are depicted on maps, graphs and charts.

Fisheries

604 **Alaska blues: a fisherman's journal.**
Joe Upton. Anchorage: Alaska Northwest Publishing, 1977. 236p. 5 maps.

These are the experiences of a seasonal commercial fisherman with a small boat (32 feet). Extensively illustrated, it treats the locations, the gear, the history, ecological issues, and the economics of fishing in Southeast Alaska.

605 **Alaska fisheries policy: economics, resources and management.**
Edited by Arlon R. Tussing, Thomas A. Morehouse, James D. Babb, Jr. Fairbanks, Alaska: Institute of Social, Economic and Government Research, University of Alaska, 1972. 470p. maps. (ISEGR Report, no. 33).

For many years this was the best introduction to the politics and public policy of managing Alaska's fisheries. Now dated, it is still a useful source.

606 **Alaska's salmon fisheries.**
Edited by Jim Rearden. Anchorage: Alaska Geographic, 1983. 123p. (*Alaska Geographic*, vol. 10, no. 3).

The five different major species of salmon constitute the most important commercial and subsistence fishery in Alaska. It is of great historical importance as mechanized canneries moved north, starting in the 1880s, and it remains important economically and politically. Rearden describes the fish and the fishery as a major sport and source of food for wildlife as well.

607 **The commercial fishing industry in Alaska's economy.**
Matthew D. Berman, Teresa Hull. Anchorage: Institute of Social and Economic Research, University of Alaska, 1987. 58p. bibliog.

This is a detailed statistical compilation of fisheries and economic statistics.

608 **Fisheries of the North Pacific: history, species, gear and processes.**
Robert J. Browning. Anchorage: Alaska Northwest, 1980. rev. ed. 423p. map.

The species of commercial fish are described, the history of the fisheries and equipment including fish processing are detailed. Although coverage is not strictly limited to Alaskan waters, most of it is relevant.

609 **Working on the edge: surviving in the world's most dangerous profession: king crab fishing on Alaska's high seas.**
Spike Walker. New York: St. Martin's Press, 1991. 279p.

As much an adventure tale as a description, this is a good source for understanding the conditions of the Bering Sea fishery during the gold-rush atmosphere of boom-and-bust fishing cycles. Walker spent nine seasons as a crew member on a crabbing boat.

Oil and gas

610 **Alaska's oil/gas and minerals industry.**
Edited by Penny Rennick. Anchorage: Alaska Geographical Society, 1982. 216p. (*Alaska Geographic*, vol. 9, no. 4).

A popular, illustrated, overview of mining geology, mining history, and the contemporary era since the discovery of the Prudhoe Bay oil field. Gravel and various strategic minerals such as tungsten, nickel, platinum, tin and antimony are covered in addition to the better-known gold, silver and petroleum industries.

611 **The Alaskan kangaroo.**
Allen Chesterfield. Seattle, Washington: Adelaide Press, 1980. 318p.

Chesterfield gives us the personal account of a native Australian who found himself in Alaska during the peak Trans-Alaska Pipeline construction years of 1975 and 1976. During that time he worked at seventeen different jobs for eleven different firms that were contracting for pipeline construction. Because his experience was so varied, he had the opportunity to observe a number of different pipeline camps and working situations.

612 **Oil and gas exploration and development in circumpolar regions of Alaska, Canada, and Greenland: an analysis of corporate involvement.**
Ecumenical Metropolitan Ministry. Seattle, Washington: Inuit Circumpolar Conference, 1977. 79p. maps. bibliog.

This is an analysis of which firms were involved in exploration and oil leases at the time of the study. It includes joint ventures and information on the ownership of the companies. The study shows that 111 firms were engaged in one country only (Alaska, Canada, Greenland), 19 were active in two, and only 4 were involved in all three. Of the 247 firms, 49 were active in Alaska and of the 217 million acres under lease, only 9.6 million were in Alaska (Canada had 205 million).

Statistics

613 Causes of death in Alaska 1950, 1980-1989: an analysis of the causes of death, years of potential life lost, and life expectancy.

Compiled by John P. Middaugh (et al.). Anchorage: Section of Epidemiology, Division of Public Health, Department of Health and Social Services, State of Alaska, 1991. 224p.

These statistics are presented in great detail, and are based upon all death certificates filed with the state for this period. They were coded for analysis by a team of physicians. Alaskans who died out of state are not included in these numbers. The report is accompanied by 42 coloured charts, graphs and diagrams.

614 Facts about Alaska: the Alaska almanac.

Compiled by Ann Chandonnet, edited by Carolyn Smith. Anchorage: Alaska Northwest Books, 1994. 18th ed. 223p.

Organized as a series of short entries on various Alaskan topics, there are a number of statistical tables including general population figures, generalized weather data such as temperature and precipitation, information on highways (route numbers, when opened, length), gold production figures (with annual prices per troy ounce), general employment totals, and a wealth of other summary information. This is a good place to look for a quick answer to a simple question, but no one topic is pursued to any depth.

615 Historical demography of Alaska's native population.

Frederick A. Milan. *Folk*, vol. 16-17 (1974/75), p. 45-54.

Although there is more recent information for current trends from the 1980 and 1990 census returns, this remains an excellent short summary of general developments from 1880 to 1970. For much of this time, before the Second World War, the number of natives was equal to, or greater than, the non-native population.

616 **Report on the population, industries and resources of Alaska.**
Ivan Petroff. Washington, DC: GPO, 1884. 189p. maps.

The 1880 census, which is the basis of this report, is a fundamental source of information on the early part of the American era in Alaska. Petroff makes reference to earlier enumerations carried out during the Russian era, from 1818 to 1863. He includes meterological data and information on fur, timber, fisheries, minerals and agriculture as they were in 1880. Petroff was a leading expert on Alaska in his day, with experience reaching back into the Russian era. This is essentially the effort of one man. His reputation suffered later, when it was discovered that he had fabricated some Russian reports that he claimed to be translating as a part of the Alaska border dispute at the turn of the century. This work, however, remains an essential part of any historical collection on Alaska.

617 **Report on population and resources of Alaska at the eleventh census: 1890.**
Robert P. Porter. Washington, DC: Department of the Interior Census Office, 1893. 282p. 3 maps.

Building upon the 1880 census (see item no. 616), this ennumeration involved more census-takers, working in seven census districts. It is illustrated with a number of photographs of people and places in Alaska. Porter extensively describes the geography and ethnography of Alaska, district by district. This remains an essential source for the study of Alaska.

618 **Suicide in Alaska from 1978 to 1985: updated data from state files.**
Norma Forbes, Vincent van der Hyde. *American Indian and Alaska Native Mental Health Research*, vol. 1, no. 3 (March 1988), p. 36-55.

The suicide rate has remained quite high in relation to the rest of the United States.

Environment

619 Alaska: challenge in conservation.
Richard A. Cooley. Madison, Wisconsin: University of Wisconsin Press, 1966. 170p. maps. bibliog.

This book has been important in the debate over the status of Alaska lands during the past several decades. It is still a good, concise, statement concerning the issues of development versus conservation. However, one must be aware that much has happened since 1966, including extensive land settlements, sweeping land withdrawals for parks, preserves and wilderness areas, and the Trans-Alaska Pipeline.

620 Alaska earthquake.
Edited by Marjorie Roberts. Anchorage: Alaska Publications, 1978. rev. ed. 64p.

This is a pictorial history of the 1964 Good Friday earthquake in Alaska. It was the strongest earthquake ever recorded on the west coast of North America. Some Anchorage streets dropped as much as 30 feet, entire coastal communities were destroyed and there were even changes in coastlines.

621 Arctic air pollution.
Edited by Bernard Stonehouse. Cambridge, England: Cambridge University Press, 1986. 328p. bibliog.

The recently recognized phenomena of arctic haze and, more recently, global warming have focused interest on the Arctic as an area for the study of global change. This conference was especially significant for the public policy issues raised. For the first time, interested laymen became aware of how industry from as far away as European Russia could affect the air over northern Alaska. These scientific presentations are of as much value to the non-specialist as to the experts.

622 **The firecracker boys.**

Daniel T. O'Neill. New York: St. Martin's Press, 1994. 388p. bibliog.

Project Chariot was a plan by the US Atomic Energy Commission under Edward Teller to blast a deep-water harbour at Cape Thomson on the Chukchi Sea. O'Neill extensively researched the politics of this project, uncovering many previously classified details. Despite the fact that there was no compelling need for a harbour, Teller pushed ahead to prove the value of nuclear explosions for civil engineering projects. One of the most revealing parts of this account is the extent to which biological research results were misrepresented. Eskimo rely upon caribou, which eat lichens, which are particularly susceptible to contamination as a result of the by-products of an atomic explosion. The project was never completed, for a number of reasons outlined by O'Neill, but in the process, the politics involved ruined several promising academic careers.

623 **In the wake of the 'Exxon Valdez': the devastating impact of the Alaska oil spill.**

Art Davidson. San Francisco, California: Sierra Club Books, 1990. 333p.

Davidson gives a straightforward account of the oil spill in March 1989, and the events that followed. It is based in part on extensive direct interviews with participants.

624 **Katmai: a true narrative.**

Wilson Fiske Erskine. London: Abelard-Schuman, 1962. 223p.

The Katmai volcanic eruption on the nearby Alaska Peninsula in June 1912 was a cataclysmic event for the town of Kodiak, where the W. J. Erskine company was engaged in commerce. The author was a fourth-generation merchant in the Alaskan trade and it was his father who directly experienced the events that he recreates as a day-to-day narrative. An immense layer of ash fell during the eruption and the population was forced to evacuate.

625 **Messages from Earth: nature and the human prospect in Alaska.**

Robert B. Weeden. Fairbanks, Alaska: University of Alaska Press, 1992. 189p. 5 maps. bibliog.

This is a thoughtful extended essay on the interaction of man and nature in Alaska by a specialist on resource management. He explores how cultural values and their evolution affect technology and man's relationship to the environment. Many natural phenomena and the ecologies within Alaska's regions are explained in spare and lucid prose.

626 **Out of the channel: the 'Exxon Valdez' oil spill in Prince William Sound.**

John Keeble. New York: Harper Collins, 1991. 290p. maps. bibliog.

This is an account of the events surrounding the spill in March 1989 and its clean-up, interwoven with the personal account and experiences of the author. The book abounds with vignettes of individuals encountered by Keeble. It is skilfully written and informative.

627 Politics and conservation: the decline of the Alaska salmon.
Richard A. Cooley. New York: Harper and Row, 1963. 230p. maps. bibliog.

Canneries were first established in Alaska in 1878. Fishing practices included some that were destructive of fish stocks, such as fish weirs and traps. These practices eventually led to the depletion of major fish populations. The commercial firms formed a powerful lobby that kept fisheries management out of the hands of the Territory of Alaska.

628 Project Chariot: Alaskan roots of environmentalism.
Peter Coates. *Alaska History*, vol. 4, no. 2 (Fall 1989), p. 1-31.

The Atomic Energy Commission, a civilian US agency, established Project Plowshare in 1957 in order to promote the peaceful use of nuclear energy. They adopted Project Chariot, a plan to create a deep-water harbour on the Chukchi Sea by using explosions. Opposition developed, on an international, national, regional, but most importantly, local level. Natives mounted a determined opposition. This was further developed by scientists and conservation organizations. Coates sees this as the real start of what would become the environmental movement. For a more detailed history of the politics of the project see O'Neill (item no. 622).

629 Season of dead water.
Edited by Helen Frost. Portland, Oregon; Dallas, Texas: Breitenbush Books, 1990. 113p.

A collection of personal reactions to the *Exxon Valdez* oil spill of 1989.

630 Spill!: the story of the 'Exxon Valdez'.
Terry Carr. New York: Franklin Watts, 1991. 64p.

An illustrated account of the March 1989 oil spill, written for children.

Education

631 **Alaska's small rural high schools: are they working?**
Judith S. Kleinfeld, G. Williamson McDiarmid, David Hagstrom. Anchorage: Institute for Social and Economic Research and the Center for Cross-Cultural Studies, University of Alaska, 1985. 149p.

This is a study of 162 rural high schools with fewer than 100 students, located in communities of fewer than 1,000 people. It was conducted nine years after the state began phasing out boarding school education and started constructing village high schools as part of the 'Molly Hooch' legal settlement (Tobeluk v. Lind, 1976).

632 **Cross-cultural issues in Alaskan education.**
Edited by Ray Barnhardt. Fairbanks, Alaska: University of Alaska, Center for Cross-Cultural Studies, 1982. 2 vols. bibliog.

Alaska began wrestling with problems of rural education and multicultural issues as it increasingly took over the old system from the Bureau of Indian Affairs. This collection of essays considers many of the continuing issues including bilingual education, native cultural values, local control of education, and practical considerations of classroom management.

633 **Fantastic Antone succeeds: experiences in educating children with fetal alcohol syndrome.**
Edited by Judith Kleinfeld, Siobhan Wescott. Fairbanks, Alaska: University of Alaska Press, 1983. 368p. bibliog.

This public health problem, which is caused by alcohol abuse during pregnancy, is especially acute in Alaska, although it is a national problem as well. This volume comprises a series of stories of how parents and teachers in Alaska have managed what had seemed to be a set of insoluble learning and behaviour problems.

634 Tannik school: the impact of education on the Eskimos of Anaktuvuk Pass.

Michael S. Cline. Anchorage: Alaska Methodist University Press, 1975. 210p. map. bibliog.

Anaktuvuk Pass is populated by an inland population of Nunamiut Eskimo. It is located halfway between Fairbanks and Point Barrow, 120 miles north of the Arctic Circle. An old hunting camp began to become the site of a permanent settlement in the early 1950s and at the time of writing there were twenty families living there. A two-room school was completed in 1961. The word 'tannik' means white man, and this is an account of the effects in this community of an outside educational institution with outside teachers. It is illustrated with numerous photographs of the village and its population.

Science and Technology

635 **Alaska Science Conference Proceedings.**

Fairbanks, Alaska: American Association for the Advancement of Science, 1950- . irregular.

Started during the era in which most scientists were based outside the state, an annual conference was held at the end of the field season. They have been held in a variety of venues and for some years, and only abstracts are published. The concept has recently been broadened to include northern Canada, and there has been some participation and joint conferences with the former Soviet Union as well.

636 **Alaska science nuggets.**

Neil Davis. Fairbanks, Alaska: Geophysical Institute, University of Alaska, 1982. 233p.

A collection of 400 articles which were distributed to newspapers in Alaska and the Yukon as a public service by the Alaska Science Forum. Grouped topically, this compilation serves as reference material in Alaskan schools. Articles are related to Alaska phenomena and cover such topics as the aurora, weather, ice, volcanoes, northern plants and animals and archaeology. A scientific perspective is also provided for common problems of northern living such as energy efficiency in housing, carbon monoxide and springtime road restrictions.

637 **Alaska's weather and climate.**

Edited by Gunter Weller. Fairbanks, Alaska: Geophysical Institute, University of Alaska, 1979. 153p. maps. bibliog.

This collection of articles was written for the educated layman by staff members of the Geophysical Institute and the National Weather Service in Alaska. There is extensive discussion of regional differences within Alaska and of phenomena peculiar to these regions such as sea ice, ice fog, sun pillars, varieties of snow, micro-climates and noctilucent clouds.

638 **Arctic dreams; imagination and desire in a northern landscape.**
Barry Lopez. New York: Charles Scribner's Sons, 1986. Bantam Books paperback edition, 1987. 417p. bibliog.

A compilation of bits and pieces of history, geology, wildlife biology and other sciences, woven together with Lopez's own experiences to form very personal impressions of the Arctic. It covers a number of specific locations within the North American Arctic, including some in Alaska. This widely read and influential book was on the *New York Times* best-seller list and was a Book-of-the-Month Club selection.

639 **Aurora borealis: the amazing northern lights.**
Syun-Ichi Akasofu. Anchorage: Alaska Geographic Society, 1979. 95p. bibliog.

This popular explanation of northern lights is written by one of the world's foremost experts.

640 **The aurora watcher's handbook.**
Neil Davis. Fairbanks, Alaska: University of Alaska Press, 1992. 230p. bibliog.

The aurora belt passes through Fairbanks, where there has been a long history of research on the 'northern lights'. Davis has spent much of his scientific career studying this phenomenon and in explaining science to the layman through the popular press. He brings these talents together in this well-illustrated guide which makes extensive use of photographs from space and of explanatory drawings.

641 **Bidarka.**
George Dyson. Edmonds, Washington: Alaska Northwest, 1986. 203p.

A bidarka is a variety of kayak traditionally used in the Aleutians and elsewhere in Alaska. These small craft are technologically suited for hunting sea otters and for travelling great distances in extreme weather conditions. Dyson has made a detailed study of the historical use and design of these vessels and has created modern versions using modern materials.

642 **Science in the Subarctic: trappers, traders, and the Smithsonian Institution.**
Debra Lindsay. Washington, DC: Smithsonian Institution, 1993. 176p. maps.

The Smithsonian Institution was an early supporter of the collection of natural science and anthropological specimens. This book covers the period from 1850 to 1870, when men such as Robert Kennicott were sent to the Mackenzie region and Russian America. This effort was organized by Spencer Baird, the assistant secretary in charge of natural history at the Smithsonian. There were a number of innovations made in fieldwork techniques, including the systematic use of native collectors.

643 **The skin boats of Saint Lawrence Island, Alaska.**
Stephen R. Braund. Seattle, Washington: University of Washington Press, 1988. 141p.

This is a study of over 30 umiaks [skin boats] conducted in 1973-74. Braund shows how the design has changed over time and how this reflected changing technological and societal needs.

644 **Where salmon come to die: an autumn on Alaska's rain coast.**
Leon Kolankiewicz. Boulder, Colorado: Pruett, 1993. 126p.

Kolankiewicz was hired as a salmon biologist to count salmon on a lake on Chichagof Island in 1982. This is the account of a naturalist, living mostly alone in a frame tent, counting salmon escapements, and observing his natural surroundings.

Literature

Selected gold-rush tales

645 **Alaska in the American literary imagination: a literary history of frontier Alaskan literature.**
Marilyn Jody. Indiana University PhD dissertation, 1969 (Available from University Microfilms International, Ann Arbor, Michigan). 255p. bibliog.

This is one of the few studies of the literature of Alaska. It is especially useful in its treatment of the 'dime novels' about Alaska and the Klondike with such characters as Diamond Dick, Jr., Klondike Kit, Nick Carter, and Fred Fearnot.

646 **The Call of the wild, White Fang, and other stories.**
Jack London. New York: Penguin, 1981. 410p.

Jack London is arguably the best known of all fiction writers of the gold-rush era. He came to Skagway in 1897, went to Dawson and Stewart in the Yukon Territory and lived in Rampart and Nome Alaska before returning south. His novels and stories have been reprinted numerous times. He published *A daughter of the snows* and *Children of the frost* in 1902. His most famous novel is *Call of the wild*, published in 1903, followed by *Seawolf* in 1904 and *White Fang* in 1905. Others followed and a number of his works have been made into motion pictures.

647 **The iron trail.**
Rex Beach. New York: Harper, 1913. 390p.

This story involves rival railroad construction efforts to forge a route to the interior of Alaska with its copper and coal. It is based upon the actual construction of the Copper River and Northwestern Railway from Cordova to the Kennicott copper mine near McCarthy. The rival town, Valdez, is here called Cortez and the names of the players and companies have been changed at will. Beach wrote a number of other novels. His themes such as gold mining, the salmon industry, and seal poaching occur in a variety of locales, including Rampart, Sitka, Bristol Bay and Glacier Bay.

648 **Short stories of Jack London: authorized one-volume edition.**
Jack London, edited by Earle Labor, Robert C. Leitz, III, I. Milo Shepard. New York: Macmillan, 1990. 738p.

London wrote much about the north country, but that was not his only subject matter. Although his short stories are not as generally well known as his novels (see item no. 646), there were many.

649 **Spawn of the North.**
Barrett Willoughby. Cambridge, Massachusetts: Riverside Press, 1932. 349p.

This novel is set in Southeast Alaska, and concerns the salmon fishery and the fish-canning industry. It has the usual cast of Willoughby heroes and villains, and the usual striking heroine, in this case one Dian Turlon.

650 **The Spell of the Yukon.**
Robert Service. New York: Dodd, Mead & Company, 1944. 126p.

This volume of poetry was first published in 1907 and has been republished in numerous volumes. Service worked in Dawson as a bank clerk. His lines have come to represent the gold rush in the Klondike and Alaska for generations of readers through such poems as 'The Shooting of Dan McGrew', 'The Cremation of Sam McGee', 'The Spell of the Yukon', and 'The Land that God forgot'.

651 **The spoilers.**
Rex Beach. New York: Burt, 1905. 313p.

One of the best of Beach's numerous novels and stories about Alaska. It is set in the Nome gold rush and involves 'claim jumping' by a group of audacious thieves who are supported by a dishonest judge, district attorney and US marshal. It is based upon a true story, with an added romantic sub-plot to heighten reader interest.

652 **The trail-eater.**
Barrett Willoughby. New York; London: G. P. Putnam's Sons, 1929. 400p.

A popular novel set in gold-rush Nome. It is about the 400-mile All-Alaska Sweepstakes sled-dog race, and is based upon the racing career of Allan Alexander Allan.

Selected fiction and poetry

653 **Alaska.**
James A. Michener. New York: Random House, 1988. 868p.

Michener's novel on Alaska has enjoyed enormous commercial success. It is no doubt the most commonly read work for those who would like a first introduction to the state. Some Alaskans are troubled by this novel, because it is never very clear where fact ends (and there are many facts) and fiction begins. Michener starts with the geological creation of what would become Alaska, moves through the lives of prehistoric beasts, to the peopling of Alaska over the Bering Land Bridge, through the discovery and exploitation of Alaska's furs by the Russians, to the gold rush, salmon fisheries and, finally, the oil boom with all of its unresolved social issues.

654 **An Alaskan reader, 1867-1967.**
Compiled and edited by Ernest Gruening. New York: Meredith Press, 1966. 443p.

This is a selection from 48 authors of fiction, non-fiction and poetry. Senator Gruening (as he was at the time of writing it) prepared this volume in celebration of the Alaska purchase centennial.

655 **Astoria, or anecdotes of an enterprise beyond the Rocky Mountains.**
Washington Irving, edited with an introduction by E. W. Todd. Norman, Oklahoma: University of Oklahoma Press, 1964. 556p. bibliog. (American Exploration and Travel Series, no. 44).

Originally published in 1836 and in numerous editions since then, this is probably the first fictional mention of Alaska in America. The inspiration for this novel was the fur trade activity of John Jacob Astor, an American entrepreneur who established a trading post in the Pacific Northwest. The novel depicts a hard-drinking and cunning Alexander Baranov, who headed the Russian establishment at Sitka.

656 **The big garage on Clear Shot: growing up, growing old, and going fishing at the End of the Road.**
Tom Bodett. New York: W. Morrow, 1990. 299p.

Bodett is a nationally broadcast radio humorist who bases his written work on a set of characters in his town of Homer, on the Kenai Peninsula. His earlier books include *As far as you can go without a passport*, *Small comforts*, and *The end of the road.*

657 **Chief Stephen's parky: one year in the life of an Athapascan girl.**
Ann Chandonnet, illustrations by Janette Kasl. Niwot, Colorado: Roberts Rhinehart, 1993. 81p.

This is fiction for children about the Tanaina Athapascans at the time that gold-rush white men first came to the Cook Inlet region in large numbers (smaller numbers of Russians had been active there for well over a century). The 18-year-old protagonist, Olga, takes a year to create an unusually elaborate and elegant squirrel-fur parka for her husband, who is 25 and a chief. This story is rich in the authentic detail of everyday life and customs.

658 **The curious eat themselves: an Alaska mystery.**
John Straley. New York: Soho Press, 1993. 264p.

This tale of mystery is set in Sitka, Ketchikan and places in between, in Southeast Alaska. It involves environmentalists, lawyers, large corporations and a cast of odd characters. It is witty and well written.

659 **Dead in the water.**
Dana Stabenow. New York: Berkley Books, 1993. 217p.

A murder mystery set on a Bering Sea crab boat. The protagonist, Kate Shugak, works undercover for the Anchorage District Attorney. This is the third book in the 'Kate Shugak mystery' series.

660 **Ice palace.**
Edna Ferber. Garden City, New York: Doubleday, 1958. 411p.

In its day a best-seller, this novel depicts Alaska on the eve of statehood. Although the names are, of course, changed, the principal characters and places are recognizable. The plot centres on the education of a girl brought up by two strongly opposed grandfathers, each representing different sides of almost every political and economic issue, including the nature and future of Alaska.

661 **Murder on the Iditarod trail.**
Sue Henry. New York: Atlantic Monthly Press, 1991. 278p.

This is a tightly written murder mystery set around a dog race. It is carefully researched and the details of mushing on the race from Anchorage to Nome ring true.

662 **The owl in the mask of the dreamer: collected poems.**
John Haines. St. Paul, Minnesota: Greywolf Press, 1993. 251p.

John Haines is probably Alaska's best-known living poet. Most, but not all, of his poetry relates to Alaska, especially to his many years as a homesteader and trapper near Fairbanks, at Richardson. In addition to his previously published poetry, he has also written essays on these topics (see item no. 670).

663 **The sea runners.**
Ivan Doig. New York: Atheneum, 1982. 279p.

This is a carefully researched novel set in Russian America in the early 1850s. A group of four Scandinavians escape their service obligations in New Archangel (Sitka) and work their way south towards the Columbia River in a canoe. The voyage proves to be a long and difficult 1,000-mile journey and only two of them make it all the way.

664 **Sitka.**
Louis L'Amour. New York: Appleton-Century-Crofts, 1957. 247p.

L'Amour was one of America's most prolific writers of 'western' novels, publishing several hundred stories and books during his career. Many have been turned into motion pictures. Although set in the last years of Russian America, the plot follows a familiar 'western' pattern. This time there are Russian princesses, dour Russian admirals, renegade fur traders, and plucky American merchants aboard schooners. Many liberties have been taken with historical accuracy.

665 **Two old women: an Alaskan legend of betrayal, courage and survival.**

Velma Wallis. Fairbanks, Alaska: Epicenter Press, 1993. 145p.

This is a Gwitch'in tale told to Wallis by her mother. It involves a period of famine, when a band chief decides that two elderly women must be left behind in order for the remainder to survive. The women survive and triumph, using their wits and courage. Without any outside help they fashion what they need, including shelter and implements such as snow-shoes and sleds. This work has sold very well and, at the time of its release, it won the 1993 Western States Book Award for creative non-fiction.

666 **The war canoe.**

Jamie S. Bryson. Anchorage: Alaska Northwest, 1990. 180p.

A work of juvenile fiction about a Tlingit youth who rediscovers his past and builds a traditional Tlingit war canoe. The tale is set in and around Wrangell, Alaska.

Essays and letters

667 **The life and letters of John Muir.**

William Frederic Badè. Boston, Massachusetts: Houghton Mifflin, 1924. 2 vols.

These letters are also to be found in *Writings of John Muir*, volumes 9 and 10 of the Sierra Edition and Manuscript Edition of Muir's works. John Muir was a leading conservationist of his day and a true ancestor of today's environmental movement. Although he spent considerable time in Alaska, most of his writings are of lower latitudes. It is interesting to compare these edited texts to those in the Engberg and Merrell edition (see item no. 156).

668 **Personal exposures.**

Rex Beach. New York: Harper, 1940. 303p.

Rex Beach wrote a number of historical novels and stories about Alaska, often with pointed political content. They include *The goose woman and other stories*, *The iron trail* (see item no. 647), *The silver horde*, *The spoilers* (item no. 651), *The winds of chance*, *Valley of thunder*, *The barrier*, and *World in his arms*. Although he eventually moved to New York, most of his reminiscences are of his life in the frontier towns and gold camps he visited in Alaska, and his various anecdotes are related to that period.

669 **A republic of rivers: three centuries of nature writing from Alaska and the Yukon.**

Compiled by John A. Murray. New York: Oxford University Press, 1990. 325p. bibliog.

These forty-eight selections are divided into three broad categories, based on chronology: 1841-1855, the age of exploration; 1867-1958, the age of exploitation;

and 1959-1989, the age of environmentalism. An index map locates the area described by each contribution. Murray's introduction and his brief explanatory notes for each selection place these readings in context. In attempting to cover all regions over several centuries, the readings are necessarily brief, but his bibliography leads the reader to longer works.

670 **The stars, the snow, the fire: twenty-five years in the northern wilderness: a memoir.**
John Meade Haines. St. Paul, Minnesota: Greywolf Press, 1989. 182p.

Haines has a well-established national reputation and is one of Alaska's leading poets. Starting in 1947, he spent twenty-five years, in several segments, at a homestead at Richardson, south of Fairbanks. He ran a trapline and observed the animals and other natural phenomena around him. He evokes a strong sense of place.

Native traditions

671 **A Dena'ina legacy-k'tl'egh'i sukudu: the collected writings of Peter Kalifornski.**
Edited by James Kari, Alan Boraas. Fairbanks, Alaska: Alaska Native Language Center, University of Alaska, 1991. 485p. maps. bibliog.

Kalifornski was one of the leading authors of native tradition of the generation just past. His tales and accounts are published here in both the Tanaina and English languages. His home was on the Kenai Peninsula and he belonged to the Kenai people. He writes especially of how they used to live, their traditions, the place-names, the language, as well as events in his own life. Songs and poems are included. Peter and his sisters were the last speakers of the Outer Inlet dialect of the Dena'ina language.

672 **The Eskimo storyteller: folktales from Noatak, Alaska.**
Edwin S. Hall. Knoxville, Tennessee: University of Tennessee Press, 1975. 491p. bibliog.

Edwin Hall, an anthropologist, and Leona Hall spent a year (1964-65) in the village of Noatak, as well as additional summers of fieldwork, in preparation for this collection of 188 folk tales. Hall includes brief autobiographies of the informants and a chapter of analysis. The book is illustrated with drawings by Alaska artist Claire Fejes.

673 **Eyak texts.**
Translated and edited by Michael E. Krauss. College, Alaska: University of Alaska and Massachusetts Institute of Technology, 1970. 250p.

The last Eyak speaker has recently passed away. Krauss makes use of and evaluates earlier efforts at collection. He then extensively expands these, using his own attempts at collection in the 1960s. The Eyak text and the English translations are printed side by side. There are 72 texts grouped into units: raven cycle, animals, people and animals, mythical beings, cautionary tales, legends of people, wars, witches and shamans, and miscellaneous ethnographic.

674 **Haa Shuk, our ancestors: Tlingit oral narratives.**

Compiled by Nora Dauenhauer, Richard Dauenhauer. Seattle, Washington: University of Washington Press and Sealaska Heritage Foundation, 1987. 514p. map.

This is a collection of fifteen narrative texts with translations from oral traditions recorded from the 1960s to 1984. A detailed biography and photograph is included for each of the twelve narrators.

675 **Haa Tumunáagu Yís, for healing our spirit: Tlingit oratory.**

Edited by Nora Marks Dauenhauer, Richard Dauenhauer. Seattle, Washington: University of Washington Press, for the Sealaska Heritage Foundation, 1990. 569p. bibliog.

Speeches form an important part of Tlingit literature. The Dauenhauers do a masterful job of introducing and annotating this body of 32 speeches, rendered in both Tlingit and English. There are photographs of many of the speakers, and the 153-page introduction provides many insights into Tlingit culture and tradition.

676 **In honor of Eyak: the art of Anna Nelson Harry.**

Compiled and edited with introduction and commentary by Michael E. Krauss. Fairbanks, Alaska: Alaska Native Language Center, University of Alaska, 1982. 157p.

Anna Nelson Harry was one of the last Eyak speakers. She was a skilled storyteller whose tales were first written down by Frederica de Laguna in 1933, although not in the Eyak language. Krauss began working intensively with Eyak during the early 1960s. This book includes ten of the sixty texts that Krauss has collected. The texts are published in both Eyak and English.

677 **People of Kauwerak: legends of the northern Eskimo.**

William A. Oquilluk with the assistance of Laurel L. Bland. Anchorage: Alaska Pacific University Press, 1981. 2nd ed. 242p.

These legends are based upon oral traditions in Northwestern Alaska written down over a lifetime and developed into a manuscript by 1971. Most of the stories come originally from Oquilluk's grandfather. He tells of the four great disasters of the past, each nearly destroying the population. The last was the great flu epidemic after the First World War. The fifth disaster would be the forgetting of the past by the Eskimo.

678 **Raven tells stories: an anthology of Alaskan Native writing.**

Edited by Joseph Bruchac. Greenfield Center, New York: Greenfield Review Press, 1991. 224p.

This is a collection from the works of twenty-three native writers. Each author's selection is prefaced by a brief autobiographical introduction and, in almost all cases, a photograph. There is one play and several essays, but most contributions are in the form of poetry.

679 **Shadow of the hunter: stories of Eskimo life.**
Richard K. Nelson. Chicago, Illinois: University of Chicago Press, 1980. 282p.

These are fictional stories written by an anthropologist who has conducted extensive fieldwork among the Eskimos of Alaska's North Slope. A full year's cycle of hunting is followed in the lives of the hunters and their families.

680 **Tales of Ticasuk: Eskimo legends and stories.**
Collected and written by Ticasuk (Emily Ivanoff Brown), illustrated by Eugene Totten, Mary Lou Totten. Fairbanks, Alaska: University of Alaska Press, 1987. 134p.

An anthology of 24 folk tales of the Unaliq Eskimos (Ticasuk's people) who originally lived on the coast of Bering Sea and a part of the Seward Peninsula. The author taught for over thirty years in rural Alaska and spent the years after her retirement studying at the University of Alaska Fairbanks and writing about matters related to her native culture.

681 **Tlingit myths and texts.**
John Reed Swanton. Washington, DC: GPO, 1909; New York: Johnson Reprint, 1970. 451p. (Smithsonian Institution, Bureau of American Ethnology, Bulletin no. 39).

These texts were gathered in Sitka and Wrangell in early 1904 and number over 100. Most were acquired in English, but an orthography was developed for printing the Tlingit language as well. This compilation has remained an essential text for the study of Tlingit literature and folklore.

682 **Ugiurangmiut Quliapyuit King Island tales: Eskimo history and legends from Bering Strait.**
Compiled and edited by Lawrence D. Kaplan with assistance from Margaret Yocom, photographs by Bernard R. Hubbard. Fairbanks, Alaska: University of Alaska Press, 1988. 259p. bibliog.

King Island is a 2½-mile-long island in the Bering Sea. It has no beaches, and the village was built on a steep rock slide. By 1960 most of the villagers had moved to Nome. These stories were gathered from King Islanders who had lived there while the village still flourished. All were born between 1904 and 1918. The tales themselves are rendered in the native language, with accompanying English translations. The photographs depict many aspects of life on King Island during the late 1930s.

Arts

683 Alaska Native arts and crafts.

Edited by Penny Rennick. Anchorage: Alaska Geographic, 1985. 209p. bibliog. (*Alaska Geographic*, vol. 12, no. 3).

Distinct regional traditions are described: the Eskimos, the Athabascans, the Aleuts, and the Northwest Coast. Coverage starts with archaeological finds and continues through contemporary living artists. This can be quite complex – for example, there are more than 20 discrete groups of Eskimo in Alaska, but the contributors are successful in indicating diversity without allowing the general account to be lost in detail.

684 Alaskan paintings of Fred Machetanz.

Introduction by Russ Riemann. New York; Toronto; London: Peacock Press, 1977. [unpaginated].

Forty plates are reproduced of typical Alaskan subjects including walrus hunting, sleds and sled dogs, old prospectors, polar bears and mountain scenery.

685 Aleut and Eskimo art: tradition and innovation in South Alaska.

Dorothy Jean Ray. Seattle, Washington: University of Washington Press, 1981. 251p. bibliog.

Another of Ray's books describing regional art among Eskimos and Aleuts. Here, she covers the decorative and sculptural arts of Aleut, Yupik and Pacific Eskimos from the first contact with Europeans up to 1979. The text is accompanied by 219 annotated illustrations, most depicting artefacts in a multitude of public and private collections.

686 Aleut art: unangam aquqaadanin, unangam of the Aleutian Archipelago.
Lydia Black. Anchorage: Aang Angagin, Aleutian/Pribilov Islands Association, 1982. 193p. bibliog.

Black's extensively illustrated study brings widely scattered collections of Aleut art together. Coverage starts with prehistoric traditions and then continues through the early contact years and beyond to contemporary artistic creations.

687 Art and Eskimo power: the life and times of Alaskan Howard Rock.
Lael Morgan. Fairbanks, Alaska: Epicenter Press, 1988. 258p.

A political biography of Rock, an Eskimo artist who was actively engaged in opposing the Atomic Energy Commission plan to build a harbour near Kotzebue by using nuclear explosions. He founded the *Tundra Times*, a state-wide native newspaper and played a major role leading to the passage of the Alaska Native Claims Settlement Act.

688 Art in the life of the Northwest coast Indians, with a catalog of the Rasmussen Collection of Northwestern Indian art at the Portland Art Museum.
Erna Gunther. Portland, Oregon: Portland Art Museum, 1966. 275p. bibliog.

Using the collection gathered by Axel Rasmussen from 1926 to 1945 as examples, Gunther describes the cultural setting of these objects, the art used in daily occupations, art's role in ceremonial life, the place of art in secret societies, art made for strangers, and the religious significance of art. There is a chapter on how the collection was assembled by Rasmussen, at one time Superintendent of Schools at Wrangell, Alaska, and later at Skagway. The book is extensively illustrated with photographs of the collection.

689 Art of the Northern Tlingit.
Aldona Jonaitis. Seattle, Washington: University of Washington Press, 1986. 188p. map. bibliog.

This anthropological study is based upon artefacts collected in Klukwan during the late nineteenth century by George Emmons and Louis Shotridge. The author is concerned about the relationship of secular art to the religious art of the shaman. She argues that there are artistic hierarchies that are counterparts to Tlingit social hierarchies.

690 Artists of the tundra and the sea.
Dorothy Jean Ray. Seattle, Washington: University of Washington Press, 1961. 170p. bibliog. Paperback edition with corrections, 1980.

Eskimo ivory carving in Northwest Alaska goes back at least 2,000 years. There was a resurgence of interest at the time of commercial whaling and the Nome gold rush in 1900, which established a commercial market for this Eskimo art form. This had a tremendous influence upon the nature of the carvings. Ray brings this long and varied tradition together, based upon her research conducted during the late 1940s and 1950s. There are numerous photographs of carvings and of the artists themselves at work.

691 **The Athapaskans: strangers of the North.**
Ottawa: National Museum of Man, National Museums of Canada, 1974. 208p. bibliog.

An international travelling exhibition was assembled from the collections of the National Museum of Man in Canada and the Royal Scottish Museum. The title essay is an excellent contribution by A. McFadyen Clark, with other contributions by William E. Taylor, Jr., Barrie Reynolds, and Dale Indiens. The catalogue is illustrated with 268 plates, some with multiple photographs. There is considerable material from the Canadian sub-arctic as well as from Alaska.

692 **The black canoe: Bill Reid and the spirit of Haida Gwaii.**
Robert Bringhurst. Seattle, Washington; Vancouver, British Columbia: University of Washington Press; Douglas & McIntyre, 1991. 173p. bibliog.

This is a description and treatise on the significance of a monumental Haida Indian bronze sculpture. About half of the book consists of photographs of the sculpture's creation, in its various versions and over a period of several years.

693 **Captured heritage: the scramble for Northwest Coast artifacts.**
Douglas Cole. Seattle, Washington: University of Washington Press, 1985. 373p. maps.

Coverage extends from British Columbia to Southeast Alaska. Cole examines the rivalry for native artefacts which was intense between 1850 and 1900 among American and European museums and private collectors. The book is superbly researched and written.

694 **The Chilkat dancing blanket.**
Cheryl Samuel. Seattle, Washington: Pacific Search Press, 1982. 234p. bibliog.

This is a history of the blankets which are woven from mountain goat wool and cedar bark and the techniques used to weave them. The blankets serve as ceremonial robes. The technique was adapted from the Tsimshian by the Tlingits. The blankets would typically take six months to weave and the right to wear them was an inherited privilege. Samuel, herself a skilled weaver, describes the entire process, accompanied by illustrative drawings and photographs. She covers the evolution of this technique in depth.

695 **Early maritime artists of the Pacific Northwest coast, 1741-1841.**
John Frazier Henry. Seattle, Washington; London: University of Washington Press, 1984. 240p.

This collection includes artists from Russian, British, French, Spanish and American voyages. Reproductions include both previously published and manuscript drawings, paintings, engravings and water-colours. Although scenes as far south as the Oregon–California border are depicted, Alaska is well represented. Many are of ethnographic interest, being the first images of Alaska Natives during the early contact era.

696 **Eskimo art.**

Dorothy Jean Ray. Seattle, Washington: University of Washington Press, 1977. 298p. bibliog. (Henry Art Gallery Index of Art in the Pacific Northwest, no. 11).

An introductory overview of art of the Alaska Eskimo. It includes 307 black-and-white reproductions of art and photographs of contemporary artists at work. The art work includes a number of ivory engravings as well as work done in other media such as crayon and water-colour sketches and whalebone carvings.

697 **Eskimo masks: art and ceremony.**

Dorothy Jean Ray, photographs by Alfred A. Blaker. Seattle, Washington: University of Washington Press, 1967. 246p. bibliog.

The core photographs are of masks housed in the extensive collection at the Lowie Museum at the University of California at Berkeley. However, Ray's text deals with Eskimo masks in general, especially with the religious significance of the objects of art. The book includes seventy plates of photographs of masks, which are accompanied by extensive descriptions and annotations.

698 **The far north: 2,000 years of American Indian and Eskimo art.**

Henry B. Collins, Frederica de Laguna, Edmund Carpenter, Peter Stone. Washington, DC: National Museum of Art for the Anchorage Historical and Fine Arts Museum, 1973. 290p. bibliog.

This is an elaborate catalogue for an exhibition which was mounted in Washington, Anchorage, Portland and Fort Worth. It serves the layman as an excellent introduction to and overview of Alaskan native art. Art and artefacts were lent by 35 museums in North America and Europe. There are 365 plates and additional illustrations.

699 **From skins, trees, quills and beads: the work of nine Athabaskans.**

Edited by Jan Steinbright. [n.p.]: Institute of Alaska Native Arts, 1985. 106p. bibliog.

There are six accounts depicting the work of nine Athabascan traditional artists. The subjects include birch-bark baskets, fish nets, snowshoes and fish traps, willow-root baskets, skin sewing, and quillwork and beadwork. In each case, photographer Charles Backus has documented the gathering and working of natural materials.

700 **Glory remembered: wooden headgear of the Alaska sea hunters.**

Lydia Black, S. V. Ivanov. Juneau: Alaska State Museum, 1991. 173p. map. bibliog.

The creation of these native wooden hats from the Aleutian Islands, Kodiak, Bristol Bay and Norton Sound involved wood working, ivory carving and painting. Black began by annotating Ivanov's 'Aleut hunting headgear and its ornamentation', first published in 1930 and reprinted here: she then expanded upon this. The authors explain the significance of the various shapes and sizes of hats, with details concerning geographical distributions and the uses and meaning of this headgear in native culture. The text is accompanied by numerous photographs and drawings.

701 **Looking at Indian art of the Northwest Coast.**
Hilary Stewart. Seattle, Washington: University of Washington Press, 1979. 111p. map. bibliog.

Two-dimensional Northwest Coast art, including that of the Alaskan Tlingits, is broken down into components, starting with form and line. Conventions for anatomical features then build when combined to form design motifs and complete animals. Three-dimensional objects with these features are also shown.

702 **Northern Athapaskan art: a beadwork tradition.**
Kate C. Duncan. Seattle, Washington: University of Washington Press, 1989. 224p. map. bibliog.

This richly illustrated text depicts the five varieties of regional styles and techniques.

703 **Painting in the North: Alaskan art in the Anchorage Museum of History and Art.**
Kesler Woodward. Anchorage: Anchorage Museum Association, 1993. 159p. bibliog.

Woodward's book serves a dual purpose. It is a description of the holdings of one of Alaska's major museums, and it is at the same time a history of Alaskan painting. Coverage starts with the first European contact in 1741, proceeds through the art of the exploring expeditions in Alaska through to the near present, which includes a number of living artists.

704 **Raven: a collection of woodcuts.**
Dale Burlison DeArmond. Anchorage: Alaska Northwest, 1975. 128p.

Alaskan artist DeArmond created these illustrations for stories adapted from John Swanton's *Tlingit myths and texts* (q.v.) originally published in 1909.

705 **Rie Muñoz, Alaskan artist.**
Introduced by Judy Shuler. Anchorage: Alaska Northwest, 1984. 74p.

Muñoz is a highly successful print-maker who produces bright and generally cheerful scenes of everyday life, frequently with native themes. Approximately seventy of her prints are reproduced.

706 **Secrets of Eskimo skin sewing.**
Edna Wilder. Anchorage: Alaska Northwest Publishing, 1976. 125p.

Wilder was the first native instructor in this speciality craft at the University of Alaska. It is a 'how to' book of instructions that includes traditional toys and a brief introduction to grass baskets and rugs.

707 **Sydney Laurence, painter of the North.**
Kesler E. Woodward. Seattle, Washington: University of Washington Press in association with the Anchorage Museum of History and Art, 1990. 140p. bibliog.

An exhibition catalogue with a wide distribution, in which 123 paintings are reproduced as colour plates. Laurence is generally considered to be Alaska's leading landscape painter of his generation, but by no means all of his paintings are of Alaska. He continued to paint Alaskan scenes while living between Los Angeles, Seattle and Anchorage until his death in 1940.

708 **Totem poles.**
Hilary Stewart. Seattle, Washington: University of Washington Press, 1980. 192p. maps.

Following a brief explanation of their general history and construction, 113 totem poles are described in detail. Each is accompanied by a drawing. These totem poles are located along the Northwest Coast in British Columbia and Alaska.

709 **Wilderness: a journal of quiet adventure in Alaska.**
Rockwell Kent. New York: Halcyon House, 1920. 217p. Numerous subsequent printings.

The journal of a year spent at Fox Island in Resurrection Bay on the Kenai Peninsula. Illustrated by 44 of the artist's drawings. He has done other work on other northern themes, most notably, Greenland.

710 **William D. Berry: 1954-1956 Alaskan field sketches.**
Compiled by Elizabeth Berry. Fairbanks, Alaska: University of Alaska Press, 1989. 230p.

This is the work of an artist and wildlife illustrator seeking insight into animals, including birds and large mammals in their habitat. These several hundred drawings, including 48 pages in colour, were selected from over 2,000 sketches that the artist made in McKinley Park, at Point Hope, and elsewhere in Alaska.

Recreation

Hunting and fishing

711 **Alaska bear tales.**

Larry Kaniut. Anchorage: Alaska Northwest, 1983. 318p. bibliog.

Selected bear hunting and bear encounter tales are told from over 200 accounts that the author gathered between 1975 and 1983.

712 **Alaska bear trails.**

Harold McCracken. Garden City, New York: Doubleday, 1931. 260p.

McCracken made a number of trips to Alaska and wrote about Alaska and the West prolifically during his lifetime. He turned increasingly from hunting with a gun to hunting with a camera. He used his photography and the collection of hunting specimens for museums to help finance his trips. This is a compilation of several of them.

713 **Alaska game trails with a master guide.**

Compiled by Charles J. Keim. Anchorage: Alaska Northwest Publishing Company, 1977. 310p.

A collection of short pieces by 38 authors concerning the master big-game guide Hal Waugh, an advocate of fair chase hunting, with its accompanying obligations for guides to abide by a set of rigorous standards.

714 **Alaska safari.**

Harold Schetzle. Anchorage: Great Northwest, 1989. 366p. bibliog.

A master big-game guide, Schetzle draws upon his experience to help novice hunters select where to hunt, learn how to hunt and know what to bring on the hunt. He begins with a brief history of big-game hunting and guiding in Alaska, which began shortly after 1900. He illustrates his advice with numerous tales and anecdotes of past hunts, both his own and those of others.

715 **Alaska–Yukon trophies won and lost.**
G. O. Young. Huntington, West Virgina: Standard Publication, 1947. 273p. bibliog.

Young travelled to Alaska in 1919 as a member of a three-man hunting party arranged through the mail. They did not all know each other previously, but details were overseen by the Territorial governor, Thomas R. Riggs. They started their hunt in McCarthy and then made their way through the Wrangell Mountains and through the Yukon Territory to Whitehorse. It was an extremely elaborate hunt and included some unexpected hardships after their hand-made boat sank while floating down a white-water river.

716 **Alaskan's how to handbook.**
Joe Dart. Fairbanks, Alaska: Interior Alaska Trappers Association, 1981. 124p.

If you ever wondered how to build a fishwheel, make snowshoes, weave a salmon net, build sleds, trap fox, make a canoe and fashion an air-tight stove, this is the place to look. This is for Alaskans and others who need practical advice for the great outdoors through the medium of diagrams, drawings, and practical explanation.

717 **Arctic hunter.**
Bud Helmericks. Boston, Massachusetts: Little, Brown, 1955. 142p.

This is a fictionalized account of two young men on a spring hunt on the Arctic coast. One is Eskimo and one Caucasian. The author lived extensively in the Arctic and has written a number of books about it. The value of this text is in the detailed descriptions of hunting techniques, with numerous drawings depicting hunting implements such as harpoons and lances, techniques such as various methods of hunting seals through the ice, and the complicated nature of sea ice.

718 **Big game trails in the far north.**
Phillip F. Neuweiler, edited with an introduction by Douglas G. LaPasta. Anchorage: Great Northwest, 1989. 316p.

These are the notes and diaries, kept over a period of fifty years and published posthumously, of a very accomplished big-game hunter. Every year he would spend a month, six weeks or even longer hunting in Alaska or Canada.

719 **Flies for Alaska: a guide to buying and tying.**
Anthony J. Route. Estes Park, Colorado: Spring Creek Press, 1991. 160p.

This is a manual for the hobby construction of artificial fishing lures. Route includes flies for trout, char and salmon.

720 **How to catch Alaska's trophy sportfish.**
Christopher Batin. Fairbanks, Alaska: Alaska Angler Publications, 1988. rev. ed. 368p.

This is a practical guide organized by species that addresses the interests of both saltwater and freshwater fishing. Numerous diagrams and sketch maps show locations.

Starting with king salmon, through small salmon varieties, and on to pike, rockfish and halibut, the appropriate gear and technique is covered in detail.

721 **Hunting in Alaska: a comprehensive guide.**
Christopher Batin. Fairbanks, Alaska: Alaska Angler Publications, 1987. 415p. maps.

Batin organizes his book by species, and then by the regions that form their habitat. He covers big game: moose, caribou, deer, elk, bear, sheep, mountain goats, bison, wolf, and musk oxen. He also discusses small game and provides a guide to planning the hunt and the care of meat and trophies during and after the hunt itself. Some of the regulatory details have changed since 1987, but this remains the best practical general hunting guide for Alaska.

722 **My lost wilderness: adventures of an Alaskan hunter and guide.**
Ralph W. Young. Piscataway, New Jersey: Winchester Press, 1983. 191p.

Young was an active big-game guide in Southeast Alaska for over thirty years. He hunted a variety of game including bears, seals, and deer. He also trapped on occasion. Along the way he encountered a number of local personalities, such as 'Sockless George'. More than a few of his clients were also interesting personalities.

723 **Oh, shoot! Confessions of an agitated sportsman, with illustrations from photographs taken by the author.**
Rex Beach. New York: Harper, 1921. 281p.

Rex Beach wrote a substantial amount of fiction with Alaskan themes. Here, he writes of his personal experiences on various hunting trips. There is only one chapter on Alaska; the other hunts occur on the eastern seaboard and in Mexico. The Alaskan bear hunt that he chronicles is typical of the sport hunting in that era. This particular hunt started in Cordova during the time the Copper River Railway was under construction.

724 **On and off Alaskan trails.**
Dow Vawter Baxter, Benjamin Labaree, Willard Hildebrand, drawings by Carleton Angell. [n.p.]: privately published, 1937. 184p.

Although privately printed, this volume has been widely distributed. These three foresters travelled to Alaska to study Alaskan forests and forest diseases. The book is written in the form of a diary or journal with numerous comments on travel conditions, the camps that the authors made, what they ate every day and the forests they studied.

725 **Shadows on the tundra: Alaskan tales of predator, prey and man.**
Tom Walker. Harrisburg, Pennsylvania: Stackpole Books, 1990. 177p.

A contemporary Alaska nature writer, Walker considers the importance of the experience of hunting with both a rifle and a camera. He raises a number of important ethical issues related to the act of hunting and the relationship of humans to wild predators. He also touches upon the changes in hunting pressure and public policy issues from the 1960s to 1990.

726 **Staying alive in Alaska's wild: true adventures with bears, wolves, wolverines, beavers, seals, dogs, volcano, williwaws on Kodiak Island, Contact Point, Kamishak Bay and River, Tugidak Island.**
Andy Nault, transcribed and edited by Tee Loftin. Washington, DC: Tee Loftin Publishers, 1980. 210p.

Feeling the near-fatal effects of a life spent indoors and smoking heavily, a Montana bartender takes to the wilderness and clean living as a trapper. He learned about the wildlife in detail, and his book is illustrated with a number of his photographs.

727 **To far western Alaska for big game: being an account of two journeys to Alaska in search of adventure.**
Theodore R. Hubback. London; New York: R. Ward; C. Scribner's Sons, 1929. 232p. 3 maps.

Hubback wrote extensively about big-game hunting all over the world, including Africa and Malaya. In Alaska, he hunted on the Kenai Peninsula, the Alaska Peninsula, and the little-known hunting grounds between the Susitna and Kuskokwim rivers in the Alaska Range. It was then still possible to find grounds that had never before seen trophy hunters. The book is full of hunting companions, life in and out of camp, weather and travel conditions, observations of animal behaviour, and there are numerous photographs.

728 **Trail of the eagle: hunting Alaska with master guide Bud Conkle.**
Bud Conkle. Anchorage: Great Northwest Publication and Distribution Company, 1990.

Conkle chronicles hunts for bear, moose, caribou, mountain sheep and mountain goats.

729 **Two Dianas in Alaska.**
Agnes Herbert, A. Shikari. London; New York: J. Land Co., 1909. 316p.

Two British women, fresh from a hunting trip to Somaliland, decided to travel across North America for an Alaskan hunting expedition, based from a sealing schooner and crew that they hired for the purpose. For various reasons, they sailed on a commercial vessel instead, hiring help where needed and coming back with a number of hunting trophies from Kodiak, the Alaska Peninsula and the Susitna River. They hunted walrus, caribou, moose, mountain sheep and wolf – and took pictures of it all.

730 **We live in the Arctic.**
Constance Helmericks, Harmon Helmericks. London: Hodder and Stoughton, 1949. 321p.

The Helmerick family wrote a number of books in the 1940s and 1950s about homesteading, hunting and trapping north of the Yukon. On several occasions they came close to starvation when game was hard to find.

Mountaineering

731 **The ascent of Denali: first complete ascent of Mt. McKinley, highest peak in North America. Containing the original diary of Walter Harper, first man to achieve Denali's true summit.**
Hudson Stuck, Walter Harper, annotations by Bradford Washburn, Yvonne Mozee. Seattle, Washington: The Mountaineers, 1977. 251p.

Stuck originally published his classic account in 1914. He describes the earlier attempts, including the James Wickersham and Frederick Cook climbs. Walter Harper was a member of Stuck's party.

732 **Dangerous steps: Vernon Tejas and the solo winter ascent of Mount McKinley.**
Lewis Freedman. Harrisburg, Pennsylania: Stackpole Books, 1990. 200p.

An Anchorage mountaineering guide, Tejas completed the first successful winter solo climb in 1988. Others had died in the attempt at winter climbs, including the famous Japanese mountaineer, Naomi Uemura, who disappeared on his way back down in 1984. The author details how he did it and his adventures along the way.

733 **Descent.**
College, Alaska: Alaska Alpine Club, 1969- . semi-annual.

The Alaska Alpine Club was founded in Fairbanks in 1952. Since then, *Descent* has been published from six times a year until 1974, and between one and four times a year since then. The newsletter contains profiles of climbers, climbing accounts, and climbing notes on particular mountains and routes. The title of this somewhat irreverent little newsletter, *Descent*, is in contrast to the better-known general mountaineering magazine, *Ascent*, published by the Sierra Club.

734 **High Alaska: a historical guide to Denali, Mount Foraker and Mount Hunter.**
Jonathan Waterman. New York: American Alpine Club, 1988. 398p. bibliog.

Waterman's account is richly illustrated with climbing photographs, from a variety of photographers, including himself, and with route photographs by Bradford Washburn. Each route is drawn on the photographs, with all of the historical variations: the northern routes, the western routes, the Northwest Buttress, the West Rib, the South Buttress, Southeast Spur and every other possible route up McKinley. In every case the historical climbs are detailed. Foraker and Hunter are treated in a similar manner.

735 **Minus 148°: the winter ascent of Mt. McKinley.**
Art Davidson. New York: Norton, 1969. 218p.

A well-prepared group of mountaineers experienced extreme conditions, severe frostbite and even death as they made the first successful winter climb of McKinley. This is a mountaineering classic.

736 **Mount McKinley, icy crown of North America.**
Fred Beckey. Seattle, Washington: The Mountaineers, 1993. 319p. bibliog.

Beckey is a seasoned mountain climber who himself was a member of a party to pioneer the Northwest Buttress route to the top of Mount McKinley in 1954. This history not only utilizes his own experience and previous publications on climbing this peak, but also includes the results of a number of personal communications with other climbers. It contains extensive advice on climbing the mountain, including matters of equipment and survival preparedness. This is not something to be taken lightly: in 1992 eleven people died while climbing on this challenging mountain.

737 **Mount McKinley, the pioneer climbs.**
Terris Moore. College, Alaska: University of Alaska Press, 1967. 202p. maps. bibliog.

Terris Moore, an experienced mountain climber himself, served as President of the University of Alaska from 1949 to 1953. This has been for many years the most widely read account of the first expeditions. There is a great deal about the Dr. Cook controversy on his claims to have climbed the mountain. Moore personally knew many of the early climbers, and refers extensively to their accounts.

738 **Mount McKinley: the conquest of Denali.**
Bradford Washburn, David Roberts, preface by Ansel Adams. New York: Abrams, 1991. 260p. maps. bibliog.

No living person has been more closely linked to this mountain than Brad Washburn, the now-retired director of the Boston Museum of Science. He has climbed the mountain a number of times, and his wife, Barbara, is the first woman to have ascended McKinley. However, it is his photography and his mapping work that has contributed the most to our knowledge. He began his photographic work in the 1930s, strapped in a small plane with a 70-pound Fairchild K-6 camera that used 9½-inch-wide film in rolls 120 feet long. His systematic and thorough coverage made possible his extremely precise 1960 map of McKinley.

739 **The organization of an Alaskan expedition.**
Boyd N. Everett, Jr. Pasadena, California: Gorak Books, 1984. 112p. bibliog.

This is an updated version of a 1966 paper, a 'how to' manual for those thinking of climbing mountains in Alaska. Of special interest are personal preparation and acclimatization, equipment choices, climbing conditions and details necessary for living comfortably for periods of time in high mountain terrain. Alaska's principal climbing mountains are rated according to difficulty.

740 **The sourdough expedition; the story of the pioneer Alaskans who climbed Mt. McKinley in 1910.**
Edited by Terrence Cole. Anchorage: Alaska Northwest, 1985. 64p. bibliog. (Northern History Library).

Four miners from the Kantishna mining district, after some boasting in Bill McPhee's Washington Saloon in Fairbanks, decided to climb McKinley – two made it to the top of the North Peak. In so doing, they substantially disproved Frederick Cook's claim to have climbed McKinley in 1909. This is a collection of brief accounts concerning the climb, with an introduction, notes and illustrations added by Cole.

741 **To the top of Denali; climbing adventures on North America's highest peak.**
Bill Sherwonit. Anchorage: Alaska Northwest Books, 1990. 347p. bibliog.

Denali has been climbed thousands of times by now, but certain expeditions are especially interesting. Sherwonit is an outdoor writer for an Anchorage newspaper, and climbed the peak himself in 1987. He starts his account with the Wickersham attempt of 1903, and the 'sourdough' expedition of 1910, and then moves through summaries of the first full ascent by the Hudson Stuck party in 1913 to the expeditions of 1932, Bradford Washburn's work on the mountain, and on to various routes and even winter climbs. This well-written, brief, overview includes information for those interested in making the attempt themselves.

Dog mushing

742 **Dog driver: a guide for the serious musher.**
Miki Collins, Julie Collins. Loveland, Colorado: Alpine Publications, 1991. 385p. bibliog.

The most thorough overall guide on how to become a successful sled-dog racer, from the training of dogs and dog psychology, through the selection of equipment, to the health of man and beast on the trail. Extensively illustrated and practical, it also reads well for someone who is simply curious and will never actually run dogs. The Collins twins are well-known outdoor writers, living in the Lake Minchumina region of Interior Alaska.

743 **Dogs of the north.**
Edited by Penny Rennick. Anchorage: Alaska Geographic Society, 1987. 117p. (*Alaska Geographic*, vol. 14, no. 1).

This is a very general, copiously illustrated, introduction to dogs who are primarily, but not exclusively, used for freighting and pulling sleds.

744 **George Attla: the legend of the sled dog trail.**
Lewis Freedman. Harrisburg, Pennsylvania: Stackpole, 1993. 204p.

This is a biography of one of the first persons to make a living from racing and breeding sled dogs in Alaska. A sprint racer, Attla won ten Fur Rendezvous (Anchorage) and eight North Americans (Fairbanks), starting in 1958. At more than sixty years of age, he is still racing, despite a knee fused because of the effects of tuberculosis as a youth, and a host of other health problems. A native of Huslia, he now lives in North Pole, near Fairbanks.

745 **Iditarod classics: tales of the trail from the men and women who race across Alaska.**
Lew Freedman. Fairbanks, Alaska: Epicenter Press, 1992. 133p. map.
These stories from 21 mushers are extensively illustrated with poster art, individual portraits of mushers, and photographs of teams on the snow.

746 **Iditarod: the great race to Nome.**
Photographed by Jeff Schultz, text by Bill Sherwonit. Bothell, Washington: Alaska Northwest, 1991. 144p.
A popularly written history, with some information on techniques and a description of the competition.

747 **Iditarod spirit.**
Kim Heacox. Portland, Oregon: Graphic Arts Center, 1991. 144p. 2 maps.
A large-format popular treatment, featuring excellent photography.

748 **The last great race.**
Tim Jones. Seattle, Washington: Madrona, 1982. 266p.
The 1979 race is described for the general reader. It is attentive to human interest, but does not neglect the equipment used, the terrain and some historical background on the territory through which the race passes. This volume continues to be one of the most popular of the general race accounts.

749 **Race across Alaska: first woman to win the Iditarod tells her story.**
Libby Riddles, Tim Jones. Harrisburg, Pennsylvania: Stackpole, 1988. 239p.
This is a first-person account in a day-by-day format. There is considerable detail about the routine involved in managing dogs and equipment on a long-distance race.

750 **The speed mushing manual: how to train racing sled dogs.**
Jim Welch. Eagle River, Alaska: Sirius, 1989. 127p.
Training dogs to win is a year-around affair that includes summer exercise and the conditioning of man and dog. This is a basic manual for medium- and short-distance racing. It details the multi-year task of creating a good team through the selective breeding of champion dogs.

751 **Travellers of the cold: sled dogs of the far north.**
Dominique Cellura. Bothell, Washington: Alaska Northwest, 1990. English ed. 160p.
Cellura begins with an historical account of dogs utilized by natives and later by explorers in the Arctic and Antarctic, but especially in Alaska. She then moves to a general description of equipment, training, and dog racing in recent times in this extensively illustrated book.

Libraries, Museums and Archives

752 **Alaska library directory.**
Juneau: Alaska Library Association, 1977- . annual.

Libraries and library staff are listed, with phone and fax numbers. The directory is very useful in finding help in tracking down local and specialized information.

753 **Alaska and Polar Regions collection at the Elmer E. Rasmuson Library.**
Marvin W. Falk. *Alaska Journal*, vol. 9 (Winter 1979), p. 65-70.

This is a short history and description of Alaska's largest historical research collection.

754 **From the land of the totem poles: the Northwest Coast Indian Art Collection at the American Museum of Natural History.**
Aldona Jonaitis. Seattle, Washington; New York: University of Washington Press and American Museum of Natural History, 1988. 269p.

Filled with photographs and colour plates, it covers the area from Yakutat in Alaska south to the Juan de Fuca Straits. It also treats the history of the American Museum of Natural History collections.

755 **Guide to museums in Alaska.**
Auke Bay, Alaska: Museum Alaska Inc., 1984.

Entries are by region for 44 museums in Alaska. Each entry includes the museum's name, address, telephone number, hours, admission charges, governing authority, type of museum, collections, activities, facilities, and a brief description. Although somewhat dated, this guide remains quite useful.

Media

756 **The Associated Press stylebook for Alaska.**
Edited by Dean M. Gottehrer. Fairbanks, Alaska: Epicenter Press, 1991. 10p. maps. bibliog.

Very brief entries for common Alaskan topics are arranged in alphabetical order. There is a short pronunciation guide for place-names, just the sort of thing a journalist might need in order to avoid embarrassing errors when filing a story facing a fast-approaching deadline.

757 **An authentic voice in the technocratic wilderness: Alaskan Natives and the *Tundra Times*.**
Patrick Daley, Beverly James. *Journal of Communication*, vol. 36, no. 3 (Summer 1986), p. 10-30.

The *Tundra Times* was established to a large degree because of native opposition to Project Chariot, a planned nuclear explosion to create an artificial harbour in Northwest Alaska. Another formative issue was the increasing pressure upon native interests brought about by the newly established state of Alaska.

758 **A guide to Alaska's newspapers.**
Compiled by Phyllis Davis. Juneau: Gastineau Channel Centennial Association and Alaska Division of State Libraries and Museums, 1976. 92p. (Alaska State Library Historical Monograph, no. 4).

Newspapers have been published in the state since 1868. There have been several earlier published lists, such as the newspaper section of Wickersham's bibliography (see item no. 789). For a number of years there has been co-operative newspaper microfilming within the state, and Davis provides some of that basic information. The Alaska State Historical Library is at present engaged in the National Endowment for the Humanities United States Newspaper project and the results of new inventories, surveys, and cataloguing are now appearing on national electronic bibliographical utilities, and there will be a new 'newspaper tree' published at the end of the project.

759 **The KNOM/Father Jim Poole story.**
Louis L. Renner. Portland, Oregon: Binford & Mort, 1985. 150p.

A Jesuit missionary priest, Poole worked to create a Catholic radio station in Nome. It started broadcasting in 1971.

760 **KYUK in Bethel: pioneering Native broadcasting in Alaska.**
Jerry Brigham, Bruce L. Smith. *Northern Review*, vol. 11 (Winter 1993), p. 101-17.

KYUK was the first Native American-owned radio and television station in the United States. Radio broadcasts began in 1971 and television started in 1973 to a Yup'ik Eskimo population of 20,000 living in the 56,000-square-mile broadcasting area, primarily treeless tundra. Bethel itself has a population of about 2,500, with 52 small villages in the surrounding area. Bethel Broadcasting also started the *Tundra Drums*, the region's only major weekly paper, in 1974. The station produces unique bilingual programming.

761 **Newsletter and publications of Alaska Native corporations: a profile of changing concerns.**
David A. Hales, Tamara Lincoln. *Native Press Research Journal*, no. 2 (Summer 1986), p. 9-12.

As of 1986, twenty-two corporate or non-profit-making newsletters were being published. They were increasingly concerned with legislation and ethnocultural matters relating to natives and with education, health and urbanization.

762 **'Stroller' White: tales of a Klondike newsman.**
Compiled and edited by Robert N. DeArmond. Skagway, Alaska: Lynn Canal Publications, 1990. 2nd ed. 237p.

Elmer J. ('Stroller') White began working in Alaska on the *Skagway News* in 1898 and moved on to Dawson. There he published a column on life in the north in the *Klondike Nugget* in 1900. He continued on other newspapers in the Yukon and Alaska for the next thirty years, ending up in Douglas and Juneau. Much of his later work looks back to the gold rush. For this book, DeArmond has gathered selections of White's work in Douglas and neighbouring Juneau.

Directories

763 **Alaska Blue Book.**

Juneau: Alaska Division of State Libraries, Museums and Archives, 1963- . biennial.

This directory of state government includes information on individual state legislators, local governments, and major federal entities in Alaska. There is miscellaneous information on the economy and the educational system.

764 **Alaska coinage through the years.**

Maurice M. Gould, Kenneth Bressett, Kaye Dethridge. Racine, Wisconsin: Whitman Publishing, 1965. 2nd ed. 176p. bibliog.

A variety of tokens and coins have been issued in Alaska over the years, starting with Indian trade tokens and the Russian-American Company – the company was allowed to issue its own money, some of it on sealskin. Trade tokens were frequently needed as the supply of bills and coins was often insufficient for the needs of trade. Small photographs are used to illustrate the tokens.

765 **Alaska Corporate Directory.**

Juneau: Department of Commerce and Economic Development, State of Alaska. various formats. 1979- . annual.

Sometimes issued as a supplement to a previous year, this directory lists corporations registered in the State of Alaska. The listing includes corporation name, date of incorporation, the registered agent for each corporation and the official address.

766 **Alaska Education Directory.**

Juneau: Office of Data Management, Department of Education, State of Alaska, 1976- . annual.

An excellent source for locating information on both public and private educational institutions in the state. There are a number of useful lists, including school districts. Details are given of superintendents, divisions within the department, business managers, numbers of schools and other statistics, specialized district personnel, educational associations, and organizations.

767 **Alaska mining history.**
Virginia Doyle Heiner. Anchorage: University of Alaska Museum and the Office of History and Archaeology, Alaska Division of Parks, 1977. 463p. bibliog. (History and Archaeology Series, no. 17).

A reference work consisting of a selected annotated bibliography on Alaskan mining, an index of mining communities with variant names, and an alphabetical listing of communities with references that document them. It is especially useful in providing information on long-abandoned settlements.

768 **Alaska Municipal Officials Directory.**
Alaska Department of Community and Regional Affairs and the Alaska Municipal League, 1991. 156p.

This is a list of officials with limited statistics for all 15 boroughs and 149 municipalities in Alaska.

769 **Alaska names and places in the Russian Orthodox *American Messenger* (1896-1973): an index and annotated bibliography.**
Compiled by Barbara Sweetland Smith, Anne C. Sudkamp. Anchorage: Alaska Historical Commission, 1984. 671p. bibliog.

Although the *Messenger* was a national publication, Alaska is prominently featured in this journal. The work consists of two parts: an index to Alaskan names, and an annotated table of contents for articles with Alaska content.

770 **Alaska Native Directory.**
Anchorage: Alaska Register, 1994. 5th ed.

This loose-leaf reference lists all of the native corporations, with addresses and names of corporate officers. It includes a list, organized by name, of all of the chief personnel of the regional and village corporations, with addresses, and telephone and fax numbers.

771 **Census Alaska: number of inhabitants, 1792-1970.**
Compiled by Alden Rollins. Anchorage: University of Alaska Anchorage Library, 1978. various paginations.

This is a compilation of facsimile reproductions of the summary statistics of the US decennial census publications on Alaska, starting with the 1880 census and continuing through to 1970. Earlier numbers referred to in the title are those summarized by Ivan Petroff in the 1880 census report, published in 1884. This can be a useful collection for those without the originals, but there is nothing new here and there are many detailed census publications that are not included in the compilation.

772 **Community profiles.**
Juneau: Alaska Department of Commerce, 1977-91.

Sixty-two separate fold-out maps were issued with information on individual towns and villages.

773 **Directory of post-secondary educational resources in Alaska.** Anchorage; Juneau: Alaska Commission on Post Secondary Education, 1976- . annual.

The directory includes descriptions of programmes and addresses for the University of Alaska system, military base programmes, private institutions, religious instruction, vocational training, and financial student aid programmes. There is also a list of out-of-state institutions authorized to operate in Alaska.

774 **Index to baptisms, marriages and deaths in the archives of the Russian Orthodox Greek Catholic Church in Alaska, 1816-1866.** Library of Congress. Washington, DC: Manuscript Division, Library of Congress, 1970. 3 vols.

No official government vital statistics were required or systematically gathered in Alaska until 1913. The Orthodox Church kept the most complete records that are now available for the pre-1913 era. Other index periods have been published separately (see below).

775 **Index to baptisms, marriages and deaths in the archives of the Russian Orthodox Greek Catholic Church in Alaska 1867-1889.** Library of Congress. Washington, DC: Manuscript Division, Library of Congress, 1973. 2 vols.

This continues the 1816-1866 coverage (q.v.).

776 **Index to baptisms, marriages and deaths in the archives of the Russian Orthodox Greek Catholic Church in Alaska 1890-1899.** Edited by Zuzanne Dagmar Ralnins. Washington, DC: Library of Congress, Manuscript Division, 1965. 258p.

This is a continuation of the 1867-1889 volume (q.v.), although published earlier, of the baptismal and other records of the Church.

777 **Index to baptisms, marriages and deaths in the archives of the Russian Orthodox Greek Catholic Church in Alaska, 1900-1936.** Compiled by John Dorosh, Elizabeth Dorosh. Washington, DC: Manuscript Division, Reference Department, Library of Congress, 1964. 267p.

A part of the extended effort to index the Church collection. See other entries above.

778 **A list of trading vessels in the maritime fur trade, 1785-1825.** F. W. Howay, edited by Richard A. Pierce. Kingston, Ontario: Limestone Press, 1973. 208p. bibliog. (Materials for the Study of Alaska History, no. 2).

Howay served as a judge in British Columbia. His consuming private interest was in regional history. This list was originally published in instalments in the Royal Society of Canada's *Proceedings and Transactions* between 1930 and 1934. His list is organized by year and includes information on the ships and documentation for voyages, including known diaries, ships' logs and sailing notices as published in newspapers.

779 **Philately below zero: a postal history of Alaska.**
James S. Couch. State College, Pennsylvania: American Philatelic Society, 1957. 81p.

This postal history concludes in 1952. At that time there were 280 discontinued and 256 active post offices in the Territory. Each of the listed post offices has a brief description of the community and its history along with the name of the then current postmaster. This is often one of the only sources available for information on these communities during the early 1950s.

780 **Population overview.**
Juneau: Alaska Department of Labor Research and Analysis Section, 1979- . annual.

These statistics are assembled for the state as a whole, but also for cities, towns and small settlements.

781 **Records of the Russian-American Company, 1802, 1817-1867.**
Raymond H. Fisher. Washington, DC: National Archives and Records Service, 1971. 195p. bibliog.

The Treaty of Cession, by which the United States acquired Alaska, provided that records and documents which remained in the former Russian America after the sale would become American property. They were shipped to Washington, and there they were occasionally consulted until such time as they were microfilmed by the National Archives and this guide produced. This is a calendar of the first six reels of microfilm (communications received 1802, 1817-29). This collection is all the more important since the home office records which had been housed in St. Petersburg were inadvertently destroyed in the late 19th century.

782 **Who's who in Alaska politics: a biographical dictionary of Alaskan political personalities, 1884-1974.**
Compiled by Evangeline Atwood, Robert N. DeArmond. Portland, Oregon: Binford & Mort for the Alaska Historical Commission, 1977. 109p.

There is quite simply no other source for information on many of these individuals.

Bibliographies

783 **Alaska: a bibliography 1570-1970.**
Elsie A. Tourville. Boston, Massachusetts: G. K. Hall & Co., 1974. 738p. bibliog.

Listing 5,040 books and pamphlets arranged alphabetically by author, this bibliography encompasses all subjects and includes promotional brochures. It excludes state and federal documents. Subject access is provided through broad categories in the index, with a numerical code designating regional coverage.

784 **Arctic Bibliography.**
Edited by Marie Tremain, Maret Martna. Montreal: Arctic Institute of North America, 1953-75. 16 vols.

Published with funding support from various government agencies in the United States and Canada (but primarily the US Department of Defense), this massive bibliography ultimately contained 108,783 citations with abstracts. It covers the entire circumpolar Arctic, with the exception of Iceland, which already had adequate bibliographical coverage. Although Alaska, and only a part of Alaska at that, is a small part of this large geographical area, there is a substantial Alaskan literature covered here. This bibliography is especially strong in its coverage of non-English titles. By the time publication ceased, over half of the entries were of Russian-language publications, including some important work done on Alaska and work related to areas off Alaska's coast.

785 **Arctic exploration and development c. 500 B.C. to 1915: an encyclopaedia.**
Clive Holland. New York; London: Garland, 1994. 704p. maps. bibliog.

Holland has devoted decades to establishing an accurate record of exploration in Canada and the Arctic in general. Alaska is well represented in this work. In addition to an entry for each major expedition, listed by date and region, there is a valuable appendix with an alphabetical listing of main expedition members. The bibliography is extensive and quite useful, but not exhaustive.

786 **Bibliography and index of Alaskan archaeology.**
C. Eugene West, Richard O. Stern. Anchorage: Alaska Anthropological Association, 1987. 333p. bibliog. (Aurora. Alaska Anthropological Association Monograph Series, no. 3).

A great deal of the archaeological research on Alaska is done by state and federal agencies directly or under contract. Much of this is written up in the report literature, or discussed through conference proceedings. Thus a majority of the actual studies would not appear in standard bibliographical databases. The bibliography is organized as an alphabetical list by author and date of publication. It is well indexed with a subject/keyword index; a geographical index, using broad regions and USGS quadrangles; and a secondary author index.

787 **Bibliography of books published in Alaska before 1868.**
Valerian Lada-Mocarski. New Haven, Connecticut: Yale University Press, 1969. 567p. bibliog.

This is the standard bibliography for the Russian period of Alaska history. Only books, not periodical articles and not maps, are described. Citations are organized in chronological order, by publication date. Each book's title page is reproduced in facsimile. A thorough bibliographical description with information on size, pagination, and collation is followed by references. Finally, there is a most useful notes section for each description which details the work's significance, publication history, and relationship to other works. A total of 160 works are described and an alphabetical index of authors, compilers, editors, pseudonyms and translators is included, in both English and Russian.

788 **Bibliography of translated Alaskan materials.**
Marvin Falk. *Alaska History*, vol. 1, no. 1 (Fall 1984), p. 53-66.

Publications about Alaska were, for the most part, not in English during the early years, especially prior to 1867. During the past several decades there has been a fast-growing body of translations which is making substantial amounts of early Alaskana available to English readers.

789 **A Bibliography of Alaskan Literature, 1724-1924; containing the Titles of all Histories, Travels, Voyages, Newspapers, Periodicals, Public Documents, etc., printed in English, Russian, German, French, Spanish, etc., relating to, descriptive of, or published in Russian America or Alaska, from 1724 to and including 1924.**
James Wickersham. Fairbanks, Alaska: Alaska Agricultural College and School of Mines, 1927. 635p. (Miscellaneous Publications of the Alaska Agricultural College and School of Mines, vol. 1).

This remains the single most useful bibliographical source for the study of early Alaska. It contains 10,380 citations which include not only monographs, but also magazine articles, government documents, a list of newspapers published in Alaska and the early promotional brochures boosting the newly founded towns of gold-rush Alaska.

790 Documenting Alaska history: a guide to Federal Archives relating to Alaska.

George Ullibarri. Fairbanks, Alaska: University of Alaska Press, 1982. 296p. bibliog.

The National Archives hold extensive collections of Alaskana. Federal agencies have always been important in Alaska, especially before statehood when there were few governmental institutions that were not a part of the federal government. This finding aid is arranged topically and it covers a variety of subject matter, including international disputes, industry, national resources, public buildings, transportation, vital statistics, military matters and scientific activities.

791 Melvin Ricks' Alaska Bibliography: an introductory guide to Alaskan historical literature.

Edited by Stephen Haycox, Betty J. Haycox. Portland, Oregon: Binford & Mort for the Alaska Historical Commission. 268p. bibliog.

Melvin Ricks privately pursued Alaska bibliography for many years, devoting the last years before his death in 1964 intensively to the topic. He left behind an extensive four-volume typescript 'index' to Alaskan history. The edited bibliography is organized by subject and author, and includes references to periodical literature as well as to monographs. For many topics, the reader is referred to other bibliographies such as Wickersham (q.v.), Tourville (q.v.) and the *Arctic Bibliography* (q.v.).

792 A sense of history: a reference guide to Alaska's women, 1896-1985.

Alaska Women's Commission. Anchorage: Alaska Women's Commission, 1985. 126p. bibliog.

This is a guide to books, articles and audio-visual materials. Information on further resources includes the oral history collections of the Alaska Community College and a guide to manuscript collections.

793 Some books about Alaska received.

Alaska Historical Library. Juneau: Alaska State Library, Alaska Department of Education. annual.

An annotated annual listing of significant books received during the year, *Some books* provides an overview of recent publication on Alaska. It is divided into three sections: juvenile, adult fiction, and adult non-fiction. Most titles are available through interlibrary load if not obtainable in a local library. Book prices are given where available. For most years, there are between 110 and 140 titles listed.

Indexes

There follow three separate indexes: authors (personal and corporate); titles; and subjects. Title entries are italicized and refer either to the main titles, or to other works cited in the annotations. The numbers refer to bibliographical entry rather than page numbers. Individual index entries are arranged in alphabetical sequence.

Index of Authors

E

F

G

H

I

J

K

L

U

V

W

Y

Z

Index of Titles

C

F

O

P

Q

R

T

U

V

W

Y

Index of Subjects

C

D

E

I

J

K

Q

R

U

V

W

Y

Z

Map of Alaska

This map shows the more important towns and other features.

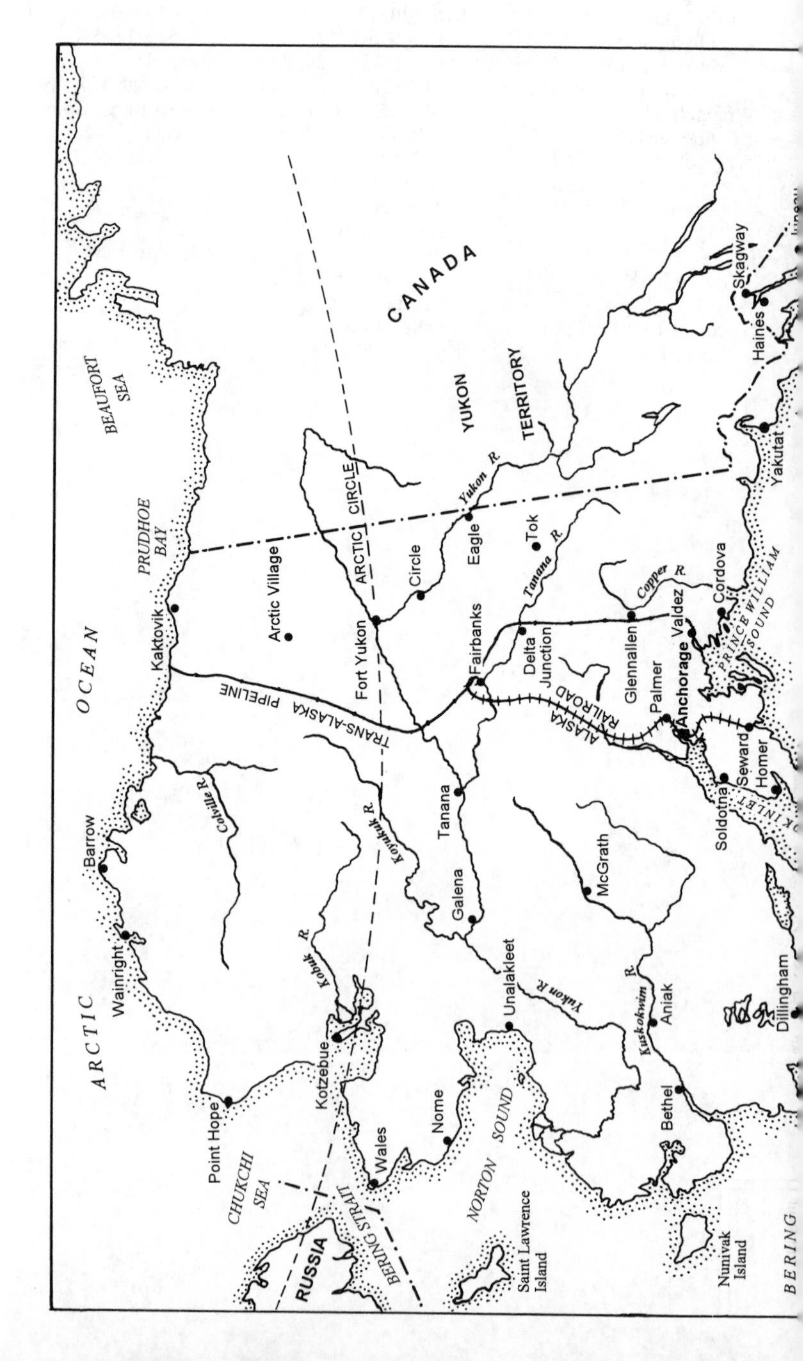

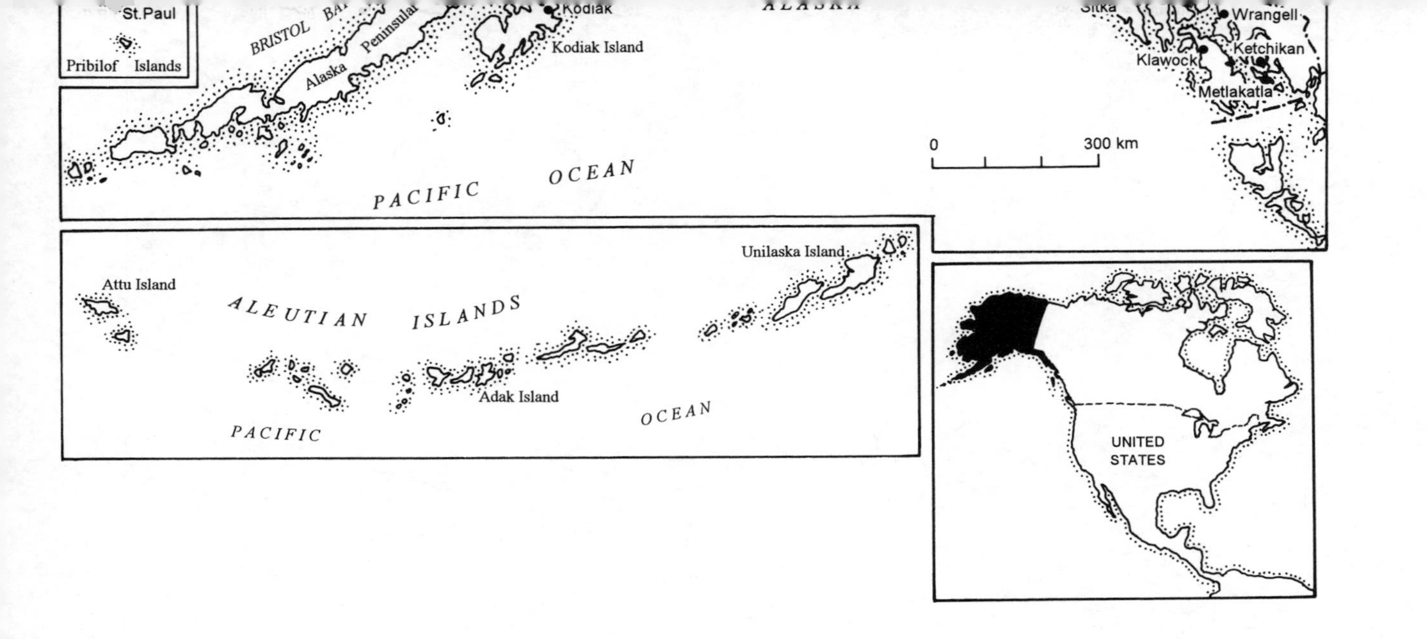
St.Paul
Pribilof Islands
BRISTOL
Alaska
Kodiak
Kodiak Island
Sitka
Wrangell
Ketchikan
Klawock
Metlakatla
0
300 km
PACIFIC OCEAN
Unilaska Island
Attu Island
ALEUTIAN ISLANDS
Adak Island
PACIFIC OCEAN
UNITED STATES

ALSO FROM CLIO PRESS

INTERNATIONAL ORGANIZATIONS SERIES

Each volume in the International Organizations Series is either devoted to one specific organization, or to a number of different organizations operating in a particular region, or engaged in a specific field of activity. The scope of the series is wide-ranging and includes intergovernmental organizations, international non-governmental organizations, and national bodies dealing with international issues. The series is aimed mainly at the English-speaker and each volume provides a selective, annotated, critical bibliography of the organization, or organizations, concerned. The bibliographies cover books, articles, pamphlets, directories, databases and theses and, wherever possible, attention is focused on material about the organizations rather than on the organizations' own publications. Notwithstanding this, the most important official publications, and guides to those publications, will be included. The views expressed in individual volumes, however, are not necessarily those of the publishers.

VOLUMES IN THE SERIES

1 *European Communities*, John Paxton
2 *Arab Regional Organizations*, Frank A. Clements
3 *Comecon: The Rise and Fall of an International Socialist Organization*, Jenny Brine
4 *International Monetary Fund*, Anne C. M. Salda
5 *The Commonwealth*, Patricia M. Larby and Harry Hannam
6 *The French Secret Services*, Martyn Cornick and Peter Morris
7 *Organization of African Unity*, Gordon Harris
8 *North Atlantic Treaty Organization*, Phil Williams
9 *World Bank*, Anne C. M. Salda
10 *United Nations System*, Joseph P. Baratta
11 *Organization of American States*, David Sheinin

TITLES IN PREPARATION

British Secret Services, Philip H. J. Davies

Israeli Secret Services, Frank A. Clements